SECOND READING
NOTABLE
AND NEGLECTED BOOKS REVISITED

Jonathan Yardley

SECOND READING
NOTABLE
AND NEGLECTED BOOKS REVISITED

Europa
editions

Europa Editions
116 East 16th Street
New York, N.Y. 10003
www.europaeditions.com
info@europaeditions.com

Library of Congress Cataloging in Publication Data is available
ISBN 978-1-60945-008-3

Yardley, Jonathan
Second Reading. Notable And Neglected Books Revisited

Book design and cover picture by Emanuele Ragnisco
www.mekkanografici.com

Prepress by Grafica Punto Print – Rome

Printed in Canada

CONTENTS

For Marisi
who saved my life

SECOND READING
NOTABLE
AND NEGLECTED BOOKS REVISITED

The five dozen pieces herein collected were published in the *Washington Post* between March 2003 and January 2010. They appeared under the same title as this book and were always accompanied by this description: "An occasional series in which the *Post*'s book critic reconsiders notable and/or neglected books from the past." Ultimately the series ran to ninety-eight books covered in ninety-seven essays; a list of the thirty-seven pieces not included in this book can be found at its end, as well as a link for reading them on-line.

Writing the column was utter pleasure for me, but that pleasure, like the column itself, came as a complete surprise. In the fall of 2002 a column I had written for the *Post* for more than two decades was yanked away from me for reasons that were never satisfactorily explained. I was bitter and angry, all the more so since I was expected to replace the column with an equal amount of work, the precise nature of which was left unspecified. Then, several months later, the inspiration for Second Reading came to me while walking home after a stimulating lunch with Deborah Heard, the new editor of the Style section. I e-mailed Deb as soon as I got there, and she immediately gave the idea her enthusiastic approval.

It didn't take long for me to realize how much fun it was to reach back into my past reading—as you'll see, the word "fun" appears frequently in these pieces—or to discover how much pleasure it gave many of the *Post*'s readers to be offered discussions of (mostly) worthy older books. The fixation of journalists on the new and the trendy is a forgivable occupational hazard, but it neglects the interests of readers who want something more substantial than the latest Flavor of the Day. My own tastes certainly are not everybody's tastes, but the steady, heavy volume of incoming e-mail convinced me that I had stumbled onto something that readers wanted. This was reconfirmed when I learned that book clubs around the *Post*'s circulation area had latched onto Second Reading as a guide to their own selections.

I also came to realize that all unwittingly I was writing what amounted to the autobiography of a lifelong reader. No one ever told me what books had to be covered in the series. It was left entirely up to me, so I followed my memory and, in many cases, my heart. You will find herein books I read (or had read to me by my parents) when I was a boy, among them Washington Irving's tales of the Catskill Mountains and C.S. Forester's Horatio Hornblower novels, as well as books and writers I came upon during my long career as a professional reviewer, among them Anita Brookner and Gabriel García Márquez.

My tastes, in the generous words of the blogger Robert Birnbaum, tend to the "idiosyncratic and wide-ranging," but they are rooted in certain constants. I am white, Anglo-Saxon, and Protestant, though the last more in name than in practice. My father spent most of his adult life as a private-school headmaster, my mother as his loyal (if occasionally vexed) helpmeet, so I grew up in a little world where serving the children of the rich was an unceasing undertaking. When I was eleven years old I was sent off for what turned out to be six years as a scholarship student at prep schools for boys most of whom were far more privileged than I. All this left me with powerful feelings about wealth, privilege, and social class, feelings that are reflected here in the pieces about John P. Marquand, Anita Brookner, F. Scott Fitzgerald and Louis Auchincloss. It also left me with a great love for the novel of manners, a love reflected in those pieces as well as several others.

I have been an ardent, constant reader since the day I was old enough to read, but I do not consider myself a literary person—first and foremost I am a journalist—and I am not ashamed to find merit in books—*Rebecca*, for example, or *Mr. Blandings Builds His Dream House*, or *The Long Season*—such as the literati scorn. Above all else I love and value the art of storytelling, now sneered at in certain quarters; I especially admire it as practiced by masters as diverse as Elizabeth Bowen, Margaret Leech, and Peter Taylor. I cherish many difficult but rewarding writers—hence William Faulkner and García Márquez—but have absolutely no taste for mere wordplay or literary games; I like puzzles in crosswords but not in novels. I savor the irony that *Ulysses*, the sine qua non of the literati but a book I simply cannot read, was admitted to these United States by my great-uncle, Federal District Judge John Woolsey. Had there been room for James Joyce in Second Reading, it would have been for *Dubliners*, not for *Ulysses* or, God knows, *Finnegans Wake*.

In the seven years of writing Second Reading the terrific word "idiosyncratic" never once popped into my head, but I did want each piece to come as a bit of a surprise to my readers and thus placed a good deal of importance on unpredictability and variety in making my selections. For the same reason I have chosen to present these sixty pieces in the order of publication.

Inevitably, in a collection of pieces such as these, there is a bit of repetition. In a few pieces I cite a book's protagonist as one of the great characters in American fiction, and in many pieces I lament the neglect into which the writer and/or his book have fallen. I considered eliminating these recurrences, but decided that to do so would take something important away from the pieces. I hope you will bear with me in this, just as I hope some of these pieces will lead you to books that will enrich your life as much as they have enriched mine.

* * *

I am deeply grateful to Kent Carroll, the publisher of Europa Editions, for allowing these Second Readings to be published by his extraordinary firm, and for giving me the opportunity to work with him after many years of friendship. At the *Washington Post*, as mentioned above, Deb Heard played a central role in getting the series into print, and she was a strong supporter of it right up to her departure from the paper (she was one among scores who took early buyouts) at the end of 2008. Rose Jacobius was the series' invaluable editor until she left, also at the end of 2008, at which point Rachel Hartigan Shea took over as my guardian angel. My thanks to all three of them.

Most of all, my thanks, like my heart, go out to my wife, Marie Arana. We are an office romance—we met in the early 1990s at the *Washington Post* Book World—and books are central to our life together. Herself the author of several brilliant books as well as, until the infamous Buyout of 2008, a fulltime editor, she always found time to read these pieces before I filed them and to catch me in the errors to which I am occasionally susceptible. Every one of these pieces was written with her foremost in mind, and dedicating this collection of them to her is only a first step toward paying my incalculable debt to her.

Washington, D.C., April 2010

H.M. Pulham, Esquire
by John P. Marquand

It is just about impossible for me to imagine beginning a series of essays about books of yesterday—books I remember with affection and admiration but have not read in many years, books I would like to encourage others to discover—with anything but a novel by John Phillips Marquand. His are not the best books I've ever read, but they are among the books I love most, and the neglect into which they have fallen is a literary outrage.

I first read Marquand half a century ago, when I was thirteen years old. It was my good fortune to be the child of parents who read incessantly and never once said that a book was "too old" for me, so when they talked with enthusiasm about their own reading, I tended to try it for myself. Nothing gave them greater pleasure than Marquand. He had, as they had, one foot on the inside of the blue-blooded WASP world and one foot on the outside; they shared his fondness for many of its people and his longing for the wealth and privilege many of them enjoyed, but they also shared his keen awareness of WASP smugness, insularity and complacency.

They found Marquand's satires of that world both hilarious and accurate, and so do I. That Marquand has almost vanished from the literary landscape is to me an unfathomable mystery. From the publication in 1937 of *The Late George Apley*, for which he won a Pulitzer Prize, until his death in 1960, Marquand was one of the most popular novelists in the country. The literati turned up their noses at him (as they do to this day) because he had done a fair amount of hackwork in his early career and continued to write, without shame, for popular magazines such as the Saturday Evening Post. But his reviews in newspapers and magazines were generally enthusiastic and his sales were spectacular. The best of his novels are *Apley* and its five immediate successors: *Wickford Point* (1939), *H.M. Pulham, Esquire* (1941), *So Little Time* (1943), *B.F.'s Daughter* (1946) and *Point of No Return* (1949). Marquand published three more in the 1950s (*Melville Goodwin, USA, Sincerely, Willis Wayde* and *Women and Thomas Harrow*) but by then his deft touch had turned a bit ham-handed, and a bitter tone had crept into his work. A possible explanation is to be found in Millicent Bell's *Marquand: An American Life* (1979), which is likely to remain the standard biography:

. . . Marquand minded that the "literary establishment" denied him the title of greatness. He would feel to the end of his career that he was penalized for achieving too supremely the identity of popularity for which he had worked so hard at the beginning. The change of character he subsequently struggled for—from the writer of magazine fodder "for the millions" to that of serious artist—was never to be completed as far as these critics were concerned: He would never join his contemporaries Hemingway and Fitzgerald and Faulkner—even Sinclair Lewis—in the literary histories. He would be bound . . . to resent this exclusion from the best company, as he knew it to be, the company of the immortals.

Bell wrote those words in the course of discussing *H.M. Pulham, Esquire,* which was "read by many Americans, not only in the serial that had run in *McCall's* and in a Reader's Digest condensation, but in printing after printing—fourteen by 1949—as well as in the separate Book-of-the-Month Club edition, a cheaper Dollar Book reprint and later paperback reprints." Like all the rest of Marquand's work, it is written with what the author himself called the "smooth technique" routinely disparaged by his critics. Its prose flows without apparent effort, which scored Marquand no points at a moment in literary history that favored Hemingway's self-conscious leanness, Fitzgerald's poetic romanticism, and Faulkner's dense complexity. Never mind that it takes a great deal of work and discipline to perfect a "smooth technique," and never mind that Marquand's prose is just about as distinctive and readily identifiable as that of other writers celebrated as stylists; in the places where literary reputations are made, he was dismissed as a slick entertainer.

Yet the truth is that *Pulham* is a work of depth and complexity. Set in Boston and environs in 1938 and 1939, with an important side trip to New York, it employs the flashback technique perfected by Marquand to explore the life of his narrator and protagonist, Harry Pulham. Now in his mid-forties (like Marquand himself at the time), Pulham has been approached—commanded is more like it—to help plan the twenty-fifth reunion of his Harvard class. The approach is made by his classmate Bo-jo Brown, football hero and perpetual schoolboy. "Our Class is the best damned class that ever came out of Harvard," Bo-jo announces, "and the reason is that we've always pulled together." So at least Bo-jo imagines; the truth is considerably more complex, not to mention more interesting and amusing.

This is because Marquand understood that "playing the game," as Bo-jo has done all his life and as Pulham is always inclined to do, is every bit as likely to complicate and diminish one's life as to enrich it. The world in which these sons of Harvard move, and into which they drag their wives and children, is at heart just a "God-damned university club," in the scornful description of an officer whom Harry encounters in the trenches of World War I. Harry likes to think that he and his crowd "do not bring our children up to be snobs" and claims that "I always like fresh points of view," yet in the same breath notes that his classmate Bill King "came from New Jersey and went to some unknown preparatory school and did not know anyone when he went to Harvard, and yet I still maintain that he is the most brilliant member of our class." Why, Harry adds, "sometimes I think I shall not mind if my son George does not make a Club at Harvard"!

The lack of self-awareness betrayed in that passage is at once hilarious and horrifying. Harry Pulham sails serenely through life, touched by the occasional moment of doubt or the even more fleeting gasp of passion, yet he always retreats into the comforts of the only world he really knows, what the cynical Bill King calls "a certain tiny, superfluous segment that is going to be nonexistent." Marquand himself held that same judgment and that same prediction, and he was right; what the late Joseph Alsop called "the WASP ascendancy" is now so far down the road to oblivion that its taillights no longer are visible. Yet Marquand also understood that the longing for familiar community is deep-rooted; the community he knew best was the WASPs', so that is what he wrote about.

Which is what the novelist of manners does: puts under his or her microscope the behavior, beliefs and mores of a specific set or class to examine individuals and groups more generally. The best-known novelists of manners often write about the upper end of the social order—Anthony Trollope, Jane Austen, William Makepeace Thackeray, Henry James, Edith Wharton, Louis Auchincloss, Peter Taylor—but every class has its own manners and all classes are fair game for the novelist. Tom Wolfe's *The Bonfire of the Vanities* is about the manners of New York society at various levels from bottom to top, much of Ralph Ellison's *Invisible Man* is about the manners of the African-American middle class, and Alice McDermott's novels are about the manners of Irish-Americans in Queens and on Long Island.

Harry Pulham, like most of us, lives in his own cocoon. There is a moment—it lasts for a few months—when it seems that he has a chance to escape it. Immediately after college he slips effortlessly into the clubby Boston investment firm of Smith and Wilding, but then he serves with distinction and bravery in the war, a war that "smashed everything," that leaves him back at home "picking up pieces of things . . . pieces of human relationships, pieces of thoughts, and when I tried to put them together again they never seemed to fit." In a wholly uncharacteristic leap into the unknown, he takes a job with the advertising agency in New York where Bill King is employed.

This gives Marquand the opportunity to take a few amusing whacks at the ad game and ad-speak, both of which he knew well, but it also puts Harry in the same office with Marvin Myles: "Certainly she was not my type, for when I was twenty-four I had no liking for girls who were aggressive or for girls who knew too much. Marvin was not my type, but there was something in her character which I grew to depend on." Soon enough he is wholly in love with her, and she with him, and—to his utter astonishment—they begin a love affair, though Harry knows it is far more than that.

Then Harry's father dies, and the responsibility for Harry's bewildered, ailing mother and his younger sister falls upon him. He knows in his heart "that everything with Marvin and me was unique, not to be placed in any single category, that nothing in this world was ever like it," but she is New York and he is Boston. He takes her to meet his family, and though everyone is polite it doesn't work: "I understood then that it was over, that it had always been impossible"—impossible not for her but for him, because "I have to live where I belong."

So he goes back to Smith and Wilding—"a gentleman's banking house run by gentlemen, a fine house with a sense of honor"—and eventually he takes a closer look at Kay Motford. He has known her for as long as he can remember and has never been drawn to her—"Kay was always sunburned and her nose kept peeling and she generally wore sneakers"—but now she offers the comforts of the familiar. As friendship turns slowly into romance, or a WASP semblance thereof, she says to him in her direct, plainspoken way: "Harry, maybe people you've always known are better. You know what they're going to do."

Here he is now, midway through his forties, settled and prosperous. He is married to Kay, has a townhouse with a George Inness landscape hanging in the parlor, a summer house in Maine and two children. "Of course Kay and I do quarrel sometimes, but when you add it all together, all of it isn't as bad as the parts of it seem. I mean, maybe that's all there is to anybody's life."

Those heartbreaking words are said over drinks to Bill King. Oblivious as ever to life's inconveniences and complexities, Harry is utterly unaware that Kay is now seeking happiness beyond the circle of "people you've always known," just as he had sought it two decades before. She and Bill are having an affair. Harry doesn't have a clue. He thinks that Bill comes to Boston for Harvard football games and that Kay goes to New York to shop.

A conversation with his sister Mary nails it all on the head. Her marriage is pro forma, and she is attracted to the man who owns her horseback-riding school. "He collects women," she tells Harry, "and it's mighty pleasant for a change," to which Harry replies with sublime predictability: "I always knew he wasn't a gentleman." Mary wraps it up: "That's what I mean. If you could ever stop being a gentleman and if I could ever stop being a lady—but we haven't got the guts to be anything else, have we? . . . We won't do anything that's really wrong, because our inhibitions will stop us, darling."

If there isn't universality to that, the word has no meaning. The price too often paid for realizing the human longing for security amid the familiar is disappointment and loss. In *The*

Late George Apley the title character falls in love with a girl from the wrong Boston neighborhood, but he comes to his senses and marries the proper one who has his father's approval. Like Harry Pulham he is left to spend the rest of his life in his ivory tower, enjoying its comforts and wondering what might have been. It is a question that many of Marquand's characters find themselves asking, and it most certainly is not a question asked only in Back Bay or Harvard Square.

Yes, Marquand had his limits, in themes, subject matter and style. So, too, do all those other American writers who enjoy the eclat that has for so long been denied him. It is ludicrous that the Library of America, which smugly proclaims itself guardian "of America's best and most significant writing," finds room on its shelves for ever less significant work yet turns up its nose at Marquand. It is equally ludicrous that until only fairly recently the publishing firm of Little, Brown and Company, for which Marquand earned millions upon millions of dollars, declined to keep his major novels consistently in print. So the next time you hear or read about some publisher or editor claiming to "serve the best interests of literature," pause a moment to reflect upon how shabbily Marquand is now served, not to mention those readers who might discover his work to their joy and reward if only they could find it.

W.C. FIELDS: HIS FOLLIES AND FORTUNES
by Robert Lewis Taylor

For years the rule among biographers has been "the bigger the better." Lately there has been a tentative move in the opposite direction—small is beautiful—but the prevailing assumption really hasn't changed: Big lives deserve big books and so, for that matter, do little lives. Every scrap of obsessively researched biographical detail demands to be included, no matter how little it may tell us about the subject, with the result that, for example, we have been given 400 pages on Hart Crane, 450 pages on Samuel Pepys and an astounding 1,150 pages in what is merely the third volume of Robert Caro's as-yet-unfinished account of the life of Lyndon Johnson.

Then there is *W.C. Fields: A Biography*, by James Curtis, which weighs in at 500 pages of text and another 100 pages of apparatus. Earnest, dutiful and encyclopedic, it pulls off what can only be called an astonishing feat: It drains just about all the humor out of the man whom one Hollywood director called "the greatest comedian that ever lived." The life of Fields calls for a Dickens, a writer with a grand and vivid style to match Fields's own, yet Curtis brings to the task the stylistic zest of a mortician.

Despair not, though, for as it happens, Fields found his Dickens more than half a century ago. He was Robert Lewis Taylor, the author of *W.C. Fields: His Follies and Fortunes*.

Published in 1949, three years after Fields's death, written without the cooperation of Fields's widow (from whom he had been estranged for years) or son, the book makes no apparent claim to being the definitive portrayal of its subject—my 1967 paperback copy has no bibliography or notes, indeed doesn't even have an index—but in fewer than 300 pages it succeeds where Curtis and too many other contemporary biographers fail: It brings its subject vividly, unforgettably back to life. Reread now, it thus serves as an accidental antidote to Curtis, and it raises important points about the biographer's task.

Taylor obviously missed some of the facts, and he probably fiddled with some of the ones he had; I have vague memories of reading somewhere a lighthearted complaint that the book is as much fiction as fact. But that complaint ignores, or denies, a fundamental truth: Biography is fiction as well as fact. When it comes to the hardest job of all—getting inside the subject's heart and soul—the qualities required have far less to do with research and collation than with imagination and empathy. Since the biographer can never truly know the subject's inner life, the best he or she can hope to do is interpret and invent.

This Taylor did with sympathy and skill. He seems to be almost totally forgotten now, though in 1959 he won a Pulitzer Prize for his novel *The Travels of Jamie McPheeters*. Born in 1912, he had an exceptionally successful career as a journalist, biographer and novelist. He published more than a dozen books, some of which were bestsellers, yet now only *Jamie McPheeters* is still in print, and it's hard to find.

This can be interpreted as evidence of the evanescence of journalism, or of the cruelty of book publishing, or of the disloyalty of readers. But whatever the explanation for Taylor's rapid disappearance from the bookstores, in the specific case of *W.C. Fields: His Follies and Fortunes* it is an injustice as well as a mystery. It is all the more so when one considers that Fields's best movies—*It's a Gift, You Can't Cheat an Honest Man, The*

Bank Dick, My Little Chickadee, Never Give a Sucker an Even Break, David Copperfield—are still widely available, and loved not merely by geezers but also by younger moviegoers.

Just how far Taylor was able to penetrate the inner Fields is itself an unsolvable mystery, but that is true of all biographers. The problem is all the more difficult for the biographer of a movie star whose on-screen persona is commonly assumed to be the real person. What Taylor nicely calls the "grandiose humbug" embodied by the on-screen Fields seems to have been central to the off-screen Fields, but the biographer must deal with deeper and more complex questions about his character and personality.

Fields had a tough start—he ran away from home in working-class Philadelphia in 1890, when he was eleven, and subsisted mostly on petty crime before discovering the gift for juggling that proved his ticket to show business. Many of his friends believed that his "personal and professional later life was dedicated to repaying society for the hurts of his childhood," Taylor writes. He made a career out of hating humanity generally, children and dogs especially, yet "despite all his bluster, he was hypersensitive, and hated to hurt anybody's feelings." For all his pool-hall conviviality, he was a lonely man who seemed incapable of human relationships beyond skin-deep male bonding. As Taylor says, "It taxes the historian's ingenuity to explain the many paradoxes of Fields."

It also taxes the writer's ingenuity to make Fields step off the printed page, but this Taylor quite triumphantly accomplishes. In part no doubt this is because he was born at a time when youngsters still read Dickens not just for schoolwork but for pleasure, and when some of those who went on to become writers fell under Dickens's influence. Like Taylor, Fields himself was one of these. He "felt an especial affinity for Dickens, in some of whose characters he saw strong traces of himself," and in time he gave the definitive screen performance of Mr.

Micawber in *David Copperfield.* Taylor captures the literary
Fields deftly:

> He loved the trappings of writing. His ritual with [his secretary]
> Miss Michael, on days when he was to work on a script or write
> something else, made him feel important. Humming cheerfully,
> he would lay things out, either on his desk or in a lawn swing
> where he liked to work. His style was extravagant, florid, influ-
> enced in large measure by Dickens, whom he knew by heart.
> "Despite his love of simplicity, he could never say, 'Hit him on the
> head,'" says Miss Michael. "He always had to make it 'Conk him
> on the noggin.'"

Taylor was a comic writer of considerable gifts, an especially useful attribute for a biographer of Fields. His description of the pool-table act that Fields worked up during his
vaudeville years is delicious, as are his accounts of Fields's golf
act and of a funeral presided over by a Philadelphia undertaker
named—Fields adored the name—Chester Snavely. But the
piece de resistance comes when Taylor describes a trip Fields
made with his friend Billy Grady:

> Grady cannot be too profuse in his praise of Fields' driving. One
> time during prohibition the comedian heard that a friend on
> Long Island had just received two cases of contraband Irish
> whiskey. He and Grady drove out immediately. They and the
> friend spent the night making sure the government would be
> unable to recover part of the whiskey, at least, and Fields and
> Grady left for home around dawn. Owing to their host's generos-
> ity, they took five or six quarts along with them, externally. Both
> Fields and Grady later recalled that it was snowing when they left,
> and they settled down for an exhausting drive. En route they took
> frequent pulls at the whiskey and remarked at the surprising
> length of Long Island. Their heads were pretty fuzzy during the
> trip. They put in at filling stations now and then, gassed up, and
> sought information about the route. However, in response to a
> question like "How far's the Queensboro Bridge?" the attendants

would only laugh, or stare stupidly. Also, as time wore on, the travelers got the cloudy impression that many people they talked to were essaying dialects, for some reason. "I don't recollect no place name of Manhasset," a man would tell them, and they would applaud, then careen on down the road, drinking his health. Their heads finally cleared, and Grady found himself looking out of a window at a palm tree. They seemed to be in a hotel room. He dressed quickly and, while Fields slept on, exhausted by the Long Island roads, went down in search of a newspaper. The first intelligence he gleaned, when he got one, was that Ocala, Florida, was expecting no more than a moderate rainfall for the time of year, and that things looked good for a big citrus crop.

Is the story true? Who knows, who cares? What matters is that Taylor's telling of the story is perfectly paced, with expert phrasing: "the surprising length of Long Island"! It passes one of the hardest tests of comic prose: Read aloud to others, it brings laughter. It also paints a miniature portrait of Fields that rings exactly, precisely true.

It should be noted that although Taylor finds much to be amused about in Fields's drinking, he writes about it honestly and ultimately in sorrow. Read a sentence such as this—"The comedian was drinking what he described as 'martinis'; he had a bottle of gin in one hand and a bottle of vermouth in the other, and he took alternate pulls, favoring the gin"—and it's impossible (for me, at least) not to laugh. But when "the long addiction to alcohol had overtaken him at last," Taylor is unsparing: "He had many of the traditional symptoms of delirium tremens—hallucinations, grotesque visitations, nostalgic evocations." Booze is what finally killed Fields, and Taylor doesn't shrink from this unpleasant truth.

In the matter of Fields's alcoholism, the truth is easily identified and described. Much of the time though the biographer works in gray areas that can only be explored with instruments subtler than those of the diligent, but unimaginative, researcher.

Robert Lewis Taylor had full command of them. He also had what so many of today's biographers so transparently lack: an ability to discriminate between material that provides illumination and material that provides padding. He was perceptive and he was selective, a felicitous combination that produced, in *W.C. Fields: His Follies and Fortunes*, an entirely wonderful book.

THE AUTUMN OF THE PATRIARCH
by Gabriel García Márquez

The second of Gabriel García Márquez's three master-works to this day remains something of a middle child: taken for granted, overlooked, misunderstood. *One Hundred Years of Solitude* (1967) is his best-known novel, his most admired, most imitated and most honored. *Love in the Time of Cholera* (1985) is his most beloved, one of the great love stories of world literature. But *The Autumn of the Patriarch* (1975) is widely believed to be difficult, inaccessible and even unpleasant.

None of this, as it happens, is true, but so many readers apparently have been scared away from the novel that it lags far behind the other two in sales and, presumably, recognition. This would be puzzling under any circumstances, but it is especially so at the present moment because *The Autumn of the Patriarch* is the definitive fictional inquiry into tyrannical government, the literature of which includes, recently, Mario Vargas Llosa's *The Feast of the Goat*. The name of the dictator who is García Márquez's protagonist is never disclosed, but it could just easily be Augusto Pinochet, Juan Vicente Gomez, Rafael Trujillo or any one of all the other Latin American dictators upon whom the author modeled this chilling figure, with a touch of Joseph Stalin and Francisco Franco thrown in for bad measure.

The reader may have noted that among those despots to the south who served as the author's models, Fidel Castro is missing. The explanation for this is simple—García Márquez is a man of the left—but it makes the author vulnerable to charges of inconsistency, if not hypocrisy. A journalist named Jorge Ramos once wrote in the *Miami Herald* that it is "difficult to believe" that the novel was based on Pinochet rather than Castro, though he acknowledged that in the mid-1970s Castro "still could dazzle and dupe writers and intellectuals on both sides of the Atlantic." This complaint, often expressed within the Cuban exile community, has merit: A tyrant is a tyrant no matter his ostensible political convictions, after all, and the picture of García Márquez cozying up to Castro is not exactly edifying.

But that complaint has to do with politics, not literature, and *The Autumn of the Patriarch* is literature above all else, a fantastic and phantasmagorical novel that at the same time is deeply grounded in reality. Forget magical realism: This is truth.

It is truth as García Márquez has observed it since his birth in March 1927 in the Colombian town of Aracataca. He studied law but soon found his way into journalism, which was, and remains, an important influence on the fiction he began writing in the early 1950s. His early work, though skillful, was limited. Then in 1965—the story, which is true, is an essential part of his legend—the world of the fictional town of Macondo came alive in his mind while he was living in Mexico City and driving south to Acapulco. He turned the car around, went home, and stayed at his desk for a year and a half, at the end of which he had the completed manuscript of *One Hundred Years of Solitude*. The novel was received with joy throughout Latin America upon its publication in 1967, and then became an international bestseller when it appeared in English in 1970. In 1982 García Márquez was awarded the Nobel Prize for Literature.

The Autumn of the Patriarch was published eight years after *Solitude* and caught many readers by surprise because it seemed, at first glance, so different. Allen B. Ruch, in his exceptionally useful modern literature Website (themodernword.com), correctly observes that its "dense but fluid prose . . . makes *Autumn of the Patriarch* García Márquez's most challenging novel; but it also makes it one of his most exciting." Ruch attributes this to the influence of James Joyce (he refers to "a winding sheet of endless words twisting through the tyrant's head like a macho version of Molly's soliloquy in *Ulysses*"). No doubt this is accurate, but American readers will be quick to recognize the hand of William Faulkner, whose powerful influence García Márquez has readily and graciously acknowledged—a reminder, in light of his frequent criticism of U.S. policy in Latin America, that political differences ultimately matter far less to him than literary affinities.

Whatever the exact inspiration for the style of *The Autumn of the Patriarch*, it is stream of consciousness. Here, though, the device is taken to new dimensions, for this is the consciousness not of a single individual but of an entire nation. With extraordinary suppleness, García Márquez moves in and out of different heads. The principal one is that of the tyrant, found dead at last "at an indefinite age somewhere between 107 and 232 years," but we hear as well from people who served him, people who feared him, people who were tortured and/or executed at his orders, people who submitted to his clumsy, brutal sexual demands and bore his thousands of nameless children.

The prose style in which this is written is elaborate, florid, expressive: to coin a usage, maximalist. Yet, interestingly, the effect on the reader is much like that of the music of a minimalist composer such as Philip Glass: a rhythm and repetitious theme are established and one submits to them, rolls along them like a surfer on a wave, accepts them on their own terms. If you don't always know whose mind it is you are entering—and you don't—it doesn't really matter, because the collective portrait of the dictator and the small Caribbean nation that he rules is more important than individual thoughts, memories and voices.

Readers who know *One Hundred Years of Solitude* and *Love in the Time of Cholera* may be unsettled by the violence and cruelty that suffuse this novel, but they will also find much they have encountered before: "the stigma of solitude," "the drain of memory," the "incapacity for love," "the lethargy of death"— all are themes García Márquez repeatedly has explored in sunnier realms than this one.

As is also true of Garcia Marquez's other masterpieces, the novel weaves back and forth in time. "The past is not dead, it's not even past," is how Faulkner put it, a notion as essential to García Márquez's work as to his own. The individual memory of the dictator and the collective memory of the nation are pinned down to no specific moment but exist in eternity. Indeed the dictator is the embodiment of time and timelessness: "the only thing that gave us security on earth was the certainty that he was there, invulnerable to plague and hurricane . . . invulnerable to time, dedicated to the messianic happiness of thinking for us, knowing that we knew that he would not take any decision for us that did not have our measure, for he had not survived everything because of his inconceivable courage or his infinite prudence but because he was the only one among us who knew the real size of our destiny."

As that passage suggests, García Márquez understands that the relationship between the suppressor and the suppressed is complex and interdependent. If there is in some of us a powerful urge to dominate, there is in others an inclination—perhaps even a desire—to submit. "These people love me," the dictator likes to tell himself, and though that is a lie and a delusion there is a grain of truth in it. The dictator and his yes men operate "an invisible service of repression and extermination," a "machine of horror," yet because it is the only existence the people have known it is also the only one they can imagine, and they submit to it.

By the same token Garcia Marquez concedes to the dictator a measure of humanity. He is a child of poverty who may for a time have had a genuine sympathy for those in like circumstances. But power has a way of feeding on itself, and so does violence. He engages the services of the sublimely satanic José Ignacio Saénz de la Barra, who employs "the most ingenious and barbarous machines of torture that the imagination could conceive of," with a toll in human lives that inexorably rises from the scores to the hundreds of thousands. When the dictator complains that "this isn't the power I wanted," the response is that it is "the only power possible in the lethargy of death."

This is gruesome business, yet because García Márquez is an uncommonly gifted comic writer there is humor in it as well—wry and morbid humor, to be sure, but humor all the same. The dictator comes to fear, as dictators always do, "that there was someone within reach of his hand," his personal Judas or Iago, and determines to strike first. He settles his complacent gaze upon "the handsome artilleryman's eyes of my soul comrade General Rodrigo de Aguilar . . . his strong right arm, his sacred accomplice," and orders the other officers closest to him to attend a banquet:

> . . . it was twelve o'clock but General Rodrigo de Aguilar was not arriving, someone started to get up, please, he said, he turned him to stone with the fatal look of nobody move, nobody breathe, nobody live without my permission until twelve o'clock finished chiming, and then the curtains parted and the distinguished Major General Rodrigo de Aguilar entered on a silver tray stretched out full length on a garnish of cauliflower and laurel leaves, steeped with spices, oven brown, embellished with the uniform of five golden almonds for solemn occasions and the limitless loops for valor on the sleeve of his right arm, fourteen pounds of medals on his chest and a sprig of parsley in his mouth,

ready to be served at a banquet of comrades by the official carvers to the petrified horror of the guests as without breathing we witness the exquisite ceremony of carving and serving, and when every plate held an equal portion of minister of defense stuffed with pine nuts and aromatic herbs, he gave the order to begin, eat hearty gentlemen.

That is in every respect an amazing piece of writing, in which cruelty and comedy are placed in perfect balance. If it is possible to be savage and witty at the same time, that is what the tyrant has done in the disposition of General Rodrigo de Aguilar. The first time I read that passage, when the novel appeared in English in 1976, I was absolutely astonished; if it no longer has the power of surprise for me, in every other respect its power and artistry are undiminished.

The same is true of the rest of the book. Its portrait of "the most solitary man on earth" is timeless and applies with equal pertinence to every man who ever has seized power by force and held onto it with force. The tyrant's "throne of illusions" rests on a foundation of lies, as we were all too painfully reminded by the tales seeping out of Iraq as yet another despotic regime crumbled into dust. When García Márquez writes about "the perfidy within the presidential palace itself . . . the greed within the adulation and the wily servility among those who flourished under the umbrella of power," he states a universal truth that each dictatorship merely reconfirms.

It should be noted, as these several quotations from the book make plain, that García Márquez is uncommonly well served by his translator. In *The Autumn of the Patriarch* as in *One Hundred Years of Solitude,* it is Gregory Rabassa. In *Basilisk's Eggs*, his seminal essay on García Márquez and *Solitude,* Alastair Reid writes: "the English translation . . . is something of a masterpiece, for it is almost matched to the tune of the Spanish, never lengthening or shortening sentences but following them measure for measure. García Márquez insists that he prefers the English translation to the original, which is tantamount to saying they are interchangeable—the near-unattainable point of arrival for any translator." The same is true of Rabassa's translation of *The Autumn of the Patriarch*, a masterpiece of translation as well as of literature.

REVEILLE IN WASHINGTON
by Margaret Leach

The best "Washington novel" isn't a novel at all. Published six decades ago, Margaret Leech's *Reveille in Washington: 1860-1865* is what academic historians condescendingly call "popular history," written with the novelist's eye for character and telling detail and with a strong command of narrative. The story of the District of Columbia during the Civil War, *Reveille in Washington* is still authoritative as history and is something of a masterpiece of storytelling.

What matters most is that *Reveille in Washington* portrays the capital city more vividly, accurately and thoroughly than any other book. Period. Its portrait of Washington transcends time. Residents no longer dump their sewage into the swamp that is now the Mall and no one rides horse-drawn streetcars from the Capitol to the White House, but the essential character of the city has not changed from that day to this. Leech got it exactly right.

The competition, to be sure, isn't much. The number of words that have been written about Washington is surely beyond human calculation, but the number of good ones is small. In his preface to the 1991 paperback edition of *Reveille in Washington,* James M. McPherson takes note of David Brinkley's *Washington Goes to War,* a look at the capital during World War II that is engaging reading but surprisingly narrow in scope. If asked to recommend a good book about the city I always cite the Federal Writers' Project's *Washington, D.C.: A Guide to the Nation's Capital,* even though it has been little revised since its original publication in 1942 and is, in any event, lamentably out of print.

Fiction? The most famous "Washington novels"—Henry Adams's *Democracy* and the historical novels by Gore Vidal—are hugely overrated and unreadable. Charles McCarry has written exceptionally intelligent spy thrillers set in and about Washington, George Pelecanos's crime novels knowingly depict the city's underside, and Edward P. Jones's short stories about the black middle class are exemplary. But their scope is rather narrow. The "Washington novels" that find their way to the bestseller lists—books by the likes of David Baldacci and the late Allen Drury—are little more than power-politics soap operas, written in execrable prose.

The prose in *Reveille in Washington,* by contrast, positively sings. It is a trifle old-fashioned, but it has immediacy and passion. Here, for example, Leech describes the city as Union casualties poured in after a terrible defeat in May 1863:

> [T]he wounded cumbered the Washington wharves, but few sightseers gathered to see the transports arriving, day after day, with the men from Chancellorsville. Now, each of those prostrate young bodies seemed the very figure of the Union itself, and people turned away from the heartsickening, habitual scene. The compact caravans of the ambulances had become a monotonous part of the pageant of the streets. The procession of the maimed, with their empty sleeves and trouser legs, no longer attracted attention. Even death had grown commonplace. . . . There was a section of the city where the rat-tat of the coffin makers' hammers sounded all day, and the stacks of long, upended boxes rose and fell outside their doors, like a fever chart of the battles. The capital had had a surfeit of misery; and, if the horror of blood beat like a wound in the back of every mind, the faces on the streets were smiling.

The woman who wrote those powerful words was born in Newburgh, on the Hudson River in New York, in 1893, less than three decades after the end of the Civil War. By the time

Margaret Leech set to work on *Reveille in Washington* in the mid-1930s, she had published three novels and a play, *Divided by Three,* had appeared briefly on Broadway in 1934. She was married to Ralph Pulitzer, publisher of the *New York World* and son of Joseph Pulitzer. She traveled in fashionable literary and journalistic circles. One prominent friend was Cass Canfield of *Harper's,* who suggested she write about Washington during the Civil War. Obviously she sensed a good story, for she seems to have gotten to work almost immediately.

In 1942 Leech was awarded the Pulitzer Prize in history for *Reveille in Washington* and eighteen years later she won a second, for *In the Days of McKinley.* She was the first woman to win the history prize, and is the only woman to win it twice. Since the Pulitzers were established by her father-in-law, the skeptical may look at this with doubting eyes, but no one who has read *Reveille in Washington* can believe that the prize was won on anything except merit.

It is a measure of her achievement that McPherson, the preeminent historian of the Civil War period, is unstinting in his praise of *Reveille in Washington.* "In only one important respect," he writes, "has subsequent scholarship modified the findings of this book. Historians no longer portray the radical Republicans in so hostile a light as they did during the 1940s, nor do they find such a large gulf between the radicals and Lincoln on issues connected with the South and slavery." Otherwise, McPherson writes, this book is "a classic in the rich field of Civil War stories," one that "can be read and appreciated at several levels," from the grand story of the war to Washington's "physical awakening from an unkempt country town to a modern city."

As McPherson says, Leech's "main protagonist is Washington itself. . . . The book not only recounts the Civil War as it was shaped in Washington and seen from Washington, but it also breathes life into the city and makes it an animate, sentient being, not merely a place." The opening chapter, a tour de force, confirms that judgment. Washington in 1860 was "an idea set in a wilderness," "pretentious and unfulfilled" in its execution of L'Enfant's design. "The vaunted buildings of Washington were the Capitol, the General Post-Office, the Patent Office, the Treasury, the Executive Mansion and the Smithsonian Institution; and, despite the distances, the tour could be made in a forenoon."

Change a few words and it could be Washington today: Pennsylvania Avenue "hummed with hacks, with the elaborate carriages of the legations and the blooded horses of the Southerners. Shops furbished their windows. Hotels and boardinghouses filled up, and so did the E Street Infirmary, the poorhouse and the county jail. Practical motives dictated the presence of all the winter sojourners. There were no parties of idle, amusement-seeking tourists. The townsfolk entertained their friends and relatives, and every winter a bevy of pretty girls came for the festivities of the social season; but, apart from these negligible few, Americans did not visit Washington for pleasure. Although it had many churches, an active Young Men's Christian Association and a dignified official society, the city bore an unwholesome name among the pious folk of the nation. It was darkly imagined as a sink of iniquity, where weak-minded bachelors were exposed to the temptations of saloons, gambling hells and light women; and the prevalence of hotel life was instanced as a proof of the city's immorality."

As the war began, "in the eyes of the North, Washington was a cherished symbol of the nation's power, to be held and defended at all costs," while in the eyes of the South, "the capital was a great prize whose capture would enhance the prestige of the rebellious government, and surely bring it recognition by foreign powers." These conflicting aspirations remained unchanged throughout the war. Washington may have been "a ramshackle town, dirty and unpaved," a place notable for "the dangers of its intrigues, and the corrupt moral atmosphere of its politics," but it had almost incalculable symbolic and military value.

"To the capital's politicians, the protection of Washington was of paramount importance," but it was protected just about as haphazardly then as it is now. "The fall of the capital was a certainty" over and over again, or so at least it seemed to residents of the city who could hear Rebel artillery in the near distance. By 1864 Confederate forces got as close as Rockville and Silver Spring in what is now suburban Maryland, but turned back without a serious engagement; still, it is nothing short of miraculous that Washington, pinned between Virginia and Maryland, never was captured or even invaded.

Matters such as that are discussed at length in all serious histories of the Civil War. They are the stuff of military and political debate unto this day. Margaret Leech's singular accomplishment is that she penetrates beneath the great events and great issues to discover the daily life of the city and the ordinary people who lived it. When Union troops finally began to arrive in Washington, for example, she tells us that "confectioners, oystermen and barbers were delighted with their trade," and the "Saturday afternoon concerts of the Marine Band were offered, just as in normal times." Later, as the novelty wore off, soldiers were "far too numerous for quiet and serenity. Children went straying after bands and regiments, and there were many accidents to little boys, whom careless officers asked to hold their horses."

The District was a mecca for African-Americans, but "troops in Washington were flagrant in their hostility to Negroes, chasing and stoning them in the streets." Discrimination was pandemic; blacks were severely punished "for pathetically childish offenses—for setting off firecrackers near a dwelling, for bathing in the canal and for flying a kite within the limits of the [city]." Leech, it should be noted, refers to blacks in terms used by

polite whites of her day—mostly "Negroes" and "colored people," far more rarely "darkies" and "pickaninnies"—but the
book leaves no doubt that she was deeply sympathetic to them
and capable of seeing beyond stereotypes.

The women of Washington come under her careful scrutiny.
Foremost among them was Mary Todd Lincoln ("She had
reached the pinnacle of worldly success, only to find it rotten
with pain and fear and hatred"), but there were also the alluring
Confederate spies Rose O'Neal Greenhow and Belle Boyd.
Women working for the government "fared badly" in hours and
pay; "there was an inexhaustible supply of them, and they were
without standing, precedent or basis for comparison." There
was also an inexhaustible supply of "fallen angels of wartime"—
prostitutes—who descended on the city in an "invasion . . . so
sensational that it was easy to exaggerate its numbers."

As so often happens, the city boomed during the war. Work
continued on the Capitol. "If people see the Capitol going on,"
Lincoln said, "it is a sign we intend the Union shall go on." An
aqueduct for the city's water supply was under construction,
and Congress authorized improvements at the Treasury, the
War Department, the Navy Department and Judiciary Square.

The Washington we know today took shape during the
Civil War. Physical shape, that is. Its social and psychological
shape had already been formed: cynicism and idealism,
pocket-lining and public service, avarice and selflessness—the
more things change, the more they remain the same. Then as
now it was a city of strivers, dealmakers and self-publicists, but
also of ordinary people going about their business without
benefit of spotlights or press clippings. Leech captures all this
within the 500-plus pages of *Reveille in Washington*, which
remains required reading for anyone who wants to know what
kind of place the nation's capital really is.

THE TWELVE CAESARS
by Suetonius,
translated by Robert Graves

Any reader interested in the corrosive effects of power would do well to read *The Twelve Caesars*, Michael Grant's authoritative synthesis of the bits and pieces that have come down to us through the ages about the men who ruled the Roman Empire from 46 B.C. through A.D. 95. But useful though this book certainly is, sooner or later the reader must turn to the original, as written by Gaius Suetonius Tranquillus, chief secretary to the Emperor Hadrian in the 2nd century A.D.

To today's reader, this may seem daunting: a book written nearly two millennia ago in a language, Latin, that is now, to all intents and purposes, dead, by an author about whom almost nothing is known. Fear not. A brilliant translation of Suetonius is easily available in what Gore Vidal has called "a good, dry, no-nonsense style." It was done in the mid-1950s by Robert Graves, who two decades earlier had leaned heavily on Suetonius in writing his immensely successful historical novels, *I, Claudius* and *Claudius the God*. It was first published in 1957 as a Penguin Classic and is still in print in the same series, revised in 1979 by Michael Grant.

Revised, that is, because Graves felt that a "literal rendering" of Suetonius in English "would be almost unreadable" and therefore took certain liberties in translation. Grant has attempted to bring Graves's translation closer to the original "without, I hope, detracting from his excellent and inimitable manner," and he has succeeded. As one who first read the

Graves translation four decades ago and has often had occasion to return to it, I can detect no significant deviations in the revised version. Graves's translation as modified by Grant still makes Suetonius immensely readable and surprisingly modern.

The collaboration of Suetonius and Graves first came to my attention thanks to an essay about it by Vidal. Though written when the translation was first published, it did not appear in print until 1972, in Vidal's essay collection *Homage to Daniel Shays.* I studied Latin in high school and college, but to the best of my knowledge had never heard of Suetonius, much less read him. Vidal explains why: "The range of vices revealed [in *The Twelve Caesars*] was considerably beyond the imagination of even the most depraved schoolboy." Previous translations had omitted or bowdlerized the juicy stuff; Graves left it all in. To wit, Augustus:

> Not even his friends could deny that he often committed adultery, though of course they said, in justification, that he did so for reasons of state, not simple passion—he wanted to discover what his enemies were at by getting intimate with their wives or daughters. Mark Antony accused him not only of indecent haste in marrying Livia, but of hauling an ex-consul's wife from her husband's dining room into the bedroom—before his eyes, too! He brought the woman back, says Antony, blushing to the ears and with her hair in disorder.

Got your attention now? Well, keep reading. Suetonius tells us that "a racy letter of Antony's survives," in which he teases Augustus: "What has come over you? Do you object to my sleeping with Cleopatra? But we are married; and it is not even as though this were anything new—the affair started nine years ago. And what about you? Are you faithful to Livia Drusilla? My congratulations if, when this letter arrives, you have not been in bed with Tertullia, or Terentilla, or Rufilla, or Salvia Titisenia—or all of them. Does it really matter so much where, or with whom, you perform the sexual act?"

They sure didn't teach that in Latin 101, at least not back when I had my nose deep in "Gallia est omnis divisa in partes tres," "Arma virumque cano" and other chestnuts of the canon. So as soon as I read the Vidal essay I got my hands on Suetonius/Graves and gobbled up every word of it. Yes, things were beginning to loosen up in the early 1970s— *Lady Chatterley's Lover* was old hat by then, and *Deep Throat* was released in 1972—but still my eyes popped open when Suetonius got around to Gaius Caesar, better known as Caligula:

> He had not the slightest regard for chastity, either his own or others'. . . . [A] young man of consular family, Valerius Catullus, revealed publicly that he had buggered the Emperor, and quite worn himself out in the process. Besides incest with his sisters, and a notorious passion for the prostitute Pyrallis, he made advances to almost every woman of rank in Rome; after inviting a selection of them to dinner with their husbands, he would slowly and carefully examine each in turn while they passed his couch. . . . Then, whenever he felt so inclined, he would send for whoever pleased him best, and leave the banquet in her company. A little while later he would return, showing obvious signs of what he had been about, and openly discuss his bed-fellow in detail, dwelling on her good and bad physical points and commenting on her sexual performance.

Each of the Caesars had his sexual peculiarities, some of them decidedly outré. Yet Vidal is correct to say that they cannot be dismissed as "abnormal men." They were in fact "a fairly representative lot," with one important twist: "They differed from us—and their contemporaries—only in the fact of power, which made it possible for each to act out his most recondite sexual fantasies. This is the psychological fascination of Suetonius. What will men so placed do? The answer, apparently, is anything and everything."

Disbelievers are referred not just to Augustus and his serial adulteries and Caligula and his cruelties but also to the much married and much cuckolded Claudius (who said, wittily, that "he seemed fated to marry wives who 'were unchaste but remained unchastened'") and the appalling Nero, who "practiced every kind of obscenity, and after defiling almost every part of his body, finally invented a novel game: He was released from a cage dressed in the skins of wild animals, and attacked the private parts of men and women who stood bound to stakes."

The business is sex, but the real subject is power, and it is for his insights into power—or the insights his evidence permits the reader to draw—that Suetonius is most usefully read. Not merely does absolute power permit a person thus inclined to indulge any sexual fantasy no matter how perverted, to eat gluttonously and drink copiously; it also permits that person to treat other human beings as disposable commodities. The amount of casual violence reported by Suetonius is simply breathtaking, even to the modern reader hardened by the various outrages of the twentieth century, from Hitler and Stalin to Saddam Hussein and the Taliban.

Augustus, noted "for courage and clemency," belied that reputation over and over. "If a cohort [of his own army] broke in battle, Augustus ordered the survivors to draw lots, then executed every tenth man." When "one Polus, a favorite freedman, was convicted of adultery with Roman matrons, Augustus ordered him to commit suicide; and sentenced Thallus, an imperial secretary, to have his legs broken for divulging the contents of a letter."

Caligula went completely over the top. He "made parents attend their sons' executions, and when one father excused himself on the ground of ill health, provided a litter for him." The "method of execution he preferred was to inflict numerous small wounds; and his familiar order: 'Make him feel that he is dying!' soon became proverbial." He "frequently had tri-als by torture in his presence while he was eating or otherwise enjoying himself; and kept an expert headsman in readiness to decapitate the prisoners brought in from gaol."

Yet, the great irony is that these merchants of death them-selves lived in constant fear of betrayal and murder. This is remarked upon by both Grant and Vidal; the latter says that all twelve Caesars were possessed by "a fear of the knife in the dark." Suetonius provides ample evidence. The days of Tiberius "were clouded with danger and fear," dangers "that threatened him from many quarters, and often led him to declare that he was holding a wolf by the ears." Claudius "was so timid and suspicious that . . . he never attended a banquet unless with an escort of javelin-bearing guards." Domitian "claimed that the lot of all Emperors is necessarily wretched, since only their assassination can convince the public that the conspiracies against their lives are real."

Grant argues that their lives were wretched not just because they were forever looking over their shoulders but because they worked so hard. "The labors that a successful emperor found himself compelled to undertake were not only terrify-ingly responsible," he writes, "but enormously extensive, and never ending." Again, the evidence provided by Suetonius is impressive. Though the duties that the Caesars assumed var-ied—Julius and Augustus were vastly more dutiful than Caligula and Nero—no one could escape their weight. Caesars acted as judge and jury over legal matters both large and triv-ial; they marched off at the head of their armies to do battle as far away as Britannia and the Rhine; they built and rebuilt (in Nero's case, burned and rebuilt) Rome and its outskirts; they dealt daily with the Senate, which though mostly toothless was meddlesome and an eternal source of rivalry and conspiracy; they staged circuses for the Roman people and fed them bread. The buck, in sum, always stopped at them.

Grant also argues that the Caesars "performed the almost superhuman task of governing many millions of men and women over a gigantic area; and on the whole, with the aid of an efficient system, they governed well. . . . The most able of them, whatever their personal peculiarities, changed the course of history for the better, and demand our awed respect and admiration."

Vidal does not address this question so directly, but one infers a different view. "In terror of their lives, haunted by dreams and omens, giddy with dominion, it is no wonder that actual insanity was often the Caesarian refuge from a reality so intoxicating," he writes, and, a few paragraphs later, reflecting upon the differences between this country during the age of Eisenhower and Rome under the Caesars, he says that "though none can deny that there is a prevailing grayness in our placid land, it is certainly better to be non-ruled by mediocrities than enslaved by Caesars."

One rather suspects that were Vidal to reconsider that passage in light of the American presidency since Eisenhower, he would want to rewrite it, and not in a way congenial to the presidency. But that is neither here nor there. The real subject is power, its uses and abuses, and in Suetonius we find an incomparable guide, made wholly accessible to today's reader in Robert Graves's compelling translation.

LUCKY JIM
by Kingsley Amis

By the early 1950s, higher education and its rich comic possibilities had barely been touched by writers of fiction. Mary McCarthy's *The Groves of Academe* was published in 1952, but there was precious little else until 1954, when two books appeared that changed everything. On this side of the Atlantic, the well-known poet and critic Randall Jarrell published *Pictures From an Institution*. Almost simultaneously, in England, the completely unknown Kingsley Amis published *Lucky Jim*.

Its initial reception was enthusiastic over there, somewhat less so here. According to Amis's biographer Eric Jacobs, his American publisher "had made a money-back offer—if readers didn't find *Lucky Jim* uproariously funny their three dollars and fifty cents would be refunded," and "copies came back in shoals." That changed. *Lucky Jim* has been translated into twenty languages and has sold millions of copies around the world. It made Amis almost instantly famous and marked the beginning of one of the truly splendid careers in postwar British fiction.

When *Lucky Jim* appeared, Amis was in his early thirties and giving a good impression of going nowhere. He had been at Oxford and known a number of people who eventually played important roles in British literature, most notably his close friend Philip Larkin (to whom *Lucky Jim* is dedicated), but the best he could find by way of employment was a lectureship at the University College of Swansea in Wales, to which he went in 1949 on the exceedingly marginal salary of

300 pounds a year. It was in the senior common room there, though, that this ambitious but frustrated novelist found, at last, his subject. Jacobs describes it, quoting in part from Amis's memoirs:

> Back in that common room, Amis had seen something he had never seen before: "Professors and lecturers sitting, standing, talking, laughing, reading, drifting in and out, drinking coffee." And he thought: "Christ. Somebody ought to do something about this. Not that it was awful—well, only a bit, it was strange and sort of developed, a whole mode of existence no one had got on to, like the SS in 1940, say." He had stumbled on a whole new world of provincial university life which had never been explored or described by an English novelist. Here was a ready-made and virgin scene, ripe for a chronicler.

It found just the man it was looking for. Amis had written one novel, which a publisher had speedily rejected, and *Lucky Jim* didn't come quickly or easily. It went through considerable revision before reaching its final form. Amis relied heavily on Larkin's counsel as he sought, among other things, to reconcile the novel's comic and serious aspects. In the end, though, he came up with a nearly perfect miniature, and he entered the phrase *Lucky Jim* into the English language, a synonym for brains, bitterness, bumbling and bibulousness.

It is entirely appropriate that the Penguin 20th-Century Classics edition of Amis's small masterpiece includes an introduction by David Lodge, for it was Amis who opened the door through which Lodge and others soon passed. *Lucky Jim* was, as Lodge writes, "the first British campus novel," and it "certainly started something. . . . My own novels of university life, and those of Malcolm Bradbury, Howard Jacobson, Andrew Davies et al., are deeply indebted to its example." Though Lodge finds darker strains in *Lucky Jim* than are commonly acknowledged—he is right to do so—Amis's comic side was what liberated Lodge to write his own classics in the genre, *Small World* and *Changing Places*, and doubtless greatly influenced the best American writer now laboring therein, James Hynes, the author of *Publish and Perish*.

The serious aspects of the novel can be found in two parallel developments: Jim Dixon's struggle toward self-definition and his relationships with two women, the neurotic Margaret and the pneumatic Christine. Lodge points out that these matters take place against the background of World War II, which to Amis, Larkin and others of their Oxbridge generation was still a very real presence in the early 1950s. Dixon is marked by the war, as are a student named Michie and a fellow renter at Jim's boardinghouse, Bill Atkinson, an "insurance salesman and ex-Army major" whom Jim "liked and revered . . . for his air of detesting everything that presented itself to his senses, and of not meaning to let this detestation become staled by custom."

Atkinson is one of the novel's many superb secondary characters, and plays an important role as Jim attempts to extricate himself from one unwanted entanglement or another. It is Atkinson who stages an elaborate faint at the climax of Jim's drunken lecture on "Merrie England" before the assembled dignitaries of the new, provincial red-brick university where Jim has obtained—and is about to lose—a provisional lectureship in medieval history, and it is Atkinson who helps Jim work his way out of Margaret's frantic clutches and into Christine's warm embrace. Every time this gruff, plain-spoken man appears on the page, the reader immediately brightens.

The novel's serious side reminds us that Amis, like all the best comic novelists, is on hand to do more than just deliver laughs, but laughs were his main business, beginning with *Lucky Jim* and continuing through two dozen works of fiction, several volumes of verse and various volumes of nonfiction, including a memoir published four years before his death (at age seventy-three) in 1995, and two celebrations of drink.

Ah yes, drink. English comic novelists approach the subject with glee, from Evelyn Waugh to William Boyd. Amis was himself a champion as well as unapologetic tippler, and so too is Jim Dixon, who suffers one of the great hangovers in all literature after his sexual advances upon Margaret are rebuffed with sudden, wholly inexplicable, vigor. Already well filled with beer, he takes a great swig from a bottle of port—"The bottle had been about three-quarters full when he started, and was about three-quarters empty when he stopped"—and in the morning pays the piper:

> Dixon was alive again. Consciousness was upon him before he could get out of the way; not for him the slow, gracious wandering from the halls of sleep, but a summary, forcible ejection. He lay sprawled, too wicked to move, spewed up like a broken spider-crab on the tarry shingle of the morning. The light did him harm, but not as much as looking at things did; he resolved, having done it once, never to move his eyeballs again. A dusty thudding in his head made the scene before him beat like a pulse. His mouth had been used as a latrine by some small creature of the night, and then as its mausoleum. During the night, too, he'd somehow been on a cross-country run and then been expertly beaten up by secret police. He felt bad.

That paragraph comes as the high moment in a two-page display of pyrotechnics—"His face was heavy, as if little bags of sand had been painlessly sewn into various parts of it, dragging the features away from the bones, if he still had bones in his face"—in which Amis draws no doubt upon extensive personal experience. Forty or more years after reading this tour de force for the first time, I read it for a second—a third? a fourth?—with undiminished laughter. Amis's delight in what the world's killjoys insist on regarding as vice was bottomless, and he loved to rub the killjoys' faces in it.

Lucky Jim appeared at a time when the world was far less familiar than it is now with the strange customs and folkways of academia, so Amis seized the opportunity to shed light in dark corners. As the novel opens Jim has completed an article to be submitted for publication in an obscure scholarly journal, publication that he hopes will enhance his curriculum vitae and help ensure another year's employment. He has been urged to write it by Professor Welch ("No other professor in Great Britain, he thought, set such store by being called Professor"), whom an unkind fate has granted "decisive power over his future." Merely contemplating the paper's title causes him to cringe:

> It was a perfect title, in that it crystallized the article's niggling mindlessness, its funereal parade of yawn-enforcing facts, the pseudo-light it threw upon non-problems. Dixon had read, or begun to read, dozens like it, but his own seemed worse than most in its air of being convinced of its own usefulness and significance. "In considering this strangely neglected topic," it began. This what neglected topic? This strangely what topic? This strangely neglected what? His thinking all this without having defiled and set fire to the typescript only made him appear to himself as more of a hypocrite and fool. "Let's see," he echoed Welch in a pretended effort of memory: "oh yes; The Economic Influence of the Developments in Shipbuilding Techniques, 1450 to 1485. After all, that's what it's . . ."

Dixon is "unable to finish his sentence," so appalled is he by his willing complicity in the mindlessness of academia at its worst. Today all of us can cite chapter and verse, mainly just by turning to the program of the annual convention of the Modern Language Association, and indeed some of us—mea culpa—cannot resist the temptation to do so. A half-century ago, though, Amis was writing about a little world about which most people knew nothing, and his depiction of it was received with astonishment and hilarity.

Remarkably, *Lucky Jim* is as fresh and surprising today as it was in 1954. It is part of the landscape, and it defines academia in the eyes of much of the world as does no other book, yet if you are coming to it for the first time you will feel, as you glide happily through its pages, that you are traveling in a place where no one else has ever been. If you haven't yet done so, you must.

THE DREADFUL LEMON SKY
by John D. MacDonald

For my money, John D. MacDonald's Travis McGee is one of the great characters in contemporary American fiction—not crime fiction; fiction, period—and millions of readers surely agree. Most of the other crime novels that MacDonald wrote over his long and astonishingly prolific career have been consigned to out-of-print oblivion—in many cases most undeservedly so—but the Travis McGee series rolls along, keeping MacDonald's memory alive and reminding us that he was a far more accomplished and important novelist than is generally recognized.

McGee was born in the early 1960s. MacDonald, then in his mid-forties, had built a substantial following for the crime novels he published in paperback originals and the short stories he published in pulp magazines, but that following was limited largely to readers of genre fiction. Then, in 1962, he somewhat reluctantly agreed to start work on a series built around a single character. The first, *The Deep Blue Goodbye,* appeared in 1964. It was followed by twenty others, the last of which, *The Lonely Silver Rain,* was published in 1985, a year before MacDonald's death.

McGee is owner of the "Busted Flush, a fifty-two foot barge-type houseboat, Slip F-18, Bahia Mar, Lauderdale." He's a World War II veteran, six feet four inches tall, solidly built. He isn't "exactly a clerical type," in the words of one of the many women for whom he does important favors: "You are huge and it is obvious you have been whacked upon, and you look as though you damn well enjoyed returning the favor." He's catnip for the ladies, but he is by his own admission "an incurable romantic who thinks the man-woman thing shouldn't be a contest."

The subject of this Second Reading could be any of the McGee novels, but I've chosen *The Dreadful Lemon Sky* because it was the first that I read. In 1976 I was the book editor of the *Miami Herald*, living and working across Florida from MacDonald's home on Siesta Key. He was about to publish *Condominium*, his first hardcover, non-genre novel, which had been chosen as a main selection of the Book-of-the-Month Club, and I had been commissioned by the club to write a brief piece about him for its newsletter.

This entailed a hurry-up course in MacDonald's fiction, which I'd never read. I mainlined a couple dozen of his novels, from early mysteries to McGees to *Condominium* itself. I was bowled over. This man whom I'd snobbishly dismissed as a paperback writer turned out to be a novelist of the highest professionalism and a social critic armed with vigorous opinions stingingly expressed. His prose had energy, wit and bite, his plots were humdingers, his characters talked like real people, and his knowledge of the contemporary world was—no other word will do—breathtaking.

MacDonald himself turned out, when I interviewed him in his comfortable, unpretentious house, to be a large, calm, genial, quiet yet talkative man: a gentleman. By then he had established himself, as I wrote in a profile of him for the *Herald*'s Sunday magazine, as "the pre-eminent 'Florida novelist,'" a distinction earned by remarkably close observation of the state: its grifters and operators and big-bucks crooks, its decent ordinary people, its overdeveloped land and polluted water. He had harsh things to say about Florida in *Condominium* and many of his other books. When I asked him about this he said: "I've always recognized that Florida is a slightly tacky state," and added, "You love it in spite of itself."

Close questioning revealed not merely that he had a complex love-hate relationship with his adopted state (he was born, in 1916, in Pennsylvania) but that he was a constant reader with high standards. He thought some genre novelists were taken too seriously, just as Thomas Pynchon was ("One is overvalued because the critic finds some elements of literacy in it, the other because he can't understand it"), and he was a tough critic who expected others' prose to have "felicity, an element of aptness." One passage from my tapes deserves full quotation:

> I just cannot read people like Leon Uris and James Michener. When you've covered one line, you can guess the next one. I like people who know the nuances of words, who know how to stick the right one in the right place. Sometimes you can laugh out loud at an exceptionally good phrase. I find it harder and harder to find fiction to read, because I either read it with dismay at how good it is or disgust at how bad it is. I do like the guys like John Cheever that have a sense of story, because, goddammit, you want to know what happens to somebody. You don't want a lot of self-conscious little logjams thrown in your way.

So, you quite properly ask, how well did MacDonald meet the standards he set for others? Very well indeed. *The Dreadful Lemon Sky* proves the point. McGee has been taking his ease in the Busted Flush when a woman steps aboard the boat at four in the morning. He had a one-night stand with her a few years ago, now sees that the "years had aged her more than she could reasonably expect and had tested and toughened her." She presses a package upon him and asks him to safeguard it; inside is nearly $95,000. Two weeks later she is killed by a truck outside a town up the Atlantic coast. "Knight-errant" that he is, McGee goes there to have a look:

> It was easy to see the shape and history of Bayside, Florida. There had been a little town on the bay shore, a few hundred people, a sleepy downtown with live oaks and Spanish moss. Then

International Amalgamated Development had moved in, bought a couple of thousand acres, and put in shopping centers, town houses, condominiums, and rental apartments, just south of town. Next had arrived Consolidated Construction Enterprises and done the same thing north of town. Smaller operators had done the same things on a smaller scale west of town. When downtown decayed, the town fathers widened the streets and cut down the shade trees in an attempt to look just like a shopping center. It didn't work. It never does. This was instant Florida, tacky and stifling and full of ugly and spurious energies. They had every chain food-service outfit known to man, interspersed with used-car lots and furniture stores.

There you have it: sharp, seamless prose, bull's-eye aim, romanticism and cynicism playing subtly off each other. The writer is MacDonald but the speaker is McGee, who is the narrator of all the novels in the series. The relationship between McGee and his creator is intimate, fascinating and a bit difficult to unravel. MacDonald doesn't seem to be projecting when he makes McGee a tender, accomplished Casanova, or when he gets McGee out of big trouble with astonishing feats of physical strength and resourcefulness; MacDonald himself seems to have been a one-woman man, happily married for nearly a half-century, and much of the violence in his novels is depicted with tongue in cheek, stylized and exaggerated.

There can be no doubt, though, that McGee speaks for MacDonald. That was made plain right off the bat in *The Deep Blue Goodbye*, when McGee introduced himself by ticking off his aversions: "credit cards, payroll deductions, insurance programs, retirement benefits, savings accounts, Green Stamps, time clocks, newspapers, mortgages, sermons, miracle fabrics, deodorants, check lists, time payments, political parties, lending libraries, television, actresses, junior chambers of commerce, pageants, progress and manifest destiny." As enemies lists go, that one is fine. But just to make things interesting, MacDonald has another voice in the McGee novels: McGee's

friend and occasional sidekick Meyer, "a semiretired economist
. . . the listening ear of a total understanding and forgiveness, a
humble wisdom." Humble, yes, but tart as well. Here—yes, one
more juicy quote—he reports to McGee after reconnoitering a
singles' apartment complex in Bayside:

> There's a kind of . . . watchful anxiety about those people. It's as
> if they're all in spring training, trying out for the team, all trying
> to hit the long ball, trying to be a star. . . . Pools and saunas and a
> gym. Four-channel sound systems. Health fads. Copper bracelets.
> *The Joy of Sex* on each and every coffee table, I would guess.
> Waterbeds, biofeedback machines. There doesn't seem to be any
> kind of murky kinky flavor about them. No group perversion
> scenes. Just a terrible urgency about finding and maintaining an
> orgasm batting average acceptable to the peer group.

Bingo. As one who quite inadvertently spent a good deal of
time in a couple of those places in Miami in the mid-seventies I
can testify that Meyer/MacDonald has hit the game-winner.
Every detail and every nuance in that passage is exactly right.
But MacDonald always got it right. He was endlessly curious,
and it didn't hurt that he'd been to Harvard Business School.
Unlike most American novelists, he knew about the real world
and viewed it with interest, with dismay perhaps, but only rarely
with contempt. He had an eye that saw everything and a memory that soaked it all up. To flesh out *The Dreadful Lemon Sky*
he had to familiarize himself with marina management, plane-
tary movement, the marijuana trade, the specs of a Beechcraft
Baron airplane, biofeedback and strategy for lane changes in
traffic—to mention only a few.

The abundance of keenly observed detail gives the McGee
series its texture, but McGee himself is the rock at its center. He
does what he calls "salvage work," described in *The Deep Blue
Goodbye* by one of his lady friends: ". . . if X has something
valuable and Y comes along and takes it away from him, and

there is absolutely no way in the world X can ever get it back, then you come in and make a deal with X to get it back, and keep half. Then you just . . . live on that until it starts to run out." As McGee says in *The Dreadful Lemon Sky*, he believes that "retirement comes when you are too old to enjoy it, so I take some of mine whenever I can," living at ease on the take from one piece of "salvage" until his funds run low and it's time to go back to work.

MacDonald concluded, after collecting a baker's dozen of his early stories (*The Good Old Stuff,* 1982) that "a precursor of Travis McGee" is to be found in Park Falkner, the protagonist of a couple he published in 1950. Perhaps so. But MacDonald refined and deepened the character; indeed about the only resemblance between the two is that each fancies himself a force for justice in a world where there's far too little of it. There's a whiff of meanness in Falkner that is nowhere to be found in McGee, who is out to do good, in his own quixotic fashion, and he does a bunch of it.

The second time around for *The Dreadful Lemon Sky*? Pure joy. Justice is done, blunt opinions are expressed, a lady or two is made happy, and the Busted Flush still floats. If you're new to McGee and wonder where to begin, any place will do, but there's a lot to be said for starting with *The Deep Blue Goodbye* and reading the books in order of publication. That way you can watch as they get better and better. You might like to know, too, that the titles are color-coded to help you tell them apart: turquoise, lavender, orange, tan, crimson, pink, purple, gold, etc. Florida colors, for the best "Florida novels" you'll ever read.

The Woman Within
by Ellen Glasgow

The court of literary opinion is no more fair or just than the court of public opinion. Writers of limited gifts and accomplishments (Ernest Hemingway, Carson McCullers, John Steinbeck) are overpraised and over-rewarded, while others of great gifts and singular accomplishments (William Humphrey, Dawn Powell, Jerome Charyn) are ignored or misunderstood. This of course is true in other endeavors, but somehow it seems especially unjust that writing, the best of which is supposed to stand the ages, so often produces such small recognition for those who do it so well.

My own list of unjustly overlooked and underrated writers is long; it includes, in addition to those mentioned above, John P. Marquand, Thomas Savage, Roxana Robinson, Harold Frederic, Elizabeth Spencer, John Oliver Killens and, at or very near the top, Ellen Glasgow. Born in 1873 to a genteel and modestly prosperous Richmond family, she published some two dozen books before her death in 1945, nineteen of which are novels. For a while during the 1920s and 1930s she enjoyed brisk sales, and in 1942 she was awarded a Pulitzer Prize for *In This Our Life,* but as is all too typical of Pulitzers in fiction, it came too late and was for a relatively minor work. Now only a handful of her novels are in print and her name rarely surfaces in discussions of American literature.

This seems more than a little odd when one considers that feminist critics and academics have made cottage industries out of other writers (Kate Chopin, Zora Neale Hurston, Sarah Orne Jewett) whose accomplishments are far more slender than Glasgow's. She was a relatively privileged white Southerner (though so was Chopin), and her principal métier (though scarcely her only one) was the novel of manners. Literary opinion in this country tends to dismiss the upper classes as irrelevant and to be suspicious of the novel of manners for the same reason. The contemporary with whom Glasgow is often compared, Willa Cather, was victim to neither of these prejudices, which may in some measure explain why her work is still admired while Glasgow's is neglected.

Glasgow (the name gives it all away) was Scottish by ancestry, and proud of it. She was Virginian, too, and proud of that as well, but in this case her pride was tempered by an utter absence of sentimentality. "She began as the most girlish of Southern romantics," Alfred Kazin wrote in *Native Ground,* published in 1942, "and later proved the most biting critic of Southern romanticism; she was at once the most traditional in loyalty to Virginia and its most powerful satirist; the most sympathetic historian of the Southern mind in modern times and a consistent satirist of that mind." The neglect now visited upon her could be explained if her work defended the Lost Cause or if her prose was old-fashioned and stilted, but neither is true; she despised the Old South mythology, and her prose is an absolute joy to read. Her chief subject is the conflict between Ol' Dixie and the rising industrial world, and she was unsparing in her criticism of the South's tendency to sentimentalize itself and its past.

For the reader who doesn't know her work, probably the logical place to start is *Barren Ground* or *The Sheltered Life,* but at a time in our literary history when memoir is all the rage, perhaps it is *The Woman Within.* Written off and on between 1934 and 1943, it was sealed in Glasgow's safe-deposit box in Richmond, preceded by a note "To My Literary Executors" that read, in part: "This rough draft is the original and only copy of my autobiography. It was written in great suffering of mind and body, and the work is as true to actual experience as I have been able to make the written word. . . . I was writing for my own release of mind and heart; and I have tried to make a completely honest portrayal of an interior world, and of that one world alone."

The manuscript was opened by Glasgow's literary executors after death in 1945 and they seem to have decided almost immediately that it had to be published—not to make money, since Glasgow had no direct descendants—but because it is "a narrative of quite extraordinary human interest." They meant not "human interest" as in a journalistic sob story, but as an exploration of the inner depths of one human heart and soul to which other humans could connect. Publication was not hasty—the book appeared in 1954—and it has remained in print off and on in the ensuing half-century, now in a paper-back from the University of Virginia Press.

This is appropriate, since the manuscript of the memoir, along with the rest of Glasgow's papers, is stored at that university's library, but it is also ironic, since Glasgow was perhaps Virginia's most astringent critic, almost certainly its most astringent native-born critic. She did love Richmond and lived in her parents' house on West Main Street all her adult life, but she saw with utter clarity the "sanctified fallacies" that Richmond and Virginia embraced. To quote Kazin again, Virginia's was "a society living perpetually in the shadow of the Civil War, a society curiously lacking in the sense of time, but oppressively fanatical when dealing with contemporary problems; obsessed by principle, but living on pluck; dedicated to 'culture' and . . . suspicious of ideas other than its own."

Here is how Glasgow herself puts it, in a passage from *The Woman Within* about an apprentice work, "Sharp Realities," that eventually she burned but that pointed her in the direction she was fated to go:

> My revolt from the philosophy of evasive idealism was seeking an outlet. I hated—I had always hated—the inherent falseness in much Southern tradition, and "Sharp Realities" was an indignant departure from the whole sentimental fallacy, not only in the South, but all over America. Those critics who classify me as "beginning in the local color school" can have read none of my earliest novels. On the contrary, my native impulse, as well as my later theories of the novel as a mirror of life, sprang directly from my dislike for what I called "little vessels of experience." Never, at any time, have little ways and means of thinking made a particular appeal to me. If I prefer fine workmanship and delicate embroideries of style, I demand that both material and pattern shall be ample in form and richly varied in texture.

She was an unlikely rebel and an unlikely realist novelist. Not merely was she in, or close to, Richmond's upper crust, she was frail, secretive, afflicted with "morbid shyness," yet even as a child she was "a social rebel." Surrounded by the wealthy and the powerful, she found herself drawn to the poor and the powerless; as a very small girl she "began to think, or to feel, that cruelty is the only sin." She was, in her parents' populous household, "the only dissenter from orthodox Christianity, and the only rebel against the Calvinist conscience."

Glasgow was deeply unhappy for much of her life. Her father was honest, decent, icily cold, rigid: "Not once in my knowledge of him had he ever changed his mind or admitted that he was wrong—or even mistaken." She adored her mother without reservation—she "was the center of my childhood's world, the sun in my universe"—but when Ellen was still young her mother "suffered the long anguish of a nervous illness." The result was that this emotionally starved girl often had nowhere to turn for succor except an older sister who was only occasionally available. Yet she "was not disposed, by temperament, to self-pity," and she was blessed with a "sardonic spirit which mocked incessantly: 'I will not be defeated! I will not look defeated!'"

A further result, of course, was that she retreated into her inner world and made a universe out of it. She became a writer, at the age of seven. She presented a lively facade to family and friends, but she was developing a real life "in the remote, hidden country of the mind" where she "ranged, free and wild, and a rebel." This passage about her early writing must be quoted at length:

> ... I wrote always in secret, but I wrote ceaselessly in dim corners, under beds, or, in the blessed summer days, under the deep shrubbery and beneath low-hanging boughs. Until my first book was finished no one, except my mother, who suspected but did not speak of it, was aware that, below the animated surface, I was already immersed in some dark stream of identity, stronger and deeper and more relentless than the external movement of living. It was not that I had so early found my vocation. At the age of seven my vocation had found me. The one permanent interest, the single core of unity at the center of my nature, was beginning to shape itself, and to harden. I was born a novelist, though I formed myself into an artist. Looking back on my life I can see that a solitary pattern has run through it, from earliest childhood. Always I have had to learn for myself, from within. Always I have persevered in the face of an immense disadvantage—in the face of illness, of partial deafness, which came later, of the necessity to blaze my own trail through the wilderness that was ignorance. To teach one's self is to be forced to learn twice. Yet, no doubt it is true, as my friends assure me, that when one hews out from rock a philosophy or an understanding, it stays fast in the mind. Only a hunger and thirst for knowledge can bring perseverance.

Glasgow went about the business of becoming a novelist with incredible single-mindedness. She was literally self-taught. Deliberately, she sought "a steady control over my ideas and my material," a "style that was balanced yet supple, a style that was touched with beauty and yet tinctured with irony," and she was always "faithful to my resolve that I would write of the universal, not of the provincial, in human nature, that I would write of characters, not of characteristics." Though "it is true that I was a born novelist, it is true also that I flung myself into my work as desperately as a man might fling himself into a hopeless battle."

This, as much as an indifference to "physical instincts" and the deafness that made conversation difficult, probably explains why she never married. She once "fell in love at first sight" with a man whom she calls Gerald B., but he was older, married and a father. For seven years, "I lived in an arrested pause between dreaming and waking," seeing him only infrequently, and then he died: "After those years, I felt love again, but never again could I feel ecstasy, never again the rush of wings in my heart. Several times I was in love with love. Twice I was engaged to be married. Always, when my senses were deeply stirred, some ghost of recollection would float between me and perfect fulfillment."

She implies that this "romantic passion" was never consummated, that "it is a law of nature that the memory of longing should survive the more fugitive memory of fulfillment." That is a keen observation, but one can only hope she found some fulfillment along with all that longing.

I first read *The Woman Within* about two decades ago, when I swallowed Glasgow's books one after another. A spree like that is fun while it lasts, but after it's over the books tend to dissolve into a blur. Read a second time, with greater care and with notepad close at hand, *The Woman Within* seems to me even better than it did at first: a classic of American autobiography and a penetrating examination of a born writer's inner life. What I have said about it here only hints at its richness, depth and implacable honesty. Read it and you surely will want to move along to Glasgow's novels, and if enough of you do, perhaps she will get the readership she so plainly deserves.

TOM JONES
by Henry Fielding

Henry Fielding's *Tom Jones* is a classic of British literature, not merely in its own right but for the incalculable influence it has had in England, the United States and wherever else English is written and read. Published in 1749 as *The History of Tom Jones, a Foundling,* it was one of the first English works of prose that we now call novels. Though it caused scandal and sensation, it soon was recognized as a masterpiece, and remains one to this day.

All of which is well and good, but when a book is as old as this one, the question inevitably arises: How accessible is it to today's reader? Is the masterpiece also a period piece, or does it offer to the contemporary reader as much pleasure and enrichment as it did to the reader of 1749?

The short answer: Yes, it does. So at least my own second reading tells me, but it is "yes" with qualifications. Though *Tom Jones* is surprisingly modern in many ways, it seems quaint by contrast with books by authors who profited from Fielding's example, from Charles Dickens to Mark Twain to Saul Bellow. Though Fielding invented both a narrative technique and a genre—or, more accurately, he transplanted the picaresque as invented by Miguel de Cervantes in *Don Quixote* from Spain to England—his methods sometimes seem rather primitive today. To enjoy *Tom Jones* to the full, one must make every effort to read it with eighteenth-century eyes.

For starters, try to imagine the shock and delight with which England greeted this tale of an abandoned bastard "who was certainly born to be hanged." Samuel Johnson, not commonly known as a prude, wrote to a lady friend: "I am shocked to hear you quote from so vicious a book . . . I scarcely know a more corrupt work." According to R.P.C. Mutter's introduction to the Penguin Classics edition, in the spring of 1750, when "London experienced two earthquake shocks, there were also those who asserted, with varying degrees of sincerity, that 'Tom Jones' was in some way responsible." Offense was taken at Fielding's candid, ribald treatment of sexual manners, his sly innuendos and double-entendres, and more deeply at his view that amatory activity between consenting adults without benefit of marital vows is unobjectionable and perhaps even commendable.

"Lookee, Mr. Nightingale," Tom says to a friend, "I am no canting hypocrite, nor do I pretend to the gift of chastity, more than my neighbours. I have been guilty with women, I own it; but I am not conscious that I have ever injured any—nor would I, to procure pleasure to myself, be knowingly the cause of misery to any human being." That may seem unexceptionable to today's reader, but eighteenth-century England was a cesspool of hypocrisy where sex was concerned, so it gasped in astonishment—and then, of course, it laughed heartily and often, for *Tom Jones* is an irrepressibly funny book.

Fielding was forty-one years old when it was published. He had written for the theater with some success until a crude attempt at censorship ended that career. He went on to become a lawyer, but writing was his calling. In 1741 he published *Shamela,* a satire of Samuel Richardson's *Pamela,* and followed it with *Joseph Andrews* in 1742. In 1744 he experienced an intolerable loss with the death of his beloved wife, but she served as inspiration for the incandescent Sophia Western in *Tom Jones,* which he began to write a couple of years later. Fielding suffered terribly from gout, but soldiered on as writer and jurist, working heroically to reduce crime and strengthen the police. He died in 1754 at the age of forty-seven.

So much has been written about *Tom Jones* that it would be pointless to subject it to lit-crit analysis. Instead my hope is to give some sense of what the novel feels like, and to suggest how a twenty-first-century reader can approach it. My suspicion is that *Tom Jones* is one of those massive literary edifices that most people have not entered. If you are one of these, I hope to persuade you to have a go at it.

My own first reading of *Tom Jones* took place sometime within the past forty years, perhaps after I saw Tony Richardson's spectacular 1963 film adaptation. I remember little about my response to it, beyond laughing a great deal, falling in love with Sophy Western, delighting in the names Fielding had invented ("the reverend Mr. Thwackum," Jemmy Tweedle, Nan Slouch, Esther Codling, Goody Brown), and following its tangled plot with astonishment.

One of the pleasures of having a sieve for a memory is that my second reading of a book is almost as fresh as my first. So I was just as surprised this time as I was many years ago when, in his preface to Book Two of the novel, Fielding makes the bold declaration that "I am, in reality, the founder of a new province of writing, so I am at liberty to make whatever laws I please therein." It is surprising to today's reader to find a novelist speaking within his text about his methods, but the real surprise is to grasp, two and a half centuries later, that Fielding knew exactly what he was doing. He was indeed making something new, a work of prose fiction that "my readers, whom I consider as my subjects, are bound to believe in and to obey."

What seems familiar to us today was something no one had read in English before 1749. That doubtless helps explain why Fielding felt it necessary to begin each of the novel's eighteen books with an explanatory preface. The reader who finds these boring or intrusive can skip them without much loss, just as the reader can skip the endless digressions in *War and Peace.* Mutter says that one critic called the film adaptation "Fielding without the waffle," and it was to these prefaces that the critic referred. Eighteenth-century readers may have needed them as guideposts to this new territory they had entered, but today's readers do not.

Concentrate instead on the characters, the humor, the labyrinthine plot and the deep moral conviction that is at the novel's core. First of course there is Tom, "a thoughtless, giddy youth, with little sobriety in his manners," who has, as his benefactor Squire Allworthy tells him, "much goodness, generosity and honor in your temper; if you will add prudence and religion to these, you must be happy." There is Sophia, who, "with all the gentleness which a woman can have, had all the spirit which she ought to have." There is the repellent Master Blifil, "sober, discreet and pious," the embodiment of hypocrisy, "capable of the basest and blackest designs," determined to scheme Tom out of his inheritance. There are the smug tutors Thwackum and Square, the lusty Molly Seagrim (and, far later in the tale, the lusty Lady Bellaston) and others too numerous to mention.

Above all there is Sophia's father, Squire Western, "a country booby" who "had not the least command over any of his passions; and that which had at any time the ascendant in his mind, hurried him to the wildest excesses." Chief among his passions are Sophia, food, drink and the hunt, though that may be in reverse order. Chasing after Sophia, who has fled his house rather than marry the odious Blifil, he complains bitterly: "Pogh! D—n the slut. I am lamenting the loss of so fine a morning for hunting." Fielding drops bons mots left and right. Blifil's father he sizes up as "one of those wise men, who . . . choose to possess every convenience of life with an ugly woman, than a handsome one without any of those conveniences." A wealthy spinster is "neither young enough nor handsome enough, to attract much wicked inclination; but she had matrimonial charms in great abundance." Mr. Dowling "had not divested himself of humanity by being an attorney," indeed "an attorney may feel all the miseries and distresses of his fellow creatures, provided he happens not to be concerned against them." Then there is one country gentleman "desiring another to kiss your a— for having just before threatened to kick his," about which Fielding observes that "no one ever desires you to kick that which belongs to himself, nor offers to kiss this part in another," and continues:

> It may likewise seem surprising, that in the many thousand kind invitations of this sort, which everyone who hath conversed with country gentlemen must have heard, no one, I believe, hath ever seen a single instance where the desire hath been complied with. A great instance of their want of politeness: for in town, nothing can be more common than for the finest gentlemen to perform this ceremony every day to their superiors, without having that favour once requested of them.

For today's reader, that brief paragraph encapsulates several aspects of this extraordinary book: its humor, which can be earthy and ribald and sly; its modernity, since the behavior in question is a fine art among ladies and gentlemen of today's town and city; its somewhat antiquated but entirely accessible language; and its deep revulsion at hypocrisy. As a traveler remarks to Tom, all over the world one encounters "the same hypocrisy, the same fraud; in short, the same follies and vices, dressed in different habits."

Yet if Fielding is merciless in his exposure of hypocrites, quacks, poseurs, opportunists, social climbers and schemers— every bit as merciless as William Makepeace Thackeray was a century later in *Vanity Fair*—at its heart *Tom Jones* is a romance, a celebration of innocence and virtue. Tom and Sophy, who possess both in abundance, are rewarded by overcoming all the obstacles Fielding throws their way and end up in each other's arms. Not merely is it a happy ending, it is an apt one, for both are given exactly what they deserve.

Tom Jones is a long book—more than 800 pages—and it took me a long time to read it. For one who has neither the time nor the inclination, there is an alternative. Though Richardson's film adaptation necessarily drops a number of secondary characters and subplots, lapses at moments into nudge-nudge, wink-wink smirking, and turns Tom's reprieve from the gallows into something quite different from Fielding's original, it captures much of the essence of the book in a mere two hours. It conveys the beauty and poverty of the countryside, the elegance and squalor of London, and the inane cruelty of the hunt; the musical score by John Addison is as witty as the novel itself; John Osborne's screenplay is a marvel.

Best of all are the actors. Albert Finney and Susannah York are lovely and engaging as Tom and Sophy, but the secondary characters are the real stars, in particular David Warner as a deliciously slimy Blifil, Peter Bull as the bloated Thwackum, Joan Greenwood as the vulpine Lady Bellaston and—ta-da!—Hugh Griffith as Squire Western. The last is a comic masterpiece. Wallowing in the haystack with whatever lass presents herself, drowning in vast oceans of strong drink, gnawing ferociously at gigantic chunks of meat, bellowing at his pigs, chickens and dogs—Griffith is Squire Western right down to the toenail. Fielding would have loved him.

PAPER TIGER
by Stanley Woodward

S tanley Woodward stood six feet three inches tall, weighed
225 pounds and was strong as the proverbial ox. He loved
sports but was injured repeatedly and had exceedingly
bad eyesight, so he had to quit long before he was ready. He
found a substitute. After World War I he got into journalism
and in the 1930s went to the *New York Herald Tribune*, where
he soon became "the best sports editor in the *Tribune*'s, or
probably any paper's, history."

That is the judgment of Richard Kluger, as expressed in
his monumental *The Paper: The Life and Death of the New
York Herald Tribune*. Today, more than four decades after
Woodward's death, it is a view near-universally held in the inner
circles of sports journalism. During his two stints at the Trib,
from 1930 to 1948 and 1959 to 1962, Kluger writes, its "sports
pages achieved an unmatched level of pungent literacy," the full
credit for which rested with Woodward. According to Frank
Graham Jr., one of the many gifted writers who worked with
him, he had "high standards and unfailing courage," including
the courage to speak his mind to bosses who didn't always like
what he said.

He was "direct, blunt, uncompromising and honest." That
is the testimony of the best writer to grace his or anyone else's
sports pages, Walter Wellesley "Red" Smith, whom Woodward
rescued from inexplicable obscurity at the *Philadelphia Record*
in 1945 and who quickly became a star of incomparable bril-
liance. Woodward said Smith "was a complete newspaper man"

who "had been through the mill and had come out with a high polish." Woodward was baffled that no other New York paper had "grabbed him," but thought he knew the reason: ". . . most writing sports editors don't want a man around who is obviously better than they. I took the opposite view on this question. I wanted no writer on the staff who couldn't beat me or at least compete with me. This was a question of policy."

That is how Woodward put it in *Paper Tiger,* a memoir first published shortly before his death in 1964. Journalism has produced surprisingly few good memoirs, perhaps because journalists tend to be reactive rather than reflective, perhaps because they are so accustomed to protecting their sources that when the opportunity arises to spill the beans, they instinctively recoil. *Paper Tiger* is the exception: candid and uncompromising, like its author, but also engaging and funny—at times uproariously so.

My copy of *Paper Tiger* is a first edition, so I assume that I read it as soon as it came out. I was living in New York then, playing out my short string at the Times, reading the Trib with admiration and envy. Woodward had retired to "a little house in the woods in Connecticut" in 1962, but his influence was still pervasive on the Trib's sports pages and his legend flourished at the health clubs where journalists gathered: the bar of the Dixie Hotel, favorite of Times people, and Bleeck's, the Trib's hangout.

I loved *Paper Tiger* then and love it now, four full decades later. It's not a period piece but a hymn to newspapering, the saga of a young man's rise from paper to paper, job to job, until he reaches the very top and then pushes the ceiling far higher than anyone before him ever had. It's a vivid portrait of newsrooms in a day long since vanished—a day of whiskey bottles in desk drawers and file cabinets, of green eyeshades and galluses, of manual typewriters and pneumatic tubes, of two-day train rides and club-car poker games, of copy boys and Western

Union—and of New York in the 1930s and forties. That era was pretty much gone by the time I got to New York, but reading *Paper Tiger* makes me ache for it all over again.

Woodward was born in 1895 in the industrial city of Worcester, Massachusetts, into comfortable but hardly privileged circumstances. He went to Amherst, which "had barely four hundred students and . . . was somewhat scrubby especially in the dead of winter." He played football—at the end of his four years "I had to have five major operations to correct the aftereffects"—but he became an astute student of the game. Football is very different now, almost incalculably more complicated, but the passages in *Paper Tiger* about formations and strategy have as much authority as when they were written.

His poor eyesight kept him out of military service during World War I, but Woodward managed to sign on with the merchant marine, which took him to "all the ports of France between Le Havre and Bordeaux," taught him "to splice and to tie a rolling hitch and a bowline-in-a-bight," and left him longing for sea duty at war's end. But his mother had liked the letters he'd written from overseas and finagled a position for him on the *Worcester Gazette*. He never looked back: "Never, from that time until I retired on April 1, 1962, was I willfully out of the newspaper business." He came under the tutelage of a city editor named Nick Skerrett whose "credo" was right out of "Front Page": "A man who gets what he is sent for is a reporter. A man who gets what he is sent for and something more is a good reporter. A man who does not get what he is sent for is a goddamned nuisance and will be fired."

It was what would now be called a learning experience: "My indoctrination into the newspaper business was based on terror." Woodward "covered everything on the paper including courts and city hall," and got to know sides of Worcester he'd never seen: "murders, robberies, strikes, symphony concerts, crap games, court trials, politics, and society." He interviewed a young touring musician named Jascha Heifetz, who couldn't remember the titles of any of the encores he'd played, and "covered labor for a year and discovered for the first time that capital is not always right."

Next stop: Boston. In 1922 he "accepted a job at fifty-five dollars a week as copyreader and make-up man on the *Herald* sports staff" and stayed at the paper for eight years, including a stint on the city staff. The reader fortunate enough to find a copy of *Paper Tiger* doubtless will agree that the highlight of this period, perhaps of the entire book, is his assignment to cover the Harvard-Yale crew race in Connecticut. His editor "believed in mobbing a good assignment when he had the men available," and in this instance decided that Woodward would be a one-man mob going up against the six sent to New London by the *Globe*. He was expected to fill an entire eight-column page with the help only of a green assistant named Steele Lindsay:

> I planned to do my big story in my room, banishing Lindsay to the Western Union office to write some kind of a lead note. [The hotel manager] was providing me with an off-duty bellhop for my special assistant. His duties would be simple but important. Each time I finished two pages he was to run them to the Western Union office. On his return to the room he was to mix me a two-ounce Tom Collins. Sugar, lemons, gin, a knife, a spoon, a high glass, and a bucket of ice already were set up. The ice would need replacement on race day.

Fueled by gin and youthful ambition, Woodward smashed the *Globe*, though at one point his copy read, "As the leading eight went by the ketch Comanche her Yale complement swarmed up her rigging like lascars on an X-E-B-E-C." His editor was thrilled—"Beat *Globe* hollow," his telegram declared—and before long Woodward was too big for Boston, so on it was to New York City: the Big Apple, the red-hot center of the known newspaper universe.

He reported to the *Herald Tribune* sports department in September 1930. The paper's character had largely been shaped by another legendary Stanley—the city editor Stanley Walker—and Woodward found it much to his liking. It was "a lively place and a really good newspaper, even though much of its business was carried on in a gin mill." He covered just about everything—he had a particular fondness for the manager of the Brooklyn Dodgers, Casey Stengel, who sometimes left a note in his hotel mailbox, "Mr. Stengel is pouring in room 806"—and in 1938 was made sports editor, a job "I held, with two years out for war correspondence, until 1948." He came to the job with assumptions that show how much the sporting world has changed in the intervening decades:

> My own theory was that there are four sports which are of paramount importance to a newspaper: baseball, horse-racing, boxing, and football. Other sports rose to prominence on occasion and faded to nothing when they were out of their active period. This could be said of tennis, golf, and yachting. There are some sports that are of comparatively little interest to the readers but are important to the paper because of their advertising connections. Among these are skiing, again yachting, horse and dog shows.

Basketball? Hockey? Small beer in what Woodward quickly turned into the best sports section around as he brought in one ace writer after another. A jealous competitor moaned: "Holy smokes! Those guys will be hiring Thomas A. Edison to turn off the lights." For a while after World War II the whole paper was on a roll—"The Sunday *Herald Tribune* hit its all-time peak in October, 1946, when it sold 748,576 copies"—but its beloved president, Ogden Reid, died the next year. Woodward was too outspoken and independent for Reid's successors, so in 1948 he was fired.

For over a decade Woodward found plenty elsewhere to

keep him busy. He presided over a short-lived magazine called *Sports Illustrated*, no kin to the present one; he edited popular annual guides to college football; he had a long tenure as sports editor of the *Miami News* and a short one in the same slot at the Newark Star- Ledger; he published several books, most notably *Sports Page,* which even now is the definitive word on the subject; he and his wife bought and ran a thriving farm in New Jersey.

Then in 1959 he returned to the Trib, which the Reids had sold to John Hay Whitney. He loved the job in Newark and hated to leave, but pride was on the line: " . . . The thing that made it necessary to go to the *Tribune* was my own vindication. I had been thrown out and now I was being asked to return. The act of returning would be a severe punch in the eye for the surviving members of the Reid family."

So return he did, to a department "in frightful shape." He whacked the deadwood, promoted able people and brought a few hotshots over from Newark. It was an instant rebirth, to which I can testify because I read every copy I could get my hands on. So did many others, but it was too late. The Trib went through a rapid succession of mostly disastrous editors in chief, and the unforgivable citywide New York newspaper strike of 1962-3 hammered several nails into its coffin. It published its last issue in 1966, staggered on as part of the *World Journal Tribune*, went out for good six months later.

Woodward was dead by then, too, gone in late 1965 at the age of seventy. He'd left the paper three years earlier—"I worked for the *New York Herald Tribune* for two stretches and left the paper in disappointment and rage both times"—and had a happy, though far too brief, retirement. Now he's gone but not forgotten, remembered only in those few places where literate, stylish sportswriting is respected and valued.

THE REIVERS
by William Faulkner

In all of American literature there is nothing—absolutely nothing—to compare with the life's work of William Faulkner. From beginning to end his achievement is at an extraordinarily high level, sustained over nearly five decades, leaving us a half dozen indisputable masterpieces—*The Sound and the Fury, As I Lay Dying, Light in August, Absalom, Absalom!, The Hamlet, Go Down, Moses*—as well as many other books of singular merit. Simply and incontrovertibly, Faulkner stands alone.

Sixty-five years ago, when Faulkner was almost completely unknown except among his fellow writers and when, incredibly, all seventeen books he had then published were out of print or almost impossible to find, Malcolm Cowley at the Viking Press came to his rescue. He combed through the immense saga of Faulkner's fictional Yoknapatawpha County and produced *The Portable Faulkner* (1946), which has been brought back into print by Penguin Classics and remains to this day the perfect introduction to that world.

In his deservedly celebrated introduction, Cowley observes that Faulkner "performed a labor of imagination that has not been equaled in our time, and a double labor: first, to invent a Mississippi county that was like a mythical kingdom, but was complete and living in all its details; second, to make his story of Yoknapatawpha County stand as a parable or legend of all the Deep South." Cowley's close analysis and astute selection from Faulkner's work helped many readers find the key to that kingdom—what Faulkner called "my own little postage stamp of native soil"—and opened the way for the belated acclaim that followed: two Pulitzer Prizes and a Nobel for literature, bestsellers and the modest wealth they produced, semi-retirement as a country squire among the First Families of Virginia.

Yet for many other readers Faulkner remains an Everest too steep and craggy to climb. His dense, at times overwrought prose; his exceedingly complex plots; the intertwined genealogies that connect his books to each other; the sheer immensity of his oeuvre—these and other challenges scare many away. What a terrible pity this is, for the riches his work yields are immeasurable, not merely its searching exploration of the great themes of Southern history—slavery, defeat, the burden of the past—but also the astonishing humor, what Cowley called "a sort of homely and sober-sided frontier humor that is seldom achieved in contemporary writing."

As an amateur student of Faulkner's work who has often praised and commented upon it in public, I am again and again asked by readers: Where should I begin? Where is the key to the kingdom? There are any number of answers—most obviously, of course, *The Portable Faulkner*—but in thinking about which book of Faulkner's to include in this series, it occurred to me that his last novel, the comparatively little-known *The Reivers,* not merely deserves rediscovery but might also provide a way into Yoknapatawpha County for eager but apprehensive readers.

I first read *The Reivers* in late 1968. I was on a sabbatical from the North Carolina newspaper where I worked and taking a graduate seminar in Faulkner. He was a writer from whom I had shied away for years, but encountering him then was a life-altering experience. Not merely did I read all the major work assigned for the course, I read everything. I became so absorbed in Yoknapatawpha that I bored everyone to distraction by talking endlessly about it. I read *The Reivers,* as I read everything else, not because I had to but because I desperately wanted to, though notes scrawled in my copy remind me that I also read it with an eye to Faulkner's treatment of black characters and racial issues, about which I wrote a paper.

The Reivers was published in 1962, barely a month before Faulkner's death that July. It is a work of fiction, but he called it "A Reminiscence." This appears to have less to do with any direct connections to his own boyhood (though doubtless there are some) than with the nostalgic mood that Faulkner found himself in during the December of his life. Faulkner's later fiction, as Cowley observes in his afterword to the 1967 edition of The Portable Faulkner, has little of the "sense of doom and outrage" in the work of "the younger possessed and unregenerate author," indeed it has "more than a touch of old-fashioned sentiment." Certainly that is true of The Reivers—its denouement comes close to being a weeper—but its overall tone is so affectingly wistful, and its humor at times is so infectious, that an old man's insistence on a happy ending certainly can be forgiven.

The title comes from an old Scottish word that means "robber." Why Faulkner chose this charming if decidedly archaic word is unclear. In his biography of Faulkner, Joseph Blotner says the original title was The Horse Stealers, but though he reports the change he does not explain it. What he does tell us is that the book was on Faulkner's mind for at least two decades. In a letter to Robert Haas at Random House in the spring of 1940, Faulkner described the story he proposed to tell:

> It is a sort of Huck Finn—a normal boy of about 12 or 13, a big, warmhearted, courageous, honest, utterly unreliable white man with the mentality of a child, an old negro family servant, opinionated, querulous, selfish, fairly unscrupulous, and in his second childhood, and a prostitute not very young anymore and with a great deal of character and generosity and common sense, and a

stolen race horse which none of them actually intended to steal. The story is how they travel for a thousand miles from hand to mouth trying to get away from the police long enough to return the horse.

Haas sent $1,000 as an advance, but Faulkner set the story aside for further contemplation. In important respects it changed remarkably little. The boy, Lucius Priest, is eleven years old rather than twelve or thirteen, but he seems very much the boy Faulkner had always imagined—a variation, perhaps slightly idealized, on himself. The white man, Boon Hogganbeck (who first appeared in four of the short stories collected in 1942 as *Go Down, Moses*), is exactly as originally described, as is Corrie, the whore. The journey is scarcely 1,000 miles—a mere 120 miles back and forth between Jefferson, the county seat of Yoknapatawpha, and Memphis—but it does involve a stolen horse and, for good measure, a stolen automobile.

The most important and revealing change is in the character of Ned McCaslin, the family retainer. As the quotation above suggests, Faulkner seems to have thought of him originally in somewhat stereotypical terms, but by the time he got around to putting the story onto paper, Ned had become, however comical and free-spirited, a figure of immense dignity: "He spoke, quiet and succinct. He was not Uncle Remus now. But then, he never was when it was just me and members of his own race around." Faulkner had always written about black characters with deep sympathy, so it seems unlikely that the civil rights stirrings of the 1950s (about which Faulkner had complicated and ambiguous feelings) had much to do with how Ned emerged once the story finally got written. One must assume that over the years Faulkner's sympathy deepened into understanding and empathy, both of which are reflected in the portrait of Ned.

What is certain is that *The Reivers* is notable for the intimate relationships between many of its black and white characters. Bear in mind that it's set in Mississippi and Tennessee in 1905, both places still very much under the thumb of Jim Crow segregation and anti-black prejudice. Yes, the N-word pops up from time to time—in the mouths of black characters as well as white, which is entirely true to life then as now—but the egalitarianism of these relationships is striking. There's more than a little Huck and Jim in the friendship between Lucius and Ned; Miss Reba, proprietress of the bordello where Corrie works, is on utterly equal terms with Minnie, who is nominally her maid but actually her friend; Ned and a white railroad man named Sam Chapman strike up a friendship based on mutual respect; Uncle Parsham, an older black man, becomes the surrogate for Lucius's adored Grandfather Priest, and something quickly develops between man and boy that is very close to love.

It is Lucius who narrates the tale from the vantage point of the early 1960s, Lucius who recalls Uncle Parsham as "the patrician . . . the aristocrat of us all and judge of us all" and who later describes dining at Uncle Parsham's table:

> "Bow your head," and we did so and he said grace, briefly, courteously but with dignity, without abasement or cringing: one man of decency and intelligence to another: notifying Heaven that we were about to eat and thanking It for the privilege, but at the same time reminding It that It had had some help, too; that if someone . . . hadn't sweated some, the acknowledgment would have graced mainly empty dishes, and said Amen and unfolded his napkin and stuck the corner in his collar exactly as Grandfather did, and we ate . . . .

This is in some ways an implacably sunny book, but any temptation Faulkner may have felt toward nostalgia is tempered by his realistic, clear-eyed view of the world. Black characters are treated indifferently or contemptuously or cruelly simply because they are black; a brutal deputy sheriff named Butch is the embodiment of rural Southern law at its worst; a nasty fifteen-year-old named Otis behaves unspeakably toward Minnie, Lucius and anyone else who crosses his path; people cheat, lie and steal, and some get away with it.

One aspect of *The Reivers* that is both interesting and unusual is that it is a coming-of-age novel written not at the beginning of its author's career but at the very end. It has the wisdom of Faulkner's age and experience. What begins as a lark for Lucius turns into the most instructive experience of his life. His parents and grandparents have gone out of town. In their absence Boon persuades Lucius to climb aboard Grandfather Priest's new automobile—a Winton Flyer that is Boon's "soul's lily maid, the virgin's love of his rough and innocent heart"—and drive off for high adventure in Memphis. Ned comes along as a stowaway, and the romp is on.

That is how it starts, but matters soon get serious. The three reivers are "innocents, complete innocents at stealing automobiles," but as one thing piles atop another, Lucius soon realizes that "I had already told more lies than I had believed myself capable of inventing." Desperately, he wishes none of it had happened, "the whole thing no more than a dream from which I could wake tomorrow." It is overwhelming: "I knew too much, had seen too much. I was a child no longer now; innocence and childhood were forever lost, forever gone from me."

Yet he knows that he can't quit. As the horse race at the novel's climax approaches, he understands that "once we were in it, I had to go on, finish it, Ned and me both even if everybody else had quit." Finish it he does, and then accepts the consequences, as administered by Grandfather Priest in the poignant closing scene.

As these extracts make plain, *The Reivers* is written in prose at once distinctly Faulknerian yet entirely accessible. It provides a way to accustom oneself to Faulkner's language without becoming immediately lost in it, as can happen to someone who wanders all innocence into *Absalom, Absalom!* or *The Bear.* It gives you an introduction to the genealogy of Yoknapatawpha without overwhelming you in its intricacies. It sets forth many of Faulkner's most important themes in clear, persuasive ways. It may not be among his masterworks, but it is a lovely book, funny and touching and Faulkner to the core.

NOTES OF A NATIVE SON
by James Baldwin

As a mature adult,—an international figure, the most prominent and venerated African-American writer of his generation—James Baldwin let fame go to his head. He could not always resist the temptation of oracular pronunciamentos, and there could be an excess of self-importance in his manner and his prose. Fame does things to people's egos, and Baldwin proved not much less susceptible to it than other authors before or since.

It was not always thus. The young Baldwin was a real heart-breaker, a man of astonishing intelligence, sensitivity and vulnerability. There is evidence of this in his first two novels—*Go Tell It on the Mountain* (1953) and *Giovanni's Room* (1956)—but there is far more in his first collection of essays, *Notes of a Native Son*, published in 1955. At the time it got a modest amount of review attention—Baldwin was still relatively unknown—much of which focused on its stinging yet nuanced exploration of "the Negro problem" and its admission "that I hated and feared white people."

This response was understandable, since black voices were still rare in American literature and the messages they sought to impart were new to most readers. In 1955 Baldwin's incredibly rich prose had a good deal of shock value, and his long, angry 1962 *New Yorker* essay—issued the next year as a book called *The Fire Next Time*—had even more. In it he took as his text "God gave Noah the rainbow sign, No more water, the fire next time!" and warned of apocalyptic violence unless America dealt honestly and aggressively with the terrible conditions in which its black citizens lived.

In subsequent years, as Baldwin became a highly skilled speaker on the lecture circuit and as he came under heavy pressure from black radicals to turn up the heat of his rhetoric, this angry eloquence became his stock in trade, and he employed it to great effect. One unintentional consequence was that it became easy to forget the young man whom readers first met in the "Autobiographical Notes" and ten additional essays collected in *Notes of a Native Son*. Meeting that young man anew, for the first time in more than four decades, has been for me incredibly moving.

I first read *Notes of a Native Son* in the winter of 1962-63, soon after coming across *The Fire Next Time*. That essay now seems overwrought, though its undeniable power is little diminished, but at the time it came as a body blow to me and to many others. White America was only beginning to awaken to the social, political and moral consequences of its repression of black America—the sit-ins in North Carolina in February 1960 had been the real wake-up call—and Baldwin was quickly becoming one of the chief bringers of the news, certainly the most prominent literary messenger.

The marginalia in my old copy of *Notes of a Native Son* make plain that in 1962 I was most struck by the ferocity of its anger. I placed a heavy pencil mark next to this passage, in which Baldwin employs strong language: "And there is, I should think, no Negro living in America who has not felt, briefly or for long periods, with anguish sharp or dull, in varying degrees and to varying effect, simple, naked and unanswerable hatred; who has not wanted to smash any white face he may encounter in a day, to violate, out of motives of the cruelest vengeance, their women, to break the bodies of all white people and bring them low, as low as that dust into which he himself has been and is being trampled; no Negro, finally, who has not had to make his own precarious adjustment to the 'nigger' who surrounds him and to the 'nigger' in himself."

Today the pitiless beauty of that passage seems to me no less arresting than it did then, and there are many other passages of comparable expressiveness and force. Baldwin could be angry, but he could also be introspective and even plaintive. In the brilliant title essay he uses the memory of his stepfather's death to touch on a number of subjects, among them the loss of his own innocence in 1943 when, at the age of nineteen, he left his native Harlem:

> I had been living in New Jersey, working in defense plants, working and living among southerners, white and black. I knew about the south, of course, and about how southerners treated Negroes and how they expected them to behave, but it had never entered my mind that anyone would look at me and expect me to behave that way. I learned in New Jersey that to be a Negro meant, precisely, that one was never looked at but was simply at the mercy of the reflexes the color of one's skin caused in other people. . . . That year in New Jersey lives in my mind as though it were the year during which, having an unsuspected predilection for it, I first contracted some dread, chronic disease, the unfailing symptom of which is a kind of blind fever, a pounding in the skull and fire in the bowels. . . . There is not a Negro alive who does not have this rage in his blood—one has the choice, merely, of living with it consciously or surrendering to it. As for me, this fever has recurred in me, and does, and will until the day I die.

No doubt Baldwin carried it with him for three more decades, until his death in 1987, yet what leaps off the page now is not so much the anger as the innocence that was wrested away from him. Picture in your mind the nineteen-year-old James Baldwin. He is short and slight, with protuberant eyes that give him a look of perpetual astonishment. He is not merely black but deeply black. He has had a hard, marginal life as one of the nine children of a loving mother and a cold, distant stepfather who "had lived and died in an intolerable bitterness of spirit." He has a passionate desire to write but was bullied by his stepfather into a brief career as a boy preacher. He is deeply uncertain about his sexual identity and is slowly moving toward open homosexuality, a subject he will explore a decade later in *Giovanni's Room.*

All in all it would be difficult to imagine someone more vulnerable to life's cruelties, random or otherwise. When he says, at the outset, that "I love America more than any other country in the world, and, exactly for this reason, I insist on the right to criticize her perpetually," one's heart aches because of all the subterranean messages that sentence contains, chief among them passionate love of country and unbearable pain at being rejected by it. Much later he tells us that "the favorite text of my father, among the most earnest of ministers, was not 'Father, forgive them, for they know not what they do,' but 'How can I sing the Lord's song in a strange land?'" and one feels, again, the anguish of alienation and rejection.

The "most difficult (and most rewarding) thing in my life has been the fact that I was born a Negro and was forced, therefore, to effect some kind of truce with this reality," Baldwin writes, and it becomes apparent as the essays in this book unfold that this has to do not merely with discrimination and rejection but also with a search for his own place in a world he did not make. In the four lovely essays in the final section about his long exile in Europe, he confronts this in various ways. One is a meditation upon the residents of a small town in Switzerland:

> The most illiterate among them is related, in a way that I am not, to Dante, Shakespeare, Michelangelo, Aeschylus, da Vinci, Rembrandt and Racine; the cathedral at Chartres says something to them which it cannot say to me, as indeed would New York's Empire State Building, should anyone here ever see it. Out of their hymns and dances come Beethoven and Bach. Go back a

few centuries and they are in their full glory—but I am in Africa, watching the conquerors arrive.

The word Baldwin uses for this condition is "disesteemed." It gnawed deeply and painfully at him. "The rage of the disesteemed is personally fruitless," he believed, "but it is also absolutely inevitable," and "no black man can hope ever to be entirely liberated from this internal warfare—rage, dissembling, and contempt having inevitably accompanied his first realization of the power of white men." The theme arises over and over again: "the injustice of the white American," "the weight of white people in the world," "the idea of white supremacy."

It's easy to read this as stock racial rhetoric, but that is a mistake. What Baldwin wanted above all else was acceptance, by blacks and whites alike. He was a member of the black community and yearned for a high place within it, which indeed he soon achieved. Among whites he wanted acceptance not because they were white—quite to the contrary—but because they were Americans and so was he. He believed that America could never be a true nation, could never achieve anything close to its potential, until black Americans were allowed to contribute as freely and fully as whites. That argument is central to *The Fire Next Time,* and is the note on which this book closes:

[The black American] is not a visitor to the West, but a citizen there, an American; as American as the Americans who despise him, the Americans who fear him, the Americans who love him— the Americans who became less than themselves, or rose to be greater than themselves by virtue of the fact that the challenge he presented was inescapable . . . The time has come to realize that the interracial drama acted out on the American continent has not only created a new black man, it has created a new white man, too . . . It is precisely this black-white experience which may prove of indispensable value to us in the world we face today. This world is white no longer, and it will never be white again.

The many decades since those words were published have proved nothing so much as that Baldwin got it prophetically, precisely right. However far we still may be from the state of grace that was Baldwin's most cherished dream, we certainly are much closer to being the "us" he envisioned than we were then. For this no small share of the credit rests with him, for he opened many eyes and changed many hearts.

He did so in prose of uncommon grace and, when the occasion called for it, wit. His influences, he thought, were "the King James Bible, the rhetoric of the store-front church, something ironic and violent and perpetually understated in Negro speech—and something of Dickens' love for bravura," and the reader will find all of that in his essays and novels. He was in fact a better essayist than novelist—more controlled, more forceful, less tempted by long-windedness—and his essays read as well now as they did when first published. It is too soon after his death for his real place in American literature to be determined, but it is certain that he will be read for many years to come, to readers' enrichment and enlightenment.

REBECCA
by Daphne du Maurier

Almost from its inception in eighteenth-century England, the gothic novel has been adored by readers and deplored by critics. For the fastidious ladies and gentlemen of the quarterly reviews and academe, its central conventions—nature red in tooth and claw; haunted castles atop windswept moors; defenseless young women at the mercy of strange, obsessed men with terrible secrets; bondage, imprisonment, sexual torment and ambiguity, raging fires—are simply too too. But readers love it, as well they should, for in the best gothic fiction, realism and romance join forces to create a territory somewhere between this world and some other in which almost everything is slightly, deliciously over the top.

Gothic fiction has produced writing that can't be credited with much more than entertainment value, stuff that usually ends up in airport bookshops and on bestseller lists. But gothic fiction also has produced a few of the indisputable masterpieces of the English language, from Mary Shelley's *Frankenstein* to Charlotte Bronte's *Jane Eyre* to William Faulkner's *Absalom! Absalom!* as well as a number of works that rise well above mere entertainment but don't quite make it all the way to the sacred halls of literature.

Among these are novels and stories by Victorian writers such as Wilkie Collins, Bram Stoker and Elizabeth Gaskell. With the twentieth century and the great literary changes it ushered in—realism, naturalism, experimentalism—gothicism lost some of its steam, but one important practitioner of the tradition had a long, fruitful career. Daphne du Maurier, born in 1907 into a distinguished Anglo-French family of artists, writers and performers, published her first novel, *The Loving Spirit*, in 1931, and promptly marched onto the bestseller lists, where she remained until her death in 1989. In all she published fifteen novels, six collections of stories and a dozen works of nonfiction, but one book stands apart from, and above, all the rest.

This is *Rebecca*, published in 1938. It was a bestseller in England and the United States, and in 1940 was produced as a movie by David O. Selznick, an exceptional work of cinematic art starring Laurence Olivier, Joan Fontaine and Judith Anderson and directed by Alfred Hitchcock, his first film for an American studio. Thanks in great measure to the movie, the book has been steadily in print ever since, in one paperback edition after another, and to this day enjoys sales that would be envied by many a Flavor of the Month author of ostensibly "serious" fiction.

It is no exaggeration to say that du Maurier was the twentieth century's Charlotte Bronte and *Rebecca* the twentieth century's *Jane Eyre*. The parallels between the two authors and the two books are obvious. Though Bronte's childhood circumstances were straitened and du Maurier's privileged, both girls lived essentially interior lives in which imagination, storytelling and fantasy were central. Both published early (Bronte under the pseudonym Currer Bell) and both became wildly successful; Michael Mason, in his introduction to the Penguin Classics edition of *Jane Eyre*, says it "may be the most read novel in English," and he may be right. Both women eventually married, du Maurier eagerly and Bronte reluctantly.

Over the years there have been countless imitations of *Jane Eyre*. Whether *Rebecca* is in fact one of these is debatable, but the similarities do tend to leap out. Jane Eyre is governess to a wealthy girl; the unnamed narrator of *Rebecca* is companion to a wealthy older woman. Both women (nineteen and twenty-one years old, respectively) are mousy in appearance (or think they are) and beleaguered by self-doubt. Both come into the employ of brooding, mysterious men in their forties—Edward Fairfax Rochester and Maxim de Winter—and both fall in love with them. Both men harbor dreadful secrets: Jane learns Rochester's on the eve of their wedding, the heroine of *Rebecca* learns de Winter's after three months of marriage. The majestic country mansions owned by both men burn to the ground in spectacular conflagrations. Happy endings are achieved, but at a high price.

It is tempting to pigeonhole *Rebecca* as "Jane Lite," but that simply is not true. If it hasn't quite the depth, if at times it lapses into conventions of the gothic novel or the English mystery novel, *Rebecca* is nonetheless a work of immense intelligence and wit, elegantly written, thematically solid, suspenseful even a second time around.

Indeed, one of the pleasures of a second reading is that though one (mostly) remembers a book's story and characters, invariably one discovers aspects of it that were missed the first time through. Utterly caught up in the novel's plot when first I read it, I simply didn't understand that this isn't just a novel about a lovesick girl's obsessive jealousy of her husband's dead first wife, it is also a book about the interweaving of past and present. Du Maurier treats memory with what can only be called delicacy and tenderness.

As the novel begins the narrator is in Monte Carlo, tending to the endless whims of her fatuous employer, Mrs. Van Hopper, and falling in love with Maxim de Winter. Looking back, she urgently tries to bring that happy past back to life: "I wanted to go back again, to recapture the moment that had gone, and then it came to me that if we did it would not be the same, even the sun would be changed in the sky, casting another shadow, and the peasant girl would trudge past us along the road in a different way, not waving this time, perhaps not even seeing us." Later, married to de Winter, relaxing at Manderley, his estate, she brings it all into focus:

> I wanted to go on sitting here, not talking, not listening to the others, keeping the moment precious for all time, because we were peaceful all of us, we were content and drowsy even as the bee who droned above our heads. In a little while it would be different, there would come tomorrow, and the next day, and another year. And we would be changed perhaps, never sitting quite like this again. Some of us would go away, or suffer, or die, the future stretched away in front of us, unknown, unseen, not perhaps what we wanted, not what we planned. This moment was safe though, this could not be touched. Here we sat together, Maxim and I, hand-in-hand, and the past and future mattered not at all. This was secure, this funny fragment of time he would never remember, never think about again. He would not hold it sacred, he was talking about cutting away some of the undergrowth in the drive, and Beatrice agreed, interrupting with some suggestion of her own, and throwing a piece of grass at Giles at the same time. For them it was just after lunch, quarter-past-three on a haphazard afternoon, like any hour, like any day. They did not want to hold it close, imprisoned and secure, as I did. They were not afraid.

A great deal happens in that paragraph, and du Maurier succeeds in telling it with exceptional skill. Obviously there is a certain degree of foreshadowing ("In a little while it would be different . . ."), but there is nothing clumsy or intrusive about it like "Little did we know that . . ." or similar hack-fiction cliches. The real heart of the passage is the narrator's poignant longing to hold on to happiness—not passion or bliss, just plain, everyday, "haphazard" happiness—and her certain knowledge that the moment will pass. Expressions of this longing arise over and over again in *Rebecca*, lending considerable thematic resonance to the narrator's desperate attempt to learn her husband's true feelings about his dead first wife and about herself.

One notable difference between du Maurier's narrator and Jane Eyre is that the latter, though unprepossessing in appearance and manner, is spunky at the core. Jane sasses and teases her master ("Mr. Rochester affirmed I was wearing him to skin and bone . . .") and starts a whole new life, all on her own, when he is forced to disclose his dreadful secret. The narrator of *Rebecca*, by contrast, recalls "that self who drove to Manderley for the first time, hopeful and eager, handicapped by a rather desperate gaucherie and filled with an intense desire to please," laments that "poise, and grace, and assurance were not qualities inbred in me," envies "someone who was never anxious, never tortured by doubt and indecision, someone who never stood as I did, hopeful, eager, frightened, tearing at bitten nails, uncertain which way to go, what star to follow."

But she doesn't stay that way. A boat comes aground on the rough coast off Manderley and she somehow senses that "I had entered into a new phase of my life and nothing would be quite the same again." She is gripped by "a latent sense of excitement at the back of my mind that I did not understand," and she steels herself not in fear but almost with joy: "The moment of crisis had come, and I must face it. My old fears, my diffidence, my shyness, my hopeless sense of inferiority, must be conquered now and thrust aside. If I failed now I should fail forever. There would never be another chance." She not merely faces up to the crisis, she emerges with a heart that, "for all its anxiety and doubt, was light and free."

That moment occurs with nearly 100 pages to go, many of which are taken up by a scene in the library of Manderley that is reminiscent of an Agatha Christie ending in which the suspects and the inspectors assemble, Clue-like, to tie up all the loose ends. It's an oddly stiff, conventional way to solve the various plotting difficulties du Maurier has posed for herself, but in fairness it must be noted that she was a mere thirty years old.

At the time du Maurier had been married for about five

years to Frederick Arthur Montague "Boy" Browning, to whom she was wildly devoted. It has been reported that one inspiration for *Rebecca* was her own jealousy of a woman to whom he had been engaged. This helps explain the real passion with which her narrator welcomes the disclosure that the dead Rebecca had been "evil and vicious and rotten." But that surely is as far as the autobiographical path leads us. *Rebecca* is strictly a work of the imagination, one that, if it does not rank quite so high as *Jane Eyre*, has pleased and mesmerized readers for more than six decades.

SOMEONE LIKE YOU
by Roald Dahl

Roald Dahl was a complicated and in some respects disagreeable man, but his many books for children remain among the world's most popular and—yes—beloved. But Dahl, whose writing career began in 1942 and lasted until his death in 1990 at age seventy-four, also wrote books for adults that are every bit as weird, droll and satisfying. These include a deliciously ribald novel, *My Uncle Oswald* (1979); two volumes of autobiography, *Boy* (1984) and *Going Solo* (1986), which are equally accessible and appealing to young and adult readers; and numerous collections of short stories, the best of which, *Someone Like You* (1953), is the one among all of Dahl's books that I treasure most.

Precisely how I came upon Dahl's work I do not recall, but it was sometime in the late 1950s, perhaps in the *New Yorker* or *Harper's*, in which his short stories occasionally appeared before the publication of *James and the Giant Peach* (1961) and the beginning of his career as a writer of children's books. My well-thumbed, loose-spined copy of *Someone Like You* is Knopf's American first edition, for which I probably paid a dollar or two at a secondhand bookstore and which can still be found at reasonable prices. It must have sold well for a short-story collection, since it went through about a dozen printings, establishing Dahl's reputation in the process.

He was a born writer. As a boy in Wales in the 1920s he despised almost everything about the public (i.e., private) schools to which he was sent, but in *Boy* he remembers being required to write an essay ("The Life Story of a Penny") and being furious when the nib of his pen broke: "I really wanted to finish that essay. I knew exactly what was going to happen to my penny through the next two pages and I couldn't bear to leave it unsaid." Still, as has been true of other writers and creative sorts, unhappiness at school laid the foundation for what came later. The lesson he was unwittingly taught at St. Peter's and Repton stayed with him for life: "Parents and schoolteachers are the enemy. The adult is the enemy of the child because of the awful process of civilizing this thing that when it is born is an animal with no manners, no moral sense at all."

At eighteen, Dahl went to work in Africa for the Shell Co. When war broke out he joined the Royal Air Force, learned to fly, and fought valiantly. He was wounded in 1942 and was posted to Washington as an air attaché, where he met the British novelist C.S. Forester, who was trying to boost support for Britain as America geared up for war. Forester proposed to interview Dahl about his combat experience, but instead Dahl wrote it out. Without changing a word, Forester sent the piece to the Saturday Evening Post, which ran it under Dahl's byline—his first—and paid him a whopping $900.

It would be exaggeration to say all was easy after that, for Dahl's career was slow getting off the ground. He was a meticulous craftsman who ran everything he wrote through several drafts, and it took him a few years to perfect his distinctive style, one that gives the sense of an intimate, wry conversation with the reader. What did become plain early on was that his unhappiness in school—as well no doubt as the early deaths of his father and an older sister—had given him a particular sensitivity to the macabre, the *outre*, the unexpected. He developed a skill at surprise endings to rival O. Henry's, though his prose style was far superior, and he slowly mastered a tone— ironic, sardonic, succinctly but painstakingly descriptive— that makes almost anything he wrote immediately identifiable.

Consider for example this passage from "Taste," the first story in *Someone Like You*:

> The man was about fifty years old and he did not have a pleasant face. Somehow it was all mouth—mouth and lips—the full, wet lips of the professional gourmet, the lower lip hanging downward in the center, a pendulous, permanently open taster's lip, shaped open to receive the rim of a glass or a morsel of food. Like a keyhole, I thought, watching it; his mouth is like a large wet keyhole.

Dahl was a close observer of faces, and the more unpleasant they were, the more he delighted in describing them: "The man's lips—like the lips of all bearded men—looked wet and naked, a trifle indecent, shining pink in among all that hair," or: "He disliked very much this man with the wide frog mouth, the broken teeth, the shifty eyes."

The first of those quotations is from "Nunc Dimittis," one of the best stories in this collection. Its narrator is Lionel Lampson, who describes himself as "a type; a rare one, mark you, but nevertheless a quite definite type—the wealthy, leisurely, middle-aged man of culture, adored (I choose the word carefully) by his many friends for his charm, his money, his air of scholarship, his generosity and, I sincerely hope, for himself also." It develops that he is not quite so adored as he imagines, that a woman with whom he frequently dines considers him a "crashing old bore." Seeking revenge—revenge being a constant in Dahl's writing, for adults and children alike—and gaining the unsuspecting connivance of a society-ladies' portrait painter, he counterattacks with "outrageous behavior"—outrageous, yes, but also entirely hilarious.

Which is to say the story is archetypal Dahl. His stories almost always are amusing. Of the eighteen stories in *Someone Like You,* only "Soldier," in which a veteran is possessed by nightmarish memories of war, is grim. Dahl loved to bring the reader right up to the edge—"Something extremely unpleasant was about to happen—I was sure of that. Something sinister and cruel and ratlike, and perhaps it really would make me sick. But I had to see it now"—and then to twist everything around with a sudden turn to the comical. The turn may be nasty and even bloody at times, but it's funny, too. He knew the hold that dread exerts on us:

> For me, after that, it was like the awful moment when you see a child running out into the road and a car is coming and all you can do is shut your eyes tight and wait until the noise tells you what has happened. The moment of waiting becomes a long lucid period of time with yellow and red spots dancing on a black field, and even if you open your eyes again and find that nobody has been killed or hurt, it still makes no difference because so far as you and your stomach were concerned you saw it all.

Reading Dahl's short stories is like that. You hold your breath, and if you didn't want to see the words on the page you'd close your eyes, too. "Man From the South," which is still perhaps my favorite among his stories—"perhaps," that is, because my favorite Dahl story tends to be the one I'm reading right now—sustains over a mere fifteen pages a remarkable level of tension, yet even reading it for the first time you sense that however close matters are brought to the edge, you're not going to fall over it.

Precisely why Dahl granted his readers this escape is unclear. He was entirely capable of unredeemed nastiness; he was, quite famously, an outspoken and unapologetic anti-Semite, and earned every ounce of the censure he received on that score. Yet he had a kind streak as well; his second wife said, "He was not an easy man, but to me he was the most stimulating man in the world and the best husband a woman could ever have." His marriage to his first wife, the actress Patricia Neal, ended unhappily in 1983, yet in the mid-1960s his round-the-clock care enabled her to make a full recovery from three massive strokes. Contradiction was his middle name. Danny DeVito, who directed a film version of Dahl's children's book *Matilda*, put it nicely: "Dahl will lead a child out onto a windy limb and then suddenly he'll place a ladder underneath and the child will be able to get safely to the ground."

He did the same for adults. Even when something quite terrible does happen—as in "Lamb to the Slaughter," the most famous of his short stories—he resolves matters with a twist, almost always ironic and usually witty. He acknowledged, indeed delighted in, the "awful magnetism" that draws us to the unknown, the unexpected, the violent, but he preferred irony to gore and laughter to screams. He pulled back from the abyss at the end of each story because he found it more agreeable to amuse than to horrify. Doubtless he understood that it is harder to be funny than to be merely sensational, which helps explain why he worked so slowly and meticulously.

Interestingly, the one story in which the ending is somewhat ambiguous—in which you are left to wonder whether this is reality or fantasy—is "The Wish," the only one in which a child is the central character. A little boy is standing in a long hallway looking at an "enormous red and black and yellow carpet." In one wonderful paragraph, Dahl's great children's books are prefigured:

> You see, he told himself, I know how it is. The red parts of the carpet are red-hot lumps of coal. What I must do is this: I must walk all the way along to it to the front door without touching them. If I touch the red I will be burnt. As a matter of fact, I will be burnt up completely. And the black parts of the carpet . . . yes, the black parts are snakes, poisonous snakes, adders mostly, and cobras, thick like tree-trunks round the middle, and if I touch one of them, I'll be bitten and I'll die before teatime. And if I get across safely, without being burnt and without being bitten, I will be given a puppy for my birthday tomorrow.

Anyone who has ever walked along a sidewalk thinking "Step on a crack, break your mother's back" (as, at my considerable age, I still sometimes do) will know immediately that in that paragraph Dahl has entered the mind of a child with total knowledge and confidence. One of the many splendid things about him is that though his inner child never deserted him, he never, as an adult, was merely childish. Whatever the age of the readers he had in mind, in his writing he combined childlike fear and wonder with adult maturity and craftsmanship. He was a marvelously gifted entertainer, make no mistake about that, but he was also a serious writer who deserves a literary reputation as large and enthusiastic as his popular acclaim.

THE LONG SEASON
by Jim Brosnan

At the dawn of the 1960s the literature of baseball was paltry. Some good fiction had been inspired by the game, notably Ring Lardner's *You Know Me Al* and Bernard Malamud's *The Natural,* but nonfiction was little more than breathless sports-page reportage: hagiographic biographies of stars written for adolescents (*Lou Gehrig: Boy of the Sandlots),* as-told-to quickies (*Player-Manager,* "by" Lou Boudreau) and once-over-lightly histories of the game (*The Baseball Story*, by Fred Lieb).

Then one book changed everything: *The Long Season,* by a little-known relief pitcher for the Cincinnati Reds named Jim Brosnan. Published in 1960, it was a diary of the 1959 season, which Brosnan began as a member of the St. Louis Cardinals and ended with the Reds. Though the book was entirely devoid of the profanity and scatology without which ballplayers can't talk, it took readers inside the clubhouse, the dugout and the bullpen—not to mention the airplane, the train and the hotel room—in ways no sportswriter ever had.

The book was greeted with astonishment outside baseball, since the notion that a ballplayer could write (not to mention write well) was beyond consideration, and with fury inside baseball, where players and sportswriters charged that by portraying the game honestly, Brosnan had violated its code of omertà. A decade and a half later, in his preface to a new edition of the book, Brosnan summed it all up:

As an active player on a big-league team I had seemingly taken undue advantage by recording an insider's viewpoint on what some professional baseball players were really like. I had, moreover, violated the idolatrous image of big leaguers who had been previously portrayed as models of modesty, loyalty and sobriety—i.e., what they were really not like. Finally, I had actually written the book by myself, thus trampling upon the tradition that a player should hire a sportswriter to do the work. I was, on these accounts, a sneak and a snob and a scab.

The reader does not need to be told what happened: après Jim, le deluge. A couple of years later Bill Veeck's splendid *Veeck as in Wreck* told the inside story of a maverick team owner, and then in 1970 Jim Bouton's Number One bestseller, *Ball Four,* did an inside number on the New York Yankees, cusswords and all. But *The Long Season* not merely changed everything, it remained the best of its kind. What Red Smith wrote in the *New York Herald Tribune*—"it is a cocky book, caustic and candid and, in a way, courageous, for Brosnan calls them as he sees them, doesn't hesitate to name names, and employs ridicule like a stiletto"—is still true today.

I was twenty years old when the book appeared, and gobbled it up as fast as I could find a copy. It's entirely possible that I'd never heard of Brosnan, since I was an American League partisan and his whole (brief) career had been in the National, but *The Long Season* made me an instant Brosnan fan and I've been one ever since. I was delighted when he and the Reds won the National League pennant in 1961 (they lost the World Series to the Yankees) and even more delighted when he told the story of that season in *Pennant Race* (1962). On giving both books what is not a second reading but more like a fifth or sixth, I find them as fresh as ever, though *The Long Season* seems to me the better of the two because its subject is an ordinary season—life as it's really lived—rather than an extraordinary one.

Brosnan was twenty-nine years old during the 1959 season; he turned thirty that October. He had been in professional baseball for a dozen years. He was called up to the Chicago Cubs in 1954 and liked the city enough to buy a house in a suburb called Morton Grove. The Cubs sent him back to the minors in 1955, brought him to Chicago in 1956 and traded him to the Cardinals in 1958. As the 1959 season began he had won twenty-two games in the majors and lost twenty-two, started thirty-five games and completed six, and, in 1958, had gotten seven saves as a relief pitcher, his chief job for the rest of his baseball career, which ended after the 1963 season. Since then he has written newspaper and magazine articles and a few baseball books for young readers, and worked in advertising (as he did during his baseball off-seasons) and broadcasting.

His fellow ballplayers seem to have liked Brosnan—a quick wit and an irreverent streak can be strong assets in the club-house—but they were clearly puzzled by him. They called him "Professor," because he almost always had a book with him, because he used big words and was curious about words unfamiliar to him, because he understood there was a larger world beyond baseball, much though he loved the game. "I maintain a small library in my locker in the clubhouse," he writes, then adds the characteristically self-mocking kicker: "Nothing like a book to keep your mind from thinking." And: "The plane ride was too quick for me to read *The Wapshot Chronicle*. When I get involved in a book my mind doesn't operate properly till I read my way back to reality."

This is a simple statement of fact, not literary posturing. Brosnan seems never to have had any pretensions about his reading or his enjoyment of intelligent conversations about matters other than the infield fly rule. He didn't think he was better than other ballplayers because he read books, and he didn't think they were inferior to him because they didn't. In fact he clearly enjoyed the company of old hands like Marv Grissom and Sal Maglie, as well as rustics like Vinegar Bend Mizell and Marshall Bridges. He chewed tobacco, too. "Can't kick the nasty habit," he admitted, though in *Pennant Race* he vowed to quit at the end of his baseball days, doubtless much to the relief of his wife, Mary Stewart, who on the evidence of both books is at least as smart, funny and irreverent as he is.

The Long Season gives pleasure on any number of levels. It conveys, as no other book ever has, the dailiness of baseball, with its season that not merely is long but provides an endless, often inexplicable, succession of ups and downs. One day in 1958, pitching against the San Francisco Giants, Brosnan gave up a homer that "cleared the back wall of the right-field bleachers, at the 425-foot mark, causing sportswriters to go dashing out of the press box with a tape measure." In 1959, with the game on the line, he faced the same batter again: "Did he hit it out again? He did not. He tapped it right back to me, like a good little boy, and we had a double play to retire the side." As he says: "This game will drive you batty." Or, as he writes a week later:

> . . . Man, that's the way it goes in this game. You make your pitch, and if it's the right pitch, it works . . . most of the time. If it's the wrong pitch, you find out soon enough, and they tell you soon enough, also. If you don't believe them, they send you somewhere else so they don't have to listen to you; and so that you can ponder by yourself the misfortune that has struck you. Etc.

Baseball is a tough game and, as that passage indicates, a merciless one as well. A couple of bad appearances—in which, as is often the case, you make all the right pitches but don't get the right results—and you're in the doghouse, or the minors, or on a plane to join another team. In late April, still with St. Louis, Brosnan sensed that "I'm not long for this clubhouse"; he'd had some bad outings and the manager, Solly Hemus, just plain didn't like him, a sentiment he returned. Sure enough on June eighth he was told to report to Cincinnati: "I sat back on the couch, half-breathing as I waited for indignation to flush good red blood to my head. Nothing happened. I took a deep breath, then exhaled slowly. It's true. The second time you're sold you don't feel a thing."

The trade turned out to be good for Brosnan. Not merely were the Reds a better team, but a month later they brought in Fred Hutchinson as manager. Brosnan had played under him the previous season in St. Louis—until Hutchinson was fired, as managers always are—and thought the world of him: "Most ballplayers respect Hutch. In fact, many of them admire him, which is even better than liking him. He seems to have a tremendous inner power that a player can sense. When Hutch gets a grip on things it doesn't seem probable that he's going to lose it. He seldom blows his top at a player, seldom panics in a game, usually lets the players work out of their own troubles if possible."

This was a different time, and managers exercised stronger control over their players than they do now, in the age of multi-trillion-dollar contracts and free agency. The game was different in other ways as well. There were only sixteen teams, and only three were west of the Mississippi. There were no play-offs; league champions went right to the World Series. Sunday doubleheaders were commonplace, and so were day games after night games. Black players had been in the majors for barely a decade, and though by the late 1950s there were many of them, race relations in the clubhouse and on the field were often testy. The American League still required pitchers to bat for themselves; the heinous designated hitter was not authorized until 1973.

Still, baseball is baseball. Today's reader may not recognize all the names that appear in *The Long Season*, but the observations they inspire about the game and how it's played are timeless. Any one of dozens could be quoted, but here is Brosnan on the formidable Don Drysdale of the Los Angeles Dodgers:

> When Drysdale is fast—on some days a pitcher throws harder than on others—his fastball pops the leather of the catcher's mitt. Like a sledgehammer slamming a fence stump. The very sound can numb a batter's hands, even before he gets out of the on-deck circle. "Got to get out in front—got to be out in front on the pitch," he says to himself. Of course, Drysdale also throws a fast curve ball. If the batter sets himself to get way out in front on the fast ball, and the pitch turns out to be a curve ball, he may suffer the embarrassment of looking like he's chasing bumblebees with a butterfly net.

That's a dandy paragraph, and there are lots more like it. *The Long Season* can be read for insights into the game, since Brosnan was an astute observer who watched carefully, asked smart questions, and was wise enough to admire skills in others that he didn't possess himself. He obviously liked ballplayers a lot, and respected their intelligence, which may seem unlettered to the chattering classes but runs deep when it comes to this most complex and nuanced of games. Over the years some players were even smart enough to grasp that *The Long Season* did them, and baseball, a favor, by capturing its human side and in so doing making them more, rather than less, interesting and admirable.

SPEAK, MEMORY
by Vladimir Nabokov

A mong the many books by Vladimir Nabokov, two are of special importance to me. The first, not surprisingly, is *Lolita*: one of the indisputably great American novels of the twentieth century, it grows ever deeper and richer not merely with each reading but also as it is reflected upon and savored within the province of memory. The other, perhaps somewhat less predictably, is *Speak, Memory,* the memoir that Nabokov wrote in bits and pieces mostly in the 1940s. It was first published in book form in 1951 (under the title *Conclusive Evidence*) and then republished, heavily edited and revised, under its current title in 1966. Precisely how many times I have read it I do not know, nor do I recall when I read it for the first time, but this can be said with certainty: It is a book that I absolutely, unconditionally love. Opening it entirely at random—to any page, any paragraph, any sentence—I feel at once in the presence of the miraculous, awakened once again to the power, the magic and the mystery of the word.

There are remarkably few pieces of writing about which I can say that: a number of poems (though I rarely read poetry anymore), James Joyce's story "The Dead," *The Great Gatsby* and *One Hundred Years of Solitude,* much Faulkner and Dickens, *Jane Eyre,* a handful of books treasured in childhood and youth. The list could go on a bit longer—Shakespeare, of course—but not much. A lifetime of reading for a living has made me difficult to satisfy, easy to displease, reluctant to give my heart to any old book or any old author.

It is true that some of Nabokov's books and the literary tricks he delighted in playing are not especially to my taste. Some of those tricks are to be found in *Speak, Memory*—word games, twinning, puns, et cetera—and those with a taste for that can read the book for the pleasures this playfulness affords them. But at heart it is a deeply humane and even old-fashioned book, and its prose from first word to last can only be called astonishing.

The memoir begins with the author's birth in St. Petersburg in 1899, though its real beginning is in 1903, when Nabokov's consciousness fully awakened and his prodigious memory clicked into place. It covers his blissful childhood as the eldest son of an almost unimaginably privileged Russian family and that family's escape from the Bolsheviks in 1918. It touches lightly on his years at Cambridge, his European exile during the 1920s and 1930s, and ends with his departure for the United States in 1940. Though it does tell a story, in structure it is episodic rather than linear, and Nabokov backs and fills as the inclination strikes him. Narrative line is almost nonexistent, so the reader is pulled along by Nabokov's effort to find the connections within his own past—"The following of such thematic designs through one's life should be, I think, the true purpose of autobiography"—and by the endless surprises of his prose.

Over the years some readers have complained that Nabokov emerges from these pages as pampered, arrogant and self-absorbed, all of which is true and none of which matters in the least. Autobiography is inherently and inescapably an act of immodesty, and don't let any autobiographer try to tell you otherwise. Its real subject is, or should be, the development of the inner and outer self, and attending properly to that task can only plunge the author into the abyss of self. The successful memoirist is the one who explores self in ways in which others can see perhaps a glimmer of their own selves and who retains throughout the redeeming quality of self-deprecation.

Nabokov was haunted and obsessed by the past. "The act of vividly recalling a patch of the past is something that I seem to have been performing with the utmost zest all my life," he writes, and, later: "I witness with pleasure the supreme achievement of memory, which is the masterly use it makes of innate harmonies when gathering to its fold the suspended and wandering tonalities of the past." Even those of us cursed with defective and/or selective memories can find, in his searches, parallels to our own attempts to figure out where we came from and who we are. Writing with passion about "the legendary Russia of my boyhood," Nabokov places each reader in his or her own childhood, no matter how different it may have been from his, spent as it was in a handsome St. Petersburg townhouse and on the three family estates fifty miles south of the city.

What matters is not that Nabokov was rich and privileged in ways few if any of his readers can comprehend—"our city household and country place," for example, had "a permanent staff of about 50 servants"—but that he brings such abiding humanity to this examination of his past. Contemplating his family's lost fortune—when the Nabokovs fled to Yalta and then to Western Europe, "except for a few jewels astutely buried in the normal filling of a talcum powder container, we were absolutely ruined"—he gets it exactly right: "The nostalgia I have been cherishing all these years is a hypertrophied sense of lost childhood, not sorrow for lost banknotes." The impulse to rediscover and reclaim childhood is deep in human nature, and thus the chord struck *Speak, Memory* is truly universal.

Nabokov can find universality in the most unlikely places. The pursuit, capture and collection of butterflies may well have been the greatest passion bestowed upon this deeply passionate man, but it is one that holds not the slightest interest for me. Yet here, in a paragraph that can (and must) be read over and over again, he places his passion in a context all of us can understand:

> I confess I do not believe in time. I like to fold my magic carpet, after use, in such a way as to superimpose one part of the pattern upon another. Let visitors trip. And the highest enjoyment of timelessness—in a landscape selected at random—is when I stand among rare butterflies and their food plants. This is ecstasy, and behind the ecstasy is something else, which is hard to explain. It is like a momentary vacuum into which rushes all that I love. A sense of oneness with sun and stone. A thrill of gratitude to whom it may concern—to the contrapuntal genius of human fate or to tender ghosts humoring a lucky mortal.

The pedants who have made it their lives' work to pick Nabokov's bones bare have no doubt critiqued that paragraph to excess. So I will merely submit it for your own scrutiny and gratification, and for the insights—both subtle and joyful—that it offers into the incredible richness of human existence. The study of butterflies—lepidopterology, to give it its proper name—is revealed under Nabokov's microscope to be yet another way to see ourselves and the world we inhabit.

It also provides Nabokov splendid opportunities for the self-mockery that makes this book as witty and funny as it is wise. "I have hunted butterflies in various climes and disguises," he writes: "as a pretty boy in knickerbockers and sailor cap; as a lanky cosmopolitan expatriate in flannel bags and beret; as a fat hatless old man in shorts." Early on he discovered "that a 'lepist' indulging in his quiet quest was apt to provoke strange reactions in other creatures," especially after he crossed the Atlantic:

> America has shown even more of this morbid interest in my retiary activities than other countries have—perhaps because I was in my forties when I came there to live, and the older the man, the queerer he looks with a butterfly net in his hand. Stern

farmers have drawn my attention to NO FISHING signs; from cars passing me on the highway have come wild howls of derision; sleepy dogs, though unmindful of the worst bum, have perked up and come at me, snarling; tiny tots have pointed me out to their puzzled mamas; broad-minded vacationists have asked me whether I was catching bugs for bait; and one morning on a wasteland, lit by tall yuccas in bloom, near Santa Fe, a big black mare followed me for more than a mile.

It would be easy to fill the rest of this essay with quotations such as that one, because *Speak, Memory* has what at times seems a bottomless supply of them. Witty, clever, self-effacing, ingenious: Nabokov is all of these things here, but he never lapses into the preciousness that was (to my taste, at least) his greatest literary weakness. Perhaps the explanation is that he deals here with matters of the utmost emotional weight for him: his beloved parents, his lost childhood, his lost Russia. It is important to emphasize that just as he had no nostalgia for lost banknotes, so he had none for lost czars. His father—assassinated in Berlin in 1922 "by a sinister ruffian" because of his liberal, anti-Bolshevik views and activities—in 1905 had "severed all connection with the tsar's government and res-olutely plunged into antidespotic politics," and Nabokov shared those convictions.

No doubt there were aspects of his lost privileged life that Nabokov did miss—who in his right mind would not?—but what most pained him once he had left Russia was that he had never known it as fully as he wanted to. "The story of my college years in England," he writes, "is really the story of my trying to become a Russian writer," and he continues:

As with smarting eyes I meditated by the fire in my Cambridge room, all the potent banality of embers, solitude and distant chimes pressed against me, contorting the very folds of my face as an airman's face is disfigured by the fantastic speed of his flight. And I thought of all I had missed in my country, of the things I would not have omitted to note and treasure, had I suspected before that my life was to veer in such a violent way.

Nabokov's entire adult life was spent in exile: in England, in Europe, in the United States, finally in Switzerland, where he died in 1977 at age seventy-eight. There were times when he thought about revisiting his native land, and by the 1970s he probably could have done so without interference or incident, but by then the Russia he knew existed only in "my rich nostalgia." Also by then, he had given it a permanent place within the pages of this book, an enduring masterpiece that assures immortality for the very Russia he had lost.

THE HOUSEBREAKER OF SHADY HILL
by John Cheever

Toward the end of his life John Cheever was festooned in honors. In 1977, his novel *Falconer* was extravagantly reviewed; it got him onto the cover of Newsweek and made the bestseller lists. The next year *The Stories of John Cheever* won it all—the Pulitzer Prize, the American Book Award, the National Book Critics Circle Award—and made the bestseller lists as well. At his death in 1982 at the age of seventy, Cheever was by any definition an American literary lion.

As so often happens in American literary careers, all the huzzahs came to Cheever long after his best work had been done. *Falconer* seems to have been celebrated more because its treatment of bisexuality was considered daring at a time when closet doors were still only slightly ajar than because of its actual literary merit, which in fact is small, especially by comparison with his two earlier novels, *The Wapshot Chronicle* (1957) and *The Wapshot Scandal* (1964). His omnium-gatherum story collection is an essential monument of American literature, but because it includes stories Cheever wrote late in his career for *Playboy*, it reminds us that in those final years, he succumbed to some of the temptations of let-it-all-hang-out trendiness, and brought little credit on himself in the process.

Instead, for an accurate understanding of Cheever's genius one must turn to the work of his mid-career, the 1950s, when—in addition to the Wapshot novels—he wrote a succession of short stories, most of them published in the *New Yorker*, that have rivals but few superiors in the national liter-

ature. The 1950s, so widely misunderstood and so stupidly
maligned, were the Golden Age of the American short story,
and the *New Yorker* was the cornucopia from which many of
its riches flowed. Though many gifted writers wrote memorably during that decade, four stood apart: Flannery
O'Connor, Peter Taylor, Eudora Welty and John Cheever.
Their individual and collective achievements are almost too
grand to describe.

Doubtless many of Cheever's admirers will insist that the
best of his story collections appeared in the next decade: *The
Brigadier and the Golf Widow* (1964), which includes his most
famous short story, "The Swimmer." That is indeed a fine
book, but then so too are *The Way Some People Live* (1942),
The Enormous Radio and Other Stories (1953), *Some People,
Places, and Things That Will Not Appear in My Next Novel*
(1961) and The *World of Apples* (1973). My own favorite is *The
Housebreaker of Shady Hill* (1959), because the cumulative
effect of its eight stories is both powerful and sublime and
because it includes "The Country Husband," Cheever's masterpiece.

Like so many of the other books that have been discussed
in this series, my copy of *The Housebreaker of Shady Hill* is a
tattered paperback, this one published in 1961 by the long-
departed firm of Hillman/MacFadden. It may well have come
to me through my parents, who were passionate admirers of
stories and novels of social manners and who instilled that passion in me. Though there is far more to Cheever than manners,
that aspect of his work—the clinical, sardonic yet sympathetic
depiction of life in leafy suburbia—first drew me to it and
remains, for me, one of its greatest attractions.

Cheever himself lived a suburban life, though he was more
observer of than participant in suburbia's cozy, charged rituals.
Born in 1912 in Massachusetts into an old New England family, he suffered lasting pain when his father left his mother after

his business was destroyed by the stock market calamity of 1929. He began a literary career in the 1930s, served in the Army in World War II, and then resumed that career at war's end. He married, had children, acknowledged convention but resisted it; he was eaten away by alcohol and late in life accepted (and practiced) his bisexuality. In his journals (published in 1991) he described his desire "to write well, to write passionately, to be less inhibited, to be warmer," and:

> To disguise nothing, to conceal nothing, to write about those things that are closest to our pain, our happiness; to write about my sexual clumsiness, the agonies of Tantalus, the depth of my discouragement—I seem to glimpse it in my dreams—my despair. To write about the foolish agonies of anxiety, the refreshment of our strength when these are ended: to write about our painful search for self, jeopardized by a stranger in the post office, a half-seen face in a train window; to write about the continents and populations of our dreams, about love and death, good and evil, the end of the world.

A tall order that, and to an extraordinary degree Cheever filled it, never more so than in these eight stories. All of them— "The Housebreaker of Shady Hill," "O Youth and Beauty!," "The Country Husband," "The Sorrows of Gin," "The Worm in the Apple," "The Five-Forty-Eight," "Just Tell Me Who It Was," and "The Trouble of Marcie Flint"—are set in Shady Hill, where everybody has "a nice house with a garden and a place outside for cooking meat," and where "there was no turpitude; there had not been a divorce since he lived there; there had not even been a breath of scandal."

The second of those quotations comes from "The Country Husband" (the first is from the title story) and describes the thoughts of Francis Weed as he contemplates the possibility of turpitude and then some: a love affair with his children's teenage babysitter. She has arrived unknown to him—he had expected "to see Mrs. Henlein, the old lady who usually stayed with the children"—and immediately she leaves him breathless: ". . . he experienced in his consciousness that moment when music breaks glass, and felt a pang of recognition as strange, deep, and wonderful as anything in his life."

He loves his wife and children, but when, as he drives the sitter home, she confesses her unhappiness with her father, he puts his arms around her, lets her cry on his shoulder and is kissed "swiftly" by her at the steps of her house. The next morning "even the smell of ink from his morning paper honed his appetite for life, and the world that was spread out around him was plainly a paradise." Yes, "the autumnal loves of middle age are well publicized, and he guessed that he was face to face with one of these, but there was not a trace of autumn in what he felt. He wanted to sport in the green woods, scratch where he itched, and drink from the same cup."

All the forgotten emotions of new love descend on him: "He would be spared nothing, then, it seemed, that a fool was not spared: ravening lewdness, jealousy, this hurt to his feelings that put tears in his eyes, even scorn—for he could see clearly the image he now presented, his arms spread over the steering wheel and his head buried in them for love." He discovers that the babysitter is engaged to a dreamy young man—"lazy, irresponsible, affected, and smelly," Francis calls him—and does something almost unimaginably cruel to the boy. He acknowledges his "wickedness" and realizes that "he had reached the point where he would have to make a choice." He makes it, and the abyss is skirted. At the end he is fashioning a coffee table in the basement of his house as the parade of suburbia marches past. Last is a neighbor's dog: "He prances through the tomato vines, holding in his generous mouth the remains of an evening slipper. Then it is dark; it is a night where kings in golden suits ride elephants over mountains."

It is close to a perfect short story. In the brief space of perhaps 10,000 words Cheever creates characters whom we see in full; he portrays the exterior and interior lives of Francis Weed with astonishing complexity and subtlety; he gets the suburban ambiance exactly right; he depicts with heartbreaking accuracy the sudden onslaught of love and the tidal wave of emotions carried with it; he gives us a man in thrall to lust—"It was his life, his boat, and, like every other man, he was made to be the father of thousands, and what harm could there be in a tryst that would make them both feel more kindly toward the world?"—but who is faithful, in the end, to his own essential decency and moral sturdiness.

Though "The Country Husband" is unique, its themes and settings are shared by the other seven stories in this book and, for that matter, by just about everything else Cheever wrote. He summarized much of it quite beautifully in his brief preface to his collected stories:

> Here is the last of that generation of chain smokers who woke the world in the morning with their coughing, who used to get stoned at cocktail parties and perform obsolete dance steps like the "Cleveland Chicken," sail for Europe on ships, who were truly nostalgic for love and happiness, and whose gods were as ancient as yours and mine, whoever you are. The constants that I look for in this sometimes dated paraphernalia are a love of light and a determination to trace some moral chain of being. Calvin played no part at all in my religious education, but his presence seemed to abide in the barns of my childhood and to have left me with some undue bitterness.

Thus we have, in the title story, Johnny Hake concluding that "money had it all over love" and doing something terrible to get the money he needs—"the moral bottom had dropped out of my world without changing a mote of sunlight"—but being called "back from death" by "the lights and signs of love and friendship"; Cash Bentley, in "O Youth and Beauty!," at the mercy of "the unbeautiful facts of life"; little Amy Lawton, in "The Sorrows of Gin," who, lying in bed, "perceived vaguely the pitiful corruption of the adult world; how crude and frail it was, like a piece of worn burlap, patched with stupidities and mistakes, useless and ugly, and yet they never saw its worthlessness, and when you pointed it out to them, they were indignant."

Over and over Cheever's characters confront "the stupendous wickedness of the world," over and over they find their own measures of hope and redemption. They make mistakes, sometimes grievous ones, and "the full force of regret" eventually crashes in on most of them, yet they persevere. Cheever knew that ultimately this is the only course for all of us, and he found honorable, appealing things in our clumsy attempts to carry on. Living as they do in the suburbs, the people of Shady Hill tend to have quieter crises and epiphanies than do those in more dramatic settings, but they have them all the same. "Urged to build bomb shelters, they plant trees and roses, and their gardens are splendid and bright." That, as Cheever understood, is a good way to carry on.

THE BOYS ON THE BUS
by Timothy Crouse

In 1972 Americans were trying to decide whether to give a controversial Republican president "four more years!" (as the Nixonites chanted) or to replace him with a relatively unknown Democrat. Emotions were high thanks to a foreign war that wasn't going well, tensions between social classes were acute, and the economy was shaky.

The press was all over the campaign. But with the exception of celebrity anchormen like Walter Cronkite, John Chancellor and Harry Reasoner, journalists were little known to the electorate. The newspaper and magazine reporters who covered the race were familiar names only to their colleagues and the few readers who paid attention to bylines. The reports they filed may (or may not) have influenced the shape of the campaigns and the outcome of the election, but the reporters themselves—even those who made occasional appearances on "Meet the Press" or "Face the Nation"—were anonymous laborers in the vineyards of political journalism.

Two books that grew out of the 1972 campaign changed all that. One was *All the President's Men* (1974), the account by Bob Woodward and Carl Bernstein of the *Washington Post* of the uncovering of the Watergate scandal; the book, and even more the film adaptation of it, made its authors famous and established celebrity as a goal to which journalists might aspire. The other, *The Boys on the Bus* (1973), by Timothy Crouse, didn't enjoy quite as much eclat (though it was a bestseller) but may have had a deeper and broader effect, for it turned the eyes of the press on the press itself, and opened the way to the age of media self-absorption.

This surely was not Crouse's intention. A mere three years out of college, he managed to talk *Rolling Stone* magazine into letting him write about the men (and the very few women) who were covering both campaigns "on the bus," though the bus was usually an airplane, and in Richard Nixon's case it rarely left the White House grounds. The pieces got a lot of attention, and when Crouse expanded them into a book, people almost immediately understood that the landscape had changed: The press itself was now a story, and it has remained one—for better, but mostly for worse—ever since.

It turned out to be Crouse's only extended venture into journalism, though he did occasional freelance pieces and was *Esquire*'s Washington columnist for a while. The son of the hugely successful Broadway producer and writer Russell Crouse (1893-1966), whose credits included *The Sound of Music, Call Me Madam* and *Life With Father,* and the brother of the respected actress Lindsay Crouse, he returned to his theatrical roots in the late 1980s by rewriting, with his friend John Weidman, his father's book for Cole Porter's *Anything Goes.* Starring Patti LuPone as Reno Sweeney, the Broadway revival ran for nearly 800 performances. Now Crouse lives in North Carolina and continues to write.

Like just about everyone else in journalism, I gobbled up the *Rolling Stone* pieces seriatim and probably reviewed the book for the newspaper in North Carolina where I worked in the early 1970s, though my files (and the paper's online morgue) don't go back that far. I know for certain that I loved it. There hadn't been anything about the press even remotely like it since Gay Talese's *The Kingdom and the Power* (1969), the celebrated fly-on-the-wall portrait of the *New York Times,* and I delighted in the journalistic gossip Crouse dished out.

There was a lot more to it than gossip, though, and it is the larger matters upon which Crouse dwells that keep the book pertinent and fresh. Rereading the book after all those years, I found myself startled from time to time by the candor with which Crouse portrays some of his dramatis personae—it is easy to imagine that R.W. "Johnny" Apple, Robert Novak and Haynes Johnson wince unto this day at their portraits in the book—but that is mostly yesterday's gossip and is likely now to matter only to those most immediately involved. Journalists are scarcely as interesting as we think we are, one of the points that *The Boys on the Bus* inadvertently underscores.

Still, some of the more trivial stuff that Crouse unearthed hasn't lost its sizzle. He has a deft way of summing people up, as in this sketch of Jules Witcover, who was then (unhappily) with the *Los Angeles Times* and whom he mostly portrays with sympathy and respect: "He had the pale, hounded look of a small liquor store owner whose shop has just been held up for the seventh time in a year." He nails "group journalism" as practiced at *Time* magazine right on the head: "The correspondents filed about 750,000 words every week, and then the editors took over. The editors worked in the New York office, and their job was to throw away about 700,000 of those words. Then they rewrote about 85 percent of the remaining copy." He perfectly captures life aboard the bus, or the plane:

> The fact that [some reporters] thought that McGovern had a chance to win showed the folly of trying to call an election from 30,000 feet in the air. . . . The reporters attached to George McGovern had a very limited usefulness as political observers, by and large, for what they knew best was not the American electorate but the tiny community of the press plane, a totally abnormal world that combined the incestuousness of a New England hamlet with the giddiness of a mid-ocean gala and the physical rigors of the Long March.

That passage is both witty and funny, but it also is true. More clearly than anyone before him, Crouse understood that journalists travel in packs. This is as true, let me hasten to say, of journalists who write book reviews as of journalists who cover political campaigns, perhaps even more so, since the pressures on the former to parrot the conventional literary wisdom are intense. But right at the outset Crouse identifies the "womblike conditions" of the bus and/or plane as giving rise to "the notorious phenomenon called 'pack journalism,'" and goes on: "They all fed off the same pool report, the same daily handout, the same speech by the candidate; the whole pack was isolated in the same mobile village. After a while, they began to believe the same rumors, subscribe to the same theories, and write the same stories."

At a precociously early age, Crouse understood some essential but little-known truths about journalists and journalism: that journalists are deathly afraid of being "wrong" and thus tend to stay within parameters set by the pack; that journalists want "to be on the Winner's Bus" because "a campaign reporter's career is linked to the fortunes of his candidate" and they don't "like to dwell on signs that their Winner [is] losing, any more than a soup manufacturer likes to admit that there is botulism in the vichyssoise"; that "journalism is probably the slowest-moving, most tradition-bound profession in America," refusing "to budge until it is shoved into the future by some irresistible external force." With regard to this last he cites the reluctance of the rest of the press to follow the Watergate trail pursued by Woodward and Bernstein until the courts got into the action; a few years later he could have cited the reluctance of the press to acknowledge the existence, much less the threat and opportunity, of the Internet.

Crouse doesn't write in a snide, condescending or superior manner. He liked most of the people he wrote about, found much that interested and impressed him in the people he didn't like, and sympathized with all of them as they tried to do good work under difficult, draining circumstances. He acknowledges that "any self-respecting journalist would sooner endorse incest than come out in favor of pack journalism" and that as long ago as 1972 "the men on the bus had more authority and independence than ever before, and many of them were searching for new ways to report on the freakish, insular existence of the press bus, and for ways to break away from the pack."

Still, he makes some damning points that are as true today as they were four decades ago. "If there was a consensus," he writes, "it was simply because all the national political reporters lived in Washington, saw the same people, used the same sources, belonged to the same background groups, and swore by the same omens. They arrived at their answers just as independently as a class of honest seventh-graders using the same geometry text—they did not have to cheat off each other to come up with the same answer." If anything, that is even more the case now, as the "inside-the-Beltway mentality" has ballooned into both a truism and the truth.

Crouse is especially tough on the White House press corps, "a strange mixture of professional witnesses, decree-promulgators, cheerleaders, hard-diggers, goldbricks and gadflies." He quotes Russell Baker, who served time there, as calling it an "airless kind of work" because "the White House was like a Stuart court, Baker thought, and all the correspondents lingered like courtiers in the antechambers." The White House is the ultimate Winner's Bus, with predictable consequences:

> Some reporters thrived in this suffocating palace atmosphere. They began to think of themselves as part of the White House, and they proudly identified themselves as being "from the White House press" instead of mentioning the paper they worked for. They forgot that they were handout artists and convinced themselves that they were somehow associates of a man who was shaping epochal events. . . . The faces of these men [in old photos on the pressroom wall] were infused with a funny expression, a

pathetic aura of pride, a sense that they were taking part in the colossal moments of history. Now most of those moments were forgotten, and no one remembered a word that any of these men had written.

"Men" is the word, all right. Women were rarities, at the White House and even more so on the bus. Crouse argues that "some of the toughest pieces on the 1972 Nixon campaign" were done by women because "having never been allowed to join in the cozy, clubby world of the men, they had developed an uncompromising detachment and a bold independence of thought which often put the men to shame." Perhaps that was true then, but women are in the club now—along with blacks and Hispanics and gays and everyone else—and guess what? The pack is bigger than ever.

THE SKETCH BOOK
by Washington Irving

Of all the books that have been and will be revisited in this series, none reaches back more deeply into my own past than Washington Irving's *The Legend of Sleepy Hollow,* originally published in 1819 as *The Sketch Book of Geoffrey Crayon, Gent.* When I was a very small boy in the early 1940s, my parents read to me about Rip Van Winkle and Ichabod Crane over and over again, and as a somewhat larger boy I read about them myself, over and over again. Their stories—Rip's twenty year snooze, Ichabod's encounter with the Headless Horseman—might as well have been bred in my bones, I know (and love) them so.

But it's been a long, long time since I've read them, maybe as many as fifty-five years. Coming to *The Sketch Book* (as I'll refer to it henceforth) after all that time has been an eye-opener, and then some. I realize now that, for all my powerful sense of intimacy with the book, I'd probably read only about a half-dozen of its nearly three dozen sketches, and probably read those—"Rip Van Winkle" and "Sleepy Hollow"—in versions that had been rewritten and edited for children. I realize as well that I'd had only a glimmering of what a splendid (if limited) writer Irving was, in particular what an ebullient humorist he was, so this Second Reading must begin with the admission that it is a discovery as well as a rediscovery.

When I was not quite three years old, in the late summer of 1942, my father took a headmaster's job at a town in the Ramapo Mountains of southeastern New York. He had a passionate love of American history and on weekends (gas rationing permitting) enjoyed taking his family to places along and near the Hudson River: the Catskills, West Point, Tarrytown, Bear Mountain. Of all my childhood memories, these are among the happiest, and they are inextricably connected to Irving's two great short stories, which are set in and about those places. Fiction and fact? I could barely distinguish them. The places where my family drove in our little Ford were Washington Irving's places, as to me they always will be.

Irving was born in New York City in 1783 into a prosperous mercantile family and named in honor of the famed general of the recently ended Revolutionary War. It was assumed that he would follow his father and brothers into business, but he studied law instead. His real love was writing, and by the time he was in his early twenties he had begun to publish newspaper pieces. His heart was broken in 1809 by the death of his young fiancée, but later that year publication of his satirical *A History of New York,* under the pseudonym Diedrich Knickerbocker, was a great success and established him as a professional writer, though for some time he continued to struggle to support himself by his pen.

The three dozen pieces in *The Sketch Book* were written while he was on an extended stay in England, motivated in part by family business and in part by his inveterate urge for travel: "I was always fond of visiting new scenes, and observing strange characters and manners." Like many educated Americans of his time, he had strongly ambivalent feelings toward England, admiring its accomplishments and traditions but resenting its snobbery and condescension. Strong strains of both are evident in *The Sketch Book,* sections of which appeared serially in England and America in 1819 and 1820. On the one hand there are lavish paeans to numerous aspects of British life, from the countryside and its churches to Westminster Abbey and its Poets' Corner, but on the other there are sharp gibes at British pretentiousness and supercil-iousness, particularly at British travelers in the United States, who "underrate a society, where there are no artificial distinc-tions, and where, by any chance, such individuals as them-selves can rise to consequence."

Irving's sketches of England led him to various tart and/or perceptive comments. What he wrote almost two centuries ago about hack writing is fully applicable today: "I have often won-dered at the extreme fecundity of the press, and how it comes to pass that so many heads, on which nature seemed to have inflicted the curse of barrenness, should teem with voluminous productions." What he has to say about great writers and their readers, inspired by visiting the monuments to the great at Poets' Corner, is similarly timeless:

> . . . there is something of companionship between the author and the reader. Other men are known to posterity only through the medium of history, which is continually growing faint and obscure; but the intercourse between the author and his fellow-men is ever new, active and immediate. He has lived for them more than for himself; he has sacrificed surrounding enjoyments, and shut himself up from the delights of social life, that he might the more intimately commune with distant minds and distant ages. Well may the world cherish his renown; for it has been pur-chased not by deeds of violence and blood, but by the diligent dispensation of pleasure. Well may posterity be grateful to his memory; for he has left it an inheritance, not of empty names and sounding actions, but whole treasures of wisdom, bright gems of thought, and golden veins of language.

The point is proved by *The Sketch Book* itself, which has survived the years with remarkable resilience and undimin-ished pertinence, notwithstanding Irving's sentimental streak. But it is for the two great short stories that we are still most likely to read it, and in which we are still most likely to detect "the diligent dispensation of pleasure." Both are believed to be based on German folk tales, relocated by Irving to the Hudson Valley he loved and knew so well. The stories of Rip Van Winkle and Ichabod Crane are as deeply ingrained in American mythology as those of George Washington and the cherry tree, Ben Franklin and his kite, Abraham Lincoln reading by firelight.

When I heard the stories as a boy of four or five, when I read them as a boy of seven or eight, I was most enthralled by their mystery and suspense: How did Rip manage to sleep through two whole decades? Was that really the Headless Horseman who chased Ichabod right out of Sleepy Hollow, or was it Brom Bones in disguise? Reading the stories now, I am most struck by their characters and their humor. Rip is "a simple, good-natured man . . . a kind neighbor, and an obedient henpecked husband" who has "an insuperable aversion to all kinds of profitable labor," "one of those happy mortals of foolish, well-oiled dispositions, who take the world easy, eat white bread or brown, whichever can be got with least thought or trouble, and would rather starve on a penny than work for a pound." His wife is a "termagant" and keeps him in a "species of despotism" called "petticoat government." Small wonder that he escapes to the mountains, where he discovers "a company of odd-looking personages playing at ninepins" and hears "the noise of the balls, which, whenever they were rolled, echoed along the mountains like rumbling peals of thunder."

As a small boy, lying abed in the Ramapos, I was both thrilled and terrified whenever a thunderstorm swept through, convinced as I was that this was "Hendrick Hudson, the first discoverer of the river and country," and his men "in their old Dutch dresses playing at nine pins in a hollow of the mountain" and that I was hearing "the sound of their balls, like distant peals of thunder." I loved that image then, and find that over six decades it has lost none of its power to move and amuse me.

Wonderful as Rip's story is, it almost pales beside Ichabod's. In his excellent introduction to the Penguin Classics edition, William L. Hedges argues that Irving in *The Sketch Book* had "given form to both the literary sketch and what was eventually to be called the short story," opening the way for Poe and Melville and innumerable others to follow. "The Legend of Sleepy Hollow" is, beyond dispute, a great American short story. It is set two miles from Tarrytown, in "a little valley, or rather lap of land among high hills, which is one of the quietest places in the whole world." A "drowsy, dreamy influence seems to hang over the land, and to pervade the very atmosphere," and strange spirits inhabit the place:

> Certain it is, the place still continues under the sway of some witching power that holds a spell over the minds of the good people, causing them to walk in a continual reverie. They are given to all kinds of marvelous beliefs, are subject to trances and visions, and frequently see strange sights, and hear music and voices in the air. The whole neighborhood abounds with local tales, haunted spots, and twilight superstitions; stars shoot and meteors glare oftener across the valley than in any other part of the country, and the nightmare, with her whole ninefold, seems to make it the favorite scene of her gambols.

No sight is stranger to the imaginations of the locals than "the apparition of a figure on horseback without a head," perhaps "the ghost of a Hessian trooper," who "rides forth to the scene of battle in nightly quest of his head," and no one is more firmly in the grip of that apparition than the schoolmaster, Ichabod Crane, who is "esteemed by the women as a man of great erudition, for he had read several books quite through, and was a perfect master of Cotton Mather's *History of New England Witchcraft*, in which, by the way, he most firmly and potently believed."

Among the women of the village, one is of special interest to Ichabod: Katrina Van Tassel, "the daughter and only child of a substantial Dutch farmer," a "blooming lass of fresh eighteen; plump as a partridge; ripe and melting and rosy cheeked as one of her father's peaches; and universally famed, not merely for her beauty, but her vast expectations." She wears "a provokingly short petticoat, to display the prettiest foot and ankle in the country round," and "from the moment Ichabod laid his eyes upon these regions of delight, the peace of his mind was at an end, and his only study was how to gain the affections of the peerless daughter of Van Tassel."

Alas for Ichabod, in his way stands Brom Van Brunt, known as Brom Bones "from his Herculean frame and great powers of limb." He too eyes this "country coquette" and the Van Tassel fortune: "This rantipole hero had for some time singled out the blooming Katrina for the object of his uncouth gallantries, and though his amorous toyings were something like the gentle caresses and endearments of a bear, yet it was whispered that she did not altogether discourage his hopes." As to the upshot of all this, you know, of course, what happens, as Irving brings his classic tale to its deliciously funny and absolutely perfect conclusion.

Irving was in his late thirties when "The Legend of Sleepy Hollow" was published. Ahead of him lay a long and astonishingly productive career that lasted almost to the moment of his death in 1859, but nothing he wrote thereafter reached the heights of this classic, essential, exquisitely American tale.

THE CATCHER IN THE RYE
by J.D. Salinger

Precisely how old I was when I first read *The Catcher in the Rye*, I cannot recall. When it was published, in 1951, I was twelve years old, and thus may have been a trifle young for it. Within the next two or three years, though, I was on a forced march through a couple of schools similar to Pencey Prep, from which J.D. Salinger's sixteen-year-old protagonist Holden Caulfield is dismissed as the novel begins, and I was an unhappy camper; what I had heard about *The Catcher in the Rye* surely convinced me that Caulfield was a kindred spirit.

By then *The Catcher in the Rye* was already well on the way to the status it has long enjoyed as an essential document of American adolescence—the novel that every high school English teacher reflexively puts on every summer reading list—but I couldn't see what all the excitement was about. I shared Caulfield's contempt for "phonies" as well as his sense of being different and his loneliness, but he seemed to me just about as phony as those he criticized as well as an unregenerate whiner and egotist. It was easy enough to identify with his adolescent angst, but his puerile attitudinizing was something else altogether.

That was then. This is half a century later. *The Catcher in the Rye* is now, you'll be told just about anywhere you ask, an "American classic," right up there with the book that was published the following year, Ernest Hemingway's *The Old Man and the Sea*. They are two of the most durable and beloved books in American literature and, by any reasonable critical standard, two of the worst. Rereading *The Catcher in the Rye* after all those years was almost literally a painful experience: The combination of Salinger's execrable prose and Caulfield's jejune narcissism produced effects comparable to mainlining castor oil.

Over that half-century I'd pretty much forgotten about *The Catcher in the Rye*, though scarcely about Salinger, whose celebrated reclusiveness had the effect of keeping him in the public eye. He published no books since *Raise High the Roof Beam, Carpenters* and *Seymour: An Introduction* in 1963, but plenty was published about him, including Ian Hamilton's decidedly unauthorized biography, *In Search of J.D. Salinger* (1988); Joyce Maynard's self-serving account of her affair with him, *At Home in the World* (1998); and his daughter Margaret A. Salinger's (also self-serving) memoir, *Dream Catcher* (2000), not to mention reams of lit crit and fanzine fawning. Rumors repeatedly made their way across the land that Salinger was busily at his writing table, that his literary fecundity remained undiminished, that bank vaults in New England contain vast stores of unpublished Salingeriana, but to date all the speculation has come to naught, for which we should—though too many people won't—be grateful.

If there's an odder duck in American literature than Salinger, his or her name doesn't come quickly to mind. He started out conventionally enough—born in Manhattan in 1919, served (valiantly) in the infantry in Europe during World War II, wrote short stories that were published in respectable magazines, notably the *New Yorker*—but he seems to have been totally undone by the fame that *The Catcher in the Rye* inflicted upon him. For nearly four decades until his extravagantly lamented death in 2010 he was a semi-hermit (he married for the third time in the late 1980s) in his New England fastness, spurning journalists and fending off adoring fans, practicing the Zen Buddhism that seems to have become an obsession with him.

It was weird, but it also was his business. If, Garbolike, he just *vanted to be alone*, he was entitled. But whether calculated or not, his reclusiveness created an aura that heightens, rather than diminishes, the mystique of *The Catcher in the Rye*. It isn't just a novel, it's a dispatch from an unknown, mysterious universe, which may help explain the phenomenal sales it enjoys to this day: about 250,000 copies a year, with total worldwide sales over—probably way over—ten million. The mass-market paperback I bought is, incredibly, from the forty-second printing; for the astonishing price of $35,000 you can buy, online, a signed copy not of the first edition—a signed copy of that, we must assume, would be almost literally priceless—but of the 1951 Book-of-the-Month Club edition.

Viewed from the vantage point of half a century, the novel raises more questions than it answers. Why is a book about a spoiled rich kid kicked out of a fancy prep school so widely read by ordinary Americans, the overwhelming majority of whom have limited means and attend, or attended, public schools? Why is Holden Caulfield nearly universally seen as "a symbol of purity and sensitivity" (as The Oxford Companion to American Literature puts it) when he's merely self-regarding and callow? Why do English teachers, whose responsibility is to teach good writing, repeatedly and reflexively require students to read a book as badly written as this one?

That last question actually is easily answered: *The Catcher in the Rye* can be fobbed off on kids as a book about themselves. It is required reading as therapy, a way to encourage young people to bathe in the warm, soothing waters of resentment (all grown-ups are phonies) and self-pity without having to think a lucid thought. Like that other (albeit marginally better) novel about lachrymose preppies, John Knowles's *A Separate Peace* (1960), *The Catcher in the Rye* touches adolescents' emotional buttons without putting their minds to work. It's easy for them, which makes it easy for teacher.

What most struck me upon reading it for a second time was how sentimental—how outright squishy—it is. The novel is commonly represented as an expression of adolescent cynicism and rebellion—a James Dean movie in print—but from first page to last Salinger wants to have it both ways. Holden is a rebel and all that—"the most terrific liar you ever saw in your life," "probably the biggest sex maniac you ever saw"— but he's a softy at heart. He's always pitying people—"I felt sorry as hell for him, all of a sudden," "You had to feel a little sorry for the crazy sonuvabitch," "Real ugly girls have it tough. I feel so sorry for them sometimes"—and he is positively a saint when it comes to his little sister, Phoebe. He buys a record for her, "Little Shirley Beans," and in the course of moping around Manhattan he does something clumsy that gives him the chance to show what a good-hearted guy he really is:

> Then something terrible happened just as I got in the park. I dropped old Phoebe's record. It broke into about fifty pieces. It was in a big envelope and all, but it broke anyway. I damn near cried, it made me feel so terrible, but all I did was, I took the pieces out of the envelope and put them in my coat pocket. They weren't good for anything, but I didn't feel like just throwing them away. Then I went in the park. Boy, was it dark.

Me, I damn near puked. That passage is flagrantly manipulative, a tug on the heartstrings aimed at bringing a tear to the eye. Ditto for Holden's brother, Allie: "He's dead now. He got leukemia and died when we were up in Maine, on July 18, 1946. You'd have liked him. He was two years younger than I was, but he was about fifty times as intelligent. He was terrifically intelligent. His teachers were always writing letters to my mother, telling her what a pleasure it was having a boy like

Allie in their class. And they weren't just shooting the crap. They really meant it."

That's just easy exploitation of the reader's emotion. Give your protagonist a dead younger brother and a cute little sister—not to mention a revered older brother, D.B., a gifted writer who sounds a whole lot like J.D. Salinger himself—and the rest is strictly downhill. From first page to last, *The Catcher in the Rye* is an exercise in button-pushing, and the biggest button it pushes is the adolescent's uncertainty and insecurity as he or she perches precariously between childhood, which is remembered fondly and wistfully, and adulthood, which is the great phony unknown. Indeed a case can be made that *The Catcher in the Rye* created adolescence as we now know it, a condition that barely existed until Salinger defined it. He established whining rebellion as essential to adolescence and it has remained such ever since. It was a short leap indeed from *The Catcher in the Rye* to *The Blackboard Jungle* to *Rebel Without a Cause* to Valley Girls to the multibillion-dollar industry that adolescent angst is today.

The cheap sentimentality with which the novel is suffused reaches a climax of sorts when Holden's literary side comes to the fore. He flunks all his courses except English. "I'm quite illiterate," he says early in the book, "but I read a lot," which establishes the mixture of self-deprecation and self-congratulation that seems to appeal to so many readers. In one of the novel's more widely quoted passages he then says:

> What really knocks me out is a book that, when you're all done reading it, you wish the author that wrote it was a terrific friend of yours and you could call him up on the phone whenever you felt like it. That doesn't happen much, though. I wouldn't mind calling this Isak Dinesen up. And Ring Lardner, except that D.B. told me he's dead.

That Ring Lardner is one of Holden's favorite writers is a

considerable, if wholly inadvertent, irony. Lardner was the master of the American vernacular who, as H.L. Mencken wrote, "set down common American with the utmost precision." Salinger, by contrast, can be seen straining at every turn to write the way an American teenager would speak, but he only produces an adult's unwitting parody of teen-speak. Unlike Lardner, Salinger has a tin ear. His characters forever say "ya" for "you," as in "ya know," which no American except perhaps a slapstick comedian ever has said. Americans say "yuh know" or "y'know," but never "ya know."

The Catcher in the Rye is a maladroit, mawkish novel, but there can be no question about its popularity or influence. My own hunch is that the reason is the utter, innocent sincerity with which it was written. It may be manipulative, but it's not phony. A better, more cynical writer than Salinger easily could write a book about a troubled yet appealing teenager, but its artifice and insincerity would be self-evident and readers would reject it as false. Whatever its shortcomings, *The Catcher in the Rye* is from the heart—not Holden Caulfield's heart, but Jerome David Salinger's. He said everything he had to say in it, which may well be why he said nothing else.

CRAZY SALAD
by Nora Ephron

It's one of the book industry's basic operating rules, so axiomatic that it ought to be capitalized: Collections Don't Sell. This has always struck me as odd, since I love to dip in and out of books by writers whose prose and ideas I admire, sampling here and there without committing to the long haul that a "real" book entails. My shelves are lined with short-story collections by the likes of Eudora Welty, John Cheever, Flannery O'Connor and Peter Taylor, and nonfiction collections by the likes of Russell Baker, A.J. Liebling, Fran Lebowitz and Joseph Epstein.

Nora Ephron, too. During the 1970s she was one of the country's best journalists and/or essayists, and during that decade she published three collections: *Wallflower at the Orgy* (1970), *Crazy Salad: Some Things About Women* (1975) and *Scribble Scribble: Notes on the Media* (1978). Apart from the wit and perspicacity of the pieces collected therein, what distinguishes Ephron from just about every writer relegated to the graveyard where collections are buried is that one of them broke the rule: It did sell.

This was *Crazy Salad,* Ephron's sympathetic but mischievous and occasionally contrarian look at American women generally and the women's movement specifically. At a moment in its history when that movement was almost aggressively humorless, Ephron wrote about it with irreverence and a merciless eye for hypocrisy and self-satisfaction. Perhaps, after surpassingly turgid feminist tomes such as Kate Millett's *Sexual*

Politics, readers were ready for a fresh, undogmatic, cheeky view of a subject about which too many people clearly had gotten entirely too solemn. Whatever the explanation, *Crazy Salad,* which takes its splendid title from William Butler Yeats—"It's certain that fine women eat / A crazy salad with their meat"—was exactly the right book for the moment, and the reading public greeted it enthusiastically.

Toward the end of it Ephron noted, in a piece about Martha Mitchell, that "there is not much call for yesterday's celebrities," and a second reading leaves no doubt that this is something of a problem for *Crazy Salad* as it nears the end of its third decade. Ephron's prose is as spare and tart as ever, and her insights remain acute, but a fair amount of stuff herein is yesterday's news. Most readers under fifty probably will have to be told that Martha Mitchell was the "slightly dizzy" estranged wife of Richard Nixon's attorney general; that Barbara Mandel was the estranged wife of the governor of Maryland; that Betty Friedan, who as author of *The Feminine Mystique* had done much to start the women's movement, by the 1970s had become something of a superannuated bore; that Rose Mary Woods was the White House secretary who did or did not erase eighteen and a half minutes from a tape recording pertaining to the Watergate investigation; that Bernice Gera was the first woman to umpire a professional baseball game.

Et cetera. These are problems most certainly not of Ephron's making, but they are problems all the same. Yet for me at least, they matter a good deal less than the pungency of Ephron's opinions and prose, her refusal to march in lockstep with feminist orthodoxy, her eye for the ludicrous and the self-righteous. I had been an admirer of Ephron's work (much of it published in *Esquire*) long before the book appeared, and I gobbled *Crazy Salad* right up, including it in my list of the best books of 1975 that I compiled for the *Miami Herald*, where I then worked.

Crazy Salad didn't come from out of the blue. Ephron wasn't exactly born with the proverbial silver spoon in her mouth, but she got off to a head start. She grew up in Beverly Hills, a daughter of prominent screenwriting parents. She hung around with the children of other Hollywood notables, attended Beverly Hills High School, then went to Wellesley College. After her graduation in 1962 she was hired as a reporter by the *New York Post*, an experience about which she writes amusingly and touchingly in *Scribble Scribble*. After that she went freelance, writing for *Esquire*, *New York*, *Rolling Stone*, the *New Yorker* and other magazines.

In *Crazy Salad* Ephron describes being photographed by Philippe Halsman, who had done "a charming book containing photographs of celebrities jumping," and being told by him that "you have only one jump in you." Subsequent developments have proved him entirely wrong. Journalism, for her, was the first of several jumps. After *Scribble Scribble* she published a funny, best-selling novel, *Heartburn* (1983), based on her spectacularly unsuccessful marriage to Carl Bernstein, and later in that decade she picked up where her parents had left off. She wrote screenplays, then moved along to producing and directing. Her best-known films are *When Harry Met Sally* (1989), *Sleepless in Seattle* (1993), *You've Got Mail* (1998) and *Julie and Julia* (2009)

At the time Ephron started movie work, I thought that Hollywood's gain was journalism's loss, and a rereading of all three of her collections leaves me even more firmly convinced of that. Journalism today has too many self-important, humorless, money-grubbing bigfeet, most of whom are far less interested in the story than in the storyteller. Ephron, as a columnist charged with expressing her own opinions, managed to strike the right balance between story and self. That she had a large and devoted readership had much to do with her ability to create a persona (one that presumably was fairly close to reality) with which readers could identify, in large measure because she was self-deprecating and actually seemed to mean it.

Thus we have Ephron writing about *Deep Throat* ("one of the most unpleasant, disturbing films I have ever seen—it is not just anti-female but anti-sexual as well"), and admitting that she is "a hung-up, uptight, middle-class, inhibited, possibly puritanical feminist who lost her sense of humor at a skin flick"; acknowledging that she would "hate to be described as a participatory journalist; but I am a writer and I am a feminist, and the two seem to be constantly in conflict"; confessing that "all I wanted in this world was to come to New York and be Dorothy Parker. The funny lady. The only lady at the table," and then admitting that "I have spent a great deal of my life discovering that my ambitions and fantasies—which I once thought of as totally unique—turn out to be cliches, so it was not a surprise to me to find that there were other young women writers who came to New York with as bad a Dorothy Parker problem as I had."

Ephron calls herself a feminist, but she scarcely prattles the party line. Taking note of the incredible rivalries and animosities among feminists in the 1970s, she says (correctly) that "the women's liberation movement at this point in history makes the American Communist Party of the 1930s look like a monolith." She takes note of "a tendency throughout the movement to overindulge in confession, to elevate The Rap to a religious end in itself, to reach a point where self-knowledge dissolves into high-grade narcissism." Writing about Phyllis Chesler's "badly written and self-indulgent" book *Women and Madness* (1973), the research in which "seems to me to be full of holes," she makes the essential but commonly overlooked point that "one of the recurring ironies of this movement [is] that there is no way to tell the truth about it without, in some small way, seeming to hurt it"—that "sisterhood . . . doesn't make for good criticism" because the movement demands praise for anything, no matter how bad, that parrots the orthodoxy.

The movement is a bit less strident now and "postfeminism" (whatever that means) is said in some quarters to be the new orthodoxy, but Ephron's views of three decades ago remain pertinent. Strictly toed party lines are for the apparatchiks of Stalinist Russia or Islamic radicals of today, not for organizations trying to advance their causes in a democracy as unruly and elastic as ours. "Movement platitudes" may come easily to those who mouth them, but they oversimplify the complex and comfort those who utter them at the expense of facing reality head-on.

Which is to say that Ephron had then and presumably has to this day no patience with ideologues, fools, poseurs and the self-deluded. The classic piece with which *Crazy Salad* ends, her evisceration of the post-sex-change Jan Morris ("James Morris has become Jan Morris, an Englishwoman who wears sweater sets and pearls, blushes frequently, bursts into tears at the littlest things, and loves having a gossip with someone named Mrs. Weatherby"), is delicious evidence that she is entirely capable of simultaneously wielding a stiletto and a bludgeon. Yet she is just as capable of doing an end run around the reader's expectations. The "frowzy, excessive, blathering" Martha Mitchell turns out, on close inspection, to be "charming" and "canny" and "moving." As for Rose Mary Woods:

> She gives the impression of being quite petite, and her friends say that she is somewhat frail physically and has suffered periodic bouts of pneumonia from overwork. She has literally worked seven-day, hundred-hour weeks, fifty-two weeks a year for twenty-three years—and in many ways she is not at all unique. There are thousands of women like her in Washington, women who come here as girls, get secretarial jobs on Capitol Hill, devote their lives to politicians, and end up elderly spinsters, living on their government pensions in apartments full of political knickknacks.

Perhaps that has changed in the intervening years, what with the acceptance of many of feminism's precepts in society and the workforce, but one rather suspects it hasn't; the self-sacrificial urge that causes some people to genuflect before others is deep in human nature and can't be erased by slogans or laws. Ditto: ". . . life for women in Washington combined the worst qualities of the South and small-town life. Washington is a city of locker-room boys, and all the old, outmoded notions apply: men and women are ushered to separate rooms after dinner, sex is dirty, and they are still serving onion-soup dip." Again, in some ways that's changed—there are now women on the Supreme Court, and no Washington host would dare separate the boys and the girls after dinner—but the essential truth about this city and its attitude toward women is unchanged.

In these matters as in so many others, Ephron got it just right. Long after its publication, *Crazy Salad* remains smart, acerbic and very much to the point. It is also a great deal of fun.

A New Life
by Bernard Malamud

P ersonal liberty is so deeply ingrained in our culture that we rarely think about it; it is as essential to the interior American landscape as amber waves of grain and purple mountain majesties are to the exterior one. The opportunity to build a new life is no less essential to our sense of who we are; not merely is it why millions of people have immigrated to America over the generations, it is also why Americans themselves are constantly on the move, seeking better prospects than the ones they were born with.

In literature as in life: From Huck Finn to Jay Gatsby to Augie March to the unnamed protagonist of Ralph Ellison's *Invisible Man,* over and over again in American literature we meet people who are in transit and looking for rebirth. As Bernard Malamud wrote in his third novel—called, appropriately enough, *A New Life*—"If this was spring, Levin knew it because he eternally hunted for it, was always nosing out the new season, the new life, 'a new birth in freedom.'" No story tells us more about ourselves than this quest for a new life, and few have told it better than Malamud did in that 1961 novel.

It is perhaps a mistake on my part, and certainly it gives me no pleasure, but my impression is that Malamud has been slowly fading from the literary landscape since his death in 1986. For three and a half decades, beginning with the publication in 1952 of his wonderful first novel, *The Natural*, Malamud was one of our most admired writers of fiction. To this date his major works are all in print thanks to the good offices of his publisher, Farrar, Straus & Giroux, but his name no longer is among the first mentioned when important American writers of the twentieth century are discussed. Presumably he is still read in university literature courses and perhaps in book clubs as well, but by contrast with his approximate contemporaries Saul Bellow and Philip Roth, he seems no longer to be at the center of our literary consciousness.

Readers old enough to remember when all three of those writers were in their prime will recognize the trinity at once: Beginning in the 1960s, Bellow, Malamud and Roth invariably were pigeonholed as the grand masters of "Jewish-American fiction." The evidence indicates that they admired each other's work and were preoccupied with many of the same themes, but they tended to regard the pigeonholing as a gross oversimplification and, indeed, as ghettoizing. Each in his own way wrote about being, simultaneously, Jewish and American, but each in his own way insisted that the larger canvas—the American one—was what mattered, and that viewing it through Jewish eyes was merely one particular slant on it, a point made implicitly by Roth in his novel *The Plot Against America.*

The same point is made in different ways by Malamud in *A New Life.* As the novelist Jonathan Lethem writes in his smart introduction to a 2004 paperback edition of it, *A New Life* is "seemingly the least Jewish of Malamud's books," in which the "word Jew is only mentioned once, practically on the last page." Its protagonist, Seymour Levin, is clearly a Jew from the moment in August 1950 that, "bearded, fatigued, lonely," he arrives at a college town in the Northwest, a stranger in "a strange land," but it matters less that he is a Jew than that he is a city boy, an outsider, a Manhattanite set down in the alien corn of a state called Cascadia, aka Oregon.

Levin is thirty years old, which was approximately my age when I first read *A New Life* in the late 1960s. As one who was beginning to fashion a career as a book reviewer, I knew it was necessary to familiarize myself with Malamud's work, as his novel *The Fixer* had swept the major prizes in 1967 and he was commonly regarded as among the most important writers of the day. Though *The Fixer* struck me as preachy, his superb short stories and his first two novels—*The Natural* and *The Assistant* (1957)—made lasting impressions on me, especially the latter, which I regard as a masterpiece in miniature.

Even in the innocence and ignorance of youth, I understood that *A New Life* was a significant departure for Malamud. Again to quote Lethem, it is Malamud's "most traditional, and least mythic," work of fiction. The fabulism and brevity that characterize almost all his writing are scarcely to be found here; *A New Life* is long, realistic and conventional. The wit of Malamud's best work is much in evidence—indeed, at times *A New Life* is laugh-out-loud funny—but the novel is grounded in quotidian reality in ways not often found elsewhere in his writings.

Beyond that, *A New Life* unquestionably is the most autobiographical of all Malamud's fiction. From 1949 until 1961 Malamud taught at what was then known as Oregon State College in Corvallis; Levin teaches (though only for one year) at Cascadia College, a "science and technology college" like Oregon State in which the liberal arts get little more than a nod. The English department in which the naive, idealistic Levin finds himself offers "a glut of composition, bonehead grammar, and remedial reading, over about a dozen skimpy literature courses."

Levin has arrived in Cascadia essentially by accident, as we learn toward the end of the novel, but he is glad to be there: "Considering that he had just got his M.A. at thirty, and had only high school teaching experience to offer, Levin felt it was the greatest good luck that he had landed an instructorship in any college." Like Malamud, who got to Oregon after fits and starts at gainful employment, Levin is ready to start over. He is "a man at thirty still running after last year's train, far behind in the world," hoping to find in this bucolic setting the things he most wants: "Order, value, accomplishment, love." Instead he finds the unexpected: a life totally unlike anything he previously had known.

Thus he encounters a woman named Laverne and heads off with her to a barn: "It was overwhelming how his life had changed in a month. You gave up the Metropolitan Museum of Art and got love in a haystack." To his surprise he "had cut himself off . . . from longing for the East." He delights in the college's "green-lawned, thickly-treed quadrangle, liking its order and beauty as he recalled the stone skyscrapers in which he had gone to college." He is in a "new world." He buys a used car, learns to drive, astonishes himself with what he can do:

> For the first time in his life Levin was on the road alone in a car—his own—carried along on his own power, so to say. Three cheers for the pioneers of the auto industry; they had put him on wheels to go where he pleased! He thought with pleasure of the many things he had learned to do in his few months here: had mowed frequent lawns, the grass still green and growing in December; raked a billion leaves, fifty percent from neighboring trees; gathered walnuts in October; picked yellow pears; regularly attended and even cleaned [the landlady's] rumbling sawdust furnace, and so on and what not. Last week he had washed and waxed his car. Levin the handy man; that is to say, man of hands.

He is a "city boy let loose" in the abundant riches of nature, and he delights in them. Not merely does he frolic in barns, he also takes long walks through the countryside and then, once he has mastered his automobile, even longer drives. But Levin is still Levin, and the propensity for getting himself into trouble that had driven him away from the East scarcely deserts him in the West. He botches things with Laverne—"Don't ever let me see you again in your whole goddam life," she shouts in farewell—and does even worse with Nadalee, a luscious coed with whom he violates the college's rule against faculty-student extracurriculars. He is sucked into campus politics as two colleagues compete to become head of the department, in the process managing to make an utter fool of himself.

Then he gets involved with Pauline Gilley, the wife of a colleague. She is "an interesting-looking woman," flat-chested but with "shapely legs" whom he finds attractive and beguiling. In spite of himself, he becomes entangled, and ends up with a lot more than he'd bargained for. What begins as sex eventually turns into love, with consequences that turn his life upside down and send him away from Cascadia to begin, quite literally, a new life, with commitments and responsibilities he certainly hadn't anticipated when he arrived there the previous year.

All of this plays out against the story of Leo Duffy, "a sort of disagreeable radical who made a lot of trouble," according to Pauline's odious husband, Gerald. Duffy ultimately was sacked. Levin now occupies his office and is haunted by him, though he never appears in the novel; for the Jewish Levin, Duffy becomes an Irish doppelganger. Pauline tells him: "Leo was different and not the slightest bit fake under any circumstances. He was serious about ideas and should have been given a fair chance to defend his. People were irritated with him because he challenged their premises." In time Levin does much the same, with results that parallel but do not replicate Duffy's.

As is made plain by Duffy's story, by the competition for the departmental chairmanship, and by Levin's frustration at the stunted curriculum he is required to follow—"I sometimes feel I'm engaged in a great irrelevancy," he says, "teaching people how to write who don't know what to write"—*A New Life* is very much a campus novel. As such it ranks with the best American examples of the genre—Randall Jarrell's *Pictures From an Institution*, Mary McCarthy's *The Groves of Academe* and James Hines's collection of novellas, *Publish and Perish*—as well as the splendid satires by the British novelist David Lodge, *Small World* and *Changing Places*, and of course Kingsley Amis's *Lucky Jim*. Seldom does one encounter in a work of literature more telling proof than Malamud offers of the old saw: Academic politics are so vicious because the stakes are so small.

Mainly, though, *A New Life* is about precisely what its title says: rebirth, regeneration, physical and psychological relocation. As such it is completely in the American grain, and exuberantly so. One can only wonder at what the people at Oregon State thought when they found themselves portrayed in its pages, but there can be no doubt that Bernard Malamud had a great deal of fun writing it. That fun, it should go without saying, is entirely infectious.

CYRANO
by Edmund Rostand,
translated by Brian Hooker

S ometime in the early 1950s, when I was in my early teens, the boarding school at which I was being held against my will decided to amuse the inmates by showing a movie one Saturday night. It was something called *Cyrano de Bergerac*, written by someone named Edmond Rostand, with someone named José Ferrer in the title role. A film version of a French play? Ouch. I went into the auditorium with all the enthusiasm of Robespierre approaching the guillotine.

Two hours later I was a changed boy. *Cyrano* had knocked me off my feet, and Ferrer had knocked me out of the park. I hadn't been to all that many movies—they weren't the obsession among the young that they are now—so my basis of comparison was narrow, but nothing since Laurence Olivier's *Henry V,* with its French sky blackened by English arrows, had so thrilled and moved me. I bought the LP recording of the soundtrack, with Ferrer declaiming the most stirring speeches, and soon after that I got my hands on the Modern Library edition of *Cyrano*, in Brian Hooker's incomparable translation (the one used in the movie). The recording got lost somewhere along the way in the half-century that followed, but the little book in its faded red binding has been with me ever since.

These words are written the morning after an umpteenth viewing of Ferrer's 1950 film, in a DVD print that shows its age but has lost none of its power to rouse, move and amuse. Watching it after rereading the play for the first time in many years, I was struck by how intelligently Carl Foreman had adapted the Rostand/Hooker text for the screen: tightening it up, in particular with regard to the comic relief provided by the poetic pastry chef Ragueneau, keeping the focus at all times on Cyrano and his frustrated love for the beautiful Roxane. A couple of years later Foreman was on the blacklist, receiving no credit for his work on the screenplay of *The Bridge on the River Kwai* and other films, but at the time he worked on *Cyrano* he was at the top, and it shows.

But this isn't a movie review, it's a second look at the play itself, as published rather than as performed. Many English translations are available, including those by Christopher Fry and Anthony Burgess, but the Hooker version is the one I grew up with, and reading any other (or watching a performance by anyone other than Ferrer) is unthinkable to me. Hooker's translation is available now only in the Bantam Classics edition, which unfortunately does not include Clayton Hamilton's introduction to the original 1923 version.

Unfortunately, that is, because Hamilton explains how Hooker's translation came to be. He is little known now except, presumably, among scholars of the theater, but in the first decades of the twentieth century Hamilton was among this country's most prominent and influential theater critics; his many books include *The Theory of the Theater and Other Principles of Dramatic Criticism* (1910), *Problems of the Playwright* (1917) and *So You're Writing a Play* (1935). Most important to the subject at hand, he was lifelong friends with Walter Hampden, the celebrated actor, theater manager and producer. As boys in the late 1890s they "used to squander the after-midnight gas, reading and rereading the magic text of this entrancing play," which had first been produced in Paris in 1897, and a quarter-century later Hamilton persuaded Hampden to mount a production with a new English translation, the existing ones failing to capture "the zest, the fire, the spontaneity, the brilliancy, the lyric rapture of Rostand."

For this Hamilton turned to Hooker, a poet who is now as forgotten as everyone else in this undertaking. Hamilton correctly writes "that Brian Hooker has succeeded in a literary task of extraordinary difficulty, that he has written a text which is both speakable and readable, and that he has made the vivid spirit of Edmond Rostand accessible . . . to English-reading lovers of belles-lettres who are not able to read French."

The "vivid spirit" to whom Hamilton refers was not yet thirty years old when his famous play appeared. Born in Marseilles in 1868, Rostand grew up in privileged circumstances that permitted him to indulge his love for writing. He published poetry and had three plays produced before *Cyrano*, but the overwhelming success of his masterpiece seems to have immobilized him. Nothing he wrote in the rest of his life came even close to *Cyrano* in either literary or commercial terms, and at his death in Paris in 1918 he seems to have been a frustrated and disappointed man.

Had it not been for Brian Hooker, it is possible that Rostand's great play might have remained little more than a bewitching rumor in the English-speaking world. Before his translation was presented on Broadway in 1923, with Hampden in the title role, only three productions of the play had appeared in New York, and only one of these in (presumably bad) English. But Hooker's *Cyrano* ran for 232 performances—an exceptionally good run for just about anything in translation—and Hampden must have loved it, because he appeared in four more productions between 1926 and 1936. Not until 1946, when Ferrer played the role (and produced the show), did Broadway see anyone else's *Cyrano*.

As one of those "English-reading lovers of belles-lettres who are not able to read French," I cannot testify with any authority to the accuracy and fidelity of Hooker's translation, but the passion with which it was embraced by Hamilton and Hampden, both of whom were fluent in French, leaves no doubt that it captures the essence of Rostand. Written in blank verse, it is as much a poem as a play. Indeed, in the most brilliant speeches—Cyrano's witty defense of his "great nose," his "No, I thank you!" declaration of independence, the balcony scene when, in the guise of Christian de Neuvillette, he professes his love for Roxane—Hooker rises to heights of romantic verse that few others have achieved in any language.

The play is set in France, Paris primarily, in the mid-seventeenth century. As just about everyone knows, Cyrano is a brave soldier, leader of the Cadets of Gascoyne, a writer and poet of sublime gifts and accomplishments who possesses every quality to which a man could aspire, except beauty: his long nose ("a rock—a crag—a cape—A cape? say rather, a peninsula!") precedes him wherever he goes, and persuades him that for all his nobility of heart and soul, he can never win the love of Roxane. Instead she tells him of her love for Christian, and he agrees to help Christian win her by writing, for him, the great romantic words that so enthrall her. Roxane and Christian marry but he soon dies in battle. A decade and a half later Cyrano, visiting Roxane in the convent to which she has repaired, himself dies from wounds inflicted in an ambush, but not before inadvertently confessing his love, to which Roxane replies in stunned sorrow, "I never loved but one man in my life, And I have lost him—twice."

Any number of excerpts could be published here for the benefit of readers who do not know Hooker's *Cyrano,* but I have chosen two of my favorites. The first comes after Cyrano is derided by an aristocratic fop as "A clown who—look at him—not even gloves! No ribbons—no lace—no buckles on his shoes," to which Cyrano replies:

I carry my adornments on my soul.
I do not dress up like a popinjay;
But inwardly, I keep my daintiness
I do not bear with me, by any chance,

An insult not yet washed away—a conscience
Yellow with unpurged bile—an honor frayed
To rags, a set of scruples badly worn.
I go caparisoned in gems unseen,
Trailing white plumes of freedom, garlanded
With my good name—no figure of a man,
But a soul clothed in shining armor, hung
With deeds for decorations, twirling—thus—
A bristling wit, and swinging at my side
Courage, and on the stones of this old town
Making the sharp truth ring, like golden spurs!

What language that is! "But inwardly, I keep my daintiness,"
"I go caparisoned in gems unseen," "With deeds for decorations"—it is difficult to imagine that Rostand's original French
could be more musical or evocative than Hooker's English.
Here it is again, in an extract from the "No thank you!"
speech, which follows Cyrano's friend Le Bret's plea that he
"stop trying to be Three Musketeers in one!" Cyrano asks:

What would you have me do?
Seek for the patronage of some great man,
And like a creeping vine on a tall tree
Crawl upward, where I cannot stand alone?
No thank you! Dedicate, as others do,
Poems to pawnbrokers? Be a buffoon
In the vile hope of teasing out a smile
On some cold face? No thank you! Eat a toad
For breakfast every morning? Make my knees
Callous, and cultivate a supple spine,—
Wear out my belly grovelling in the dust?
No thank you! . . . Shall I labor night and day
To build a reputation on one song,
And never write another? Shall I find
True genius only among Geniuses,
Palpitate over little paragraphs,
And struggle to insinuate my name
In the columns of the Mercury?

No thank you! Calculate, scheme, be afraid,
Love more to make a visit than a poem,
Seek introductions, favors, influences?—
No thank you! No, I thank you! And again
I thank you!

Is there, anywhere in any language, a more devastating repudiation of toadying and apple-polishing than that? In the District of Columbia, where those practices have been raised to something approximating high art, every word of that speech should be posted on every office wall on K Street and Capitol Hill, not to mention the White House. With eloquence that almost literally takes the breath away, Rostand/Hooker constructs a great avalanche of words, each one of them exactly right, each target hit dead center.

Cyrano the man and *Cyrano* the play are romantic to the core: romantic in the grand manner rather than in the simpering Hollywood style. Romance on such a scale has long been out of literary fashion, with the result that many self-appointed arbiters of literary and cultural fashion look down their own (very short) noses at *Cyrano*. The last word belongs to Clayton Hamilton:

> This gallant play is still as thrillingly alive as it was in 1898. Rostand was like Shakespeare in one respect at least; for he wrote "not of an age but for all time." It is only the realists, who write about contemporary manners and contemporary morals, who grow speedily old-fashioned: the romantics, who escape from their own period, remain forever young and forever new.

THE HOUSE ON COLISEUM STREET
by Shirley Ann Grau

It took an inexcusably long time to happen, but in the mid-1990s I made my first visit to New Orleans after years of knowing it only through novels, plays and movies. My eldest son was living in an apartment on the fringes of the Garden District, which I soon set out to explore. Taking my time—nobody does anything fast in New Orleans—I rambled along the quiet, beautiful streets, admiring the old houses, somehow elegant and funky at the same time, with their wrought-iron porch railings and their bright gardens and their palpable sense of laid-back exclusivity. Then a street sign stopped me cold: Coliseum Street, it said, and right away I knew exactly where I was. Looking at the houses along the street, I knew that one had to be the house on Coliseum Street. Just about any one of them could have fit the description:

> Like all the others on that street the house was narrow and three stories tall, white painted and black shuttered. The first two floors had porches straight across the front, narrow porches edged and ornamented with light lacy ironwork. A slender delicate house of the sort that had been popular in the 1840s. In front was a tiny lawn divided exactly in two by a brick walk and edged by the scrolls and feathers of a low iron fence. In one of those smooth tiny patches of grass, misplaced and hideous, was a fountain, a bubbling fountain.

Lovers of *The House on Coliseum Street*, by Shirley Ann Grau, will know at once that this is where the family of Aurelie Caillet lives: Aurelie herself, now middle-aged; her present husband, Herbert Norton; her twenty-year-old daughter, Joan Claire Mitchell, by a previous marriage; and her younger daughter, Doris, by yet another husband. Grau is now best known for *The Keepers of the House*, for which she won a Pulitzer Prize in 1965, and is perhaps most highly regarded by literary critics for her splendid short stories, many of which are collected in *Selected Stories* (2003), but *The House on Coliseum Street*, published in 1961, remains the book of hers of which I am most fond.

No doubt this has something to do with its setting, as I have revisited New Orleans many times and, like uncountable others, fallen permanently in love with it, in particular the Garden District and the adjacent Uptown clustered around Magazine Street, along which Ignatius J. Reilly rides in John Kennedy Toole's *A Confederacy of Dunces*. But *The House on Coliseum Street* has much more to it than atmosphere. It is an understated but powerful study of a young woman whose sheltered, modestly fortunate life is interrupted by an event that takes on traumatic dimensions and leaves her struggling between her instinct for convention and her deep longing to break away.

When I first read Grau's novel in 1969, among the many things that interested me was that it didn't seem particularly "Southern." Yes, it was set in New Orleans, and strongly tied to that particular place as well as to Louisiana's Gulf Coast, but it didn't seem tied to the South the way William Faulkner's fiction is, or Flannery O'Connor's, or Elizabeth Spencer's. The reason, it turns out, is that Grau doesn't think of herself as a "Southern writer" and dislikes being pigeonholed as one. Now in her early eighties, living comfortably in the plush New Orleans suburb of Metairie, she still takes offense at it. When an Associated Press reporter asked her about it in December 2003, he wrote that "she sneers and rolls her eyes at the phrase." It is one that critics frequently apply to her, but then she says (and who's to argue with her?), "Logic is not the strong point of critics."

Forty years ago, in another interview, she addressed the question in a less heated way:

> It seems to me that the whole definition of regional novel is quite misleading. No novel is really a regional novel. A novel has to be set somewhere. A Southern writer has a harder time because everybody says immediately "Southern regionalist." They have finally stopped saying this about Faulkner, but only after the Nobel Prize. This term is misleading and it is impossible, because a good novel isn't a regional study and it isn't sociology. . . . It's fiction; it's a thing in itself. This confusion leads people very far astray. You will find reviewers saying, "This is exactly the way things are." Well, of course they aren't! It is an imaginary picture of some people who happen to live here in the South. I would love to get away from the Southern label. I would like once in my life to have something I write taken as fiction, not as Southern sociology.

Consider it done. *The House on Coliseum Street* could take place anywhere. Its location is specific and lends it a certain New Orleans flavor, but what happens to Joan Mitchell could happen anywhere. In her low-key but forceful way, Grau writes about themes that transcend time and place, but then so did Faulkner and O'Connor and Welty and all the others with whom she resists comparison. It should be said, though, that much of Grau's fiction is deeply informed by Southern history and experience, especially as to questions of race. It is just about impossible to imagine a writer from elsewhere writing *The Keepers of the House* or the short stories of *The Black Prince* (1955), works that treat race in various ways, though certainly not didactically. Grau may just be a little more "Southern" than she wants us to believe.

Indeed if the only person you met in the pages of *The House on Coliseum Street* was Aurelie Caillet, you might think you'd somehow wandered into a Tennessee Williams play. She is a classic New Orleans eccentric who looks in the mirror and recoils at the wrinkles she sees—"To cheer herself up, she made a series of appointments at the very best beauty salon"—and who is horrified when Joan buys a secondhand black Pontiac: "My dear," she says, "you're not going to leave it parked out front?" There's a funny scene in which, back from a visit with her cousins in Tennessee, all of them gardeners, Aurelie decides that "it was part of a lady's life, this gardening; and it was a part she was missing." So she orders "a set of copper gardening tools from Hammacher Schlemmer" and eventually halfheartedly uses them. "Such pretty tools," Joan tells her, "seems a shame to get them dirty," to which Aurelie replies: "Just hold them under the faucet, and they will be good as new."

That moment occurs shortly after Joan learns that she is pregnant, not by her dull, decent steady, Fred Aleman, but by Michael Kern, a teacher at the university where she works in the library. She is worried but happy: "This is how you tell, she thought. It's a feeling after all. Heavy and lazy and smug and full." Out there in the garden she tells Aurelie, "I've got to do something, and I don't know what to do." When she tells Aurelie that "I'm pregnant" and that the father is not good old reliable Fred, Aurelie marches her inside and announces that she will go to the coast to visit her aunt—"it can be done easier" there—and Joan sadly realizes: "It's all decided for me . . . . I knew it would be."

The pregnancy is terminated, leaving Joan feeling "crispy and brittle." Aurelie, her aunt tells Joan, has explained her trip to the beach to Fred: "She told him the truth, of course—that you were very tired and nervous and a bit overwrought. A common complaint of young females." With a rush of anger and horror, Joan realizes that "they were all going to pretend that it hadn't happened, that nothing had happened. But it had. Of course it had." She is appalled; the most important thing ever to happen to her is going to be treated as if it never occurred. She drifts into a state of suspension. She misses three meetings at her sorority and is asked to resign. "I was a founding member," Aurelie says. "They can't do this." Joan thinks:

> Aurelie can fix it up. . . . Daughters of founding members don't get thrown out, no matter what they do. Aurelie will have it all fixed by tomorrow. And everybody will forget it. Aurelie knows so many people. Fix up anything. And what do they do with the little shrimp child? Red and stringy. What do they do? Do they bury it? But you couldn't do that. It isn't a person. The grave of a shrimp, the grave of a seaweed. What to put on the marker? And that would be silly.

Joan is sad, hurt, bewildered, empty. She feels a "quivering shaking uncertainty." She thinks: "the hurt will stop when I'm pregnant. When all that empty space is filled up. . . . I want to be great and round, she thought. And rest my hands on my belly. Folded hands resting and waiting. Feeling your body grow great and large and expand and fill the world. Filling the world with your seed." She resumes dating Fred and sometimes finds herself happy with him, which surprises her "because she knew he wasn't the right man at all." She wants Michael, even though she knows quite well that he's a cad, but he's dating her sister Doris. So she decides upon an act of retribution that will ruin his life as surely as he has ruined hers.

Her life changes, and Michael's changes, but the house goes on: "The house had a definite smell, she thought. And all the cleaning in the world would never get it out. Because it wasn't a smell of dirt. It wasn't a smell of cooking. Or of anything in particular. It was the smell of everything. Of everything that had gone on in the house for the past hundred and twenty years. It was the smell of the people and the things. Of the living that had gone on between the walls." Joan "wanted none of the things that have happened" but is powerless to stop them. Life goes on, and "will go on happening when I'm dead." And "instead of being frightened, she felt comforted."

There's nothing "Southern" about that at all, except that it happens in the South and is told by a writer who happens to be Southern. It is a tiny human drama that in one form or another could be visited upon anyone, anywhere, and in Grau's telling it achieves genuine universality. Reading *The House on Coliseum Street* for the second time, I am struck far more than I was the first time by its maturity, wisdom and psychological acuity. It, like its outspoken author, has aged very well indeed.

Pogo
by Walt Kelly

For many years it has been my passionate conviction that the greatest monument of American literature is Yoknapatawpha, the fictional Mississippi county created by William Faulkner. But when I was young—too young to understand Faulkner, for sure—another southern place a few hundred miles to the east seemed to me at once the most magical and believable in all America. It was an actual place, the Okefenokee Swamp in southern Georgia, but in the hands of an amazingly gifted man named Walt Kelly it had been transformed into a universe all its own, a microcosm of America populated by a vast cast of wild, crazy, goofy, fantastic and utterly lovable characters.

Okefenokee had been on the map for ages, though little known outside Georgia. In 1936 the Okefenokee National Wildlife Refuge was established, with nearly half a million acres of pristine freshwater swampland, but it is no exaggeration to say that it was Walt Kelly who really put Okefenokee on the map, made it a part of the national consciousness. He did so through a hugely popular comic strip called *Pogo* and through the dozens of books in which the stories he told were recycled and granted a somewhat more permanent existence.

Permanence in the world of newspapers and books too often being a sometime thing, Pogo Possum and his many friends (a few enemies, too) now seem about to fall right off the map. Fewer than a half-dozen of Kelly's books are still in print, and most of those are hard if not impossible to find. Because the Pogo books sold well in their time, used copies are fairly easy to come by, but because most appeared as paperback originals they often are in poor condition, doubtless from being lovingly and laughingly read over and over.

The original Pogo collection, *Pogo*, the one under reconsideration here, was published in 1951, and followed soon thereafter by that landmark campaign document, *I Go Pogo*. I was just entering my teens at the time, in a family that disdained comics in any form, but somehow I found my way to *Pogo* (the book cost all of one dollar!) and, in the years to come, many of Kelly's other books. Eventually I built up a substantial collection of Kellyana, but sometime during the 1970s or 1980s, in the course of one of my many moves, it disappeared, leaving—as I now understand after reading *Pogo* for the first time in many years—a larger hole in my life than I realized at the time.

At the height of the comic strip's popularity, in the late 1950s, *Pogo* circulated in about 600 newspapers and exercised an influence far beyond the comic pages. Kelly had decided political opinions and didn't hesitate to express them in print. He was a liberal of the Adlai Stevenson variety, as I was, too, and he was merciless to those whom he regarded as bugbears, most notably Sen. Joe McCarthy, whom he made into a nasty bobcat called Simple J. Malarkey. By laughing at McCarthy, Kelly almost certainly played a significant role in that demagogue's eventual disgrace, and in later years he took well-aimed whacks at many others, including Richard Nixon, Spiro Agnew, Fidel Castro and Nikita Khrushchev—and by singling out the last two made plain that he was as capable of laughing at those on the left as on the right.

In 1951, though, all that was ahead of him. Pogo was an innocent possum hanging out in the Okefenokee with Albert Alligator, Howland Owl, the turtle Churchy-la-Femme, Porky Pine, the cow Horrors Greeley, the fetching skunk Mam'zelle

Hepzibah, Beauregard the houn' dog, Mallard de Mer ("the seasick duck"), Deacon Muskrat and Wiley Cat. Kelly had been drawing the strip for only a couple of years and was still feeling his way, though evidence of the more complex and outspoken *Pogo* of later years can be found in the last few chapters of this first volume.

Kelly was in his mid-thirties when he began *Pogo,* but he had a long and fruitful apprenticeship. Born in 1913—for biographical details I am indebted to the excellent Books and Writers Web site, http://kirjasto.sci.fi/kelly.htm—he began working on newspapers in Connecticut before he finished high school, skipped college, did newspapering and cartooning in New York and then animation for Walt Disney in California, illustrated manuals for the army during World War II, and at the *New York Star* started *Pogo,* which lived a lot longer than the *Star.*

Precisely how it is that a Connecticut Yankee was inspired to do a comic strip set in the Deep South is probably an unfathomable mystery, though it is useful to bear in mind that Southern folklore and popular literature—in particular the *Uncle Remus* stories of Joel Chandler Harris—had a heavy influence on Disney, which may have been passed along to Kelly. The language spoken by Pogo et al. is, as Books and Writers quite accurately puts it, a mixture of "Elizabethan English, French, and white and black Southern." Kelly had a keen feeling for language, and he delighted in seeing what he could make it do. Thus for example Howland Owl and Churchy-la-Femme hatch a plot to build "Adam bombs," which involves crossing "a geeranium plant an' a li'l baby yew tree," at the end of which, as the wise owl puts it, "you gits a yew-ranium bush!"

That comes from a story—and story is the right word, for Kelly was a master storyteller—called "Upon Adom." In the previous tale, "Some Gentlemen of the Fourth Escape," Pogo and Albert propose to go into newspapering, which mainly involves sharpening pencils until a little fellow floats into view using a book as his boat. The sendup that ensues is delicious, as he announces:

> Good afternoon, young man, I'm a bookworm by trade, ready to review a book, run errands or answer the telephone. . . . Take this book I ride on, it's the wrong color . . . and cheap at that. See, it RUNS! Doesn't resist water. . . . Now this page chosen at random is LUMPY with punctuation . . . HARD on the teeth . . . crawling with consonants. . . . UGH! what shoddy material!

Whereupon the book sinks, leaving the bookworm to speak truth: "Ah, me! Modern literature has no staying power! See, it went down like a STONE."

In that as in so much else, Kelly's universe occupies a territory that embraces both utter nonsense and utter common sense. In the story titled "My Love Is a Rose / Our Violence Blue, / A Young Man's Fancy / And So Dear Are You," Porky Pine—prickly, cantankerous, plainspoken and obviously dear to Kelly's heart—proposes to court Mam'zelle Hepzibah, explaining to the assembled doubters: "How gracefully she steps . . . how dainty her tread . . . yes, her carriage is a thing of beauty," which sets off the following dialogue:

> Albert: "Hot dog! If yo' lady friend got a carriage, let's all go for a ride!"
> Porky: "I only said, 'Her carriage is a thing of beauty.' I mean she walks well."
> Churchy: "Why she walk if she got a carriage?"
> Beauregard: "Gadzooks! Maybe the pony died."

Readers lucky enough to know the nonsense plays of Ring Lardner will find much that's familiar in dialogue such as this, with its lovely mixture of the logical and the illogical. In these early stories, still testing his powers, Kelly clearly delighted in seeing what he could make the language do, and he often left the doing to that immortal troubadour Churchy-la-Femme, who, as Churchy puts it, "recites 'propriate stirrin' poetry," to wit:

I was stirrin' up a stirrup cup
In a stolen sterling stein,
When I chanced upon a ladle
Who was once my Valentine . . .
(Natural this was a ladle I used to spoon with.)

When Christmas nears, Churchy has the 'propriate carol—"Good King Sourkraut looked out on his feets uneven!"—and follows it up with the lines that Kelly eventually incorporated in another of his most memorable songs, set to the tune of "Deck the Halls": "Nora's freezin' on the trolley, / Swaller dollar collar-flower alley-GA-ROO." One can only imagine the pleasure that Kelly, whose photographs suggest nothing so much as impishness, must have gotten out of writing that. It's as inspired as anything in Lewis Carroll, and deserves to be recognized as such.

Kelly was as common-sensically wise as he was funny, as when Porky Pine advises the characteristically overwrought Albert, "Don't take life so serious, son . . . it ain't no how permanent." Later, in a poster for Earth Day 1970, Kelly had Pogo famously observe, "We have met the enemy and he is us," and as the strip aged he was given more and more to somewhat bloated aphorisms. Perhaps not surprisingly, many of Kelly's admirers find the later, more political strips superior to the earlier, more innocent ones, but this probably reflects their own politics more than the strips' actual merits. Though I read *Pogo* assiduously right up to Kelly's unhappily early death in 1973 and often sympathized with the sentiments he expressed as he raked George Wallace, J. Edgar Hoover et al. over his very hot coals, to my taste the early Kelly is best. Since laughter is always the best medicine for whatever ails us, this doctor's prescription in these troubled times is *Pogo* of any vintage, twice in the morning and twice at bedtime.

THE HABIT OF BEING: LETTERS OF FLANNERY O'CONNOR
edited by Sally Fitzgerald

The God Flannery O'Connor worshiped so devoutly put her faith to a severe test. In 1950, when she was twenty-five years old, she developed lupus, the same autoimmune disease that had killed her father when she was a teenager; with characteristic stoicism, she called the disease "no great hardship." Six years later she was on crutches, which she laughed off: "I will henceforth be a structure with flying buttresses," which, she said in the Southern vernacular she enjoyed using, "don't bother me none." Then in August 1964 she died, at the age of thirty-nine; in the last letter she wrote, mailed by her mother after her death, she apologized to a friend for not sending some short stories because "I've felt too bad to type them."

All of those quotations are to be found in *The Habit of Being,* the collection of her letters edited by her close friend Sally Fitzgerald. During her lifetime O'Connor published two novels—*Wise Blood* (1952) and *The Violent Bear It Away* (1960)—and two collections—*A Good Man Is Hard to Find* (1955) and *Three by Flannery O'Connor* (1964)—all of which secured the high reputation she enjoys to this day. Two posthumous books further embellished it: the story collection *Everything That Rises Must Converge* (1965) and a volume of occasional prose, *Mystery and Manners* (1969). *The Habit of Being,* though, added a new dimension to our understanding of her: It gave us Flannery O'Connor the person, and what an extraordinary one she turned out to have been.

This very large book (more than 600 pages) was published in March 1979, a few months after I had joined the *Washington Star* as its book editor. I revered O'Connor's fiction and essays, and leaped at the opportunity to read and review her letters. I fully expected to like and admire them but never bargained for falling in love with them. That is exactly what happened. The review I wrote bordered on the ecstatic:

> She was, these letters tell us in ways her other writings cannot, a great woman. Like all of us, she had her vanities, her moods, her fits of petulance and selfishness—but these only made her more human. She had saintly qualities, but she was no saint. She was a great writer who, out of a clear and unwavering vision, told stories that at moments reach the luminous borders of perfection. These letters must be counted among her finest and most durable work; they will be read so long as there is room in the world for love, faith, courage and laughter.

Rereading these letters now, after a quarter of a century, I find no reason to alter anything in that judgment except, perhaps, to make it even more emphatic. *The Habit of Being* is a great American book by one of the greatest American writers. Meticulously edited by Fitzgerald (who died in 2000) with a minimum of editorial intrusion, the letters are not so much correspondence as conversation, between the reader and a woman who turns out to be the perfect conversationalist: a bit gabby, hugely funny, reflective, informative, impudent, wise and—yes—inspiring.

O'Connor's life was brief and, apart from her writing and her illness, doesn't come with much in the way of plot. She was born in Savannah in 1925, the only child of a modestly prominent and prosperous family that moved to the small town of Milledgeville when she was twelve. She went to college in Georgia and then in Iowa, did some time in writing colonies and New York City, but essentially remained in Milledgeville for the rest of her life. She never married. Her rural South and her Catholicism are essential: "To my way of thinking, the only thing that keeps me from being a regional writer is being a Catholic and the only thing that keeps me from being a Catholic writer (in the narrow sense) is being a Southerner."

She began writing when she was young and proved prodigious at it: She was twenty-one when her first story was published, and twenty-seven at the publication of *Wise Blood.* Her gifts were quickly recognized and her works were received enthusiastically, though too many critics mistook the violence in her work for "Southern Gothic" and overlooked the deeper currents that flow through it. She believed in grace, the action of which "changes a character," and she understood that too many readers missed this in her work:

> Part of the difficulty of all this is that you write for an audience who doesn't know what grace is and don't recognize it when they see it. All my stories are about the action of grace on a character who is not very willing to support it, but most people think of these stories as hard, hopeless, brutal, etc.

Those words were written to a woman known only, by her own insistence, as "A.," who wrote to O'Connor in 1955 inquiring about religious themes in her work and became, in the nine years remaining to O'Connor, what Fitzgerald calls an "almost uniquely important friend." We know now that "A." was a woman named Betty Hester, who died in 1998 and whose papers—opened in 2007—were willed to Emory University. We also know a bit more about this friendship thanks to Brad Gooch's useful biography, *Flannery* (2009), but it is unauthorized because O'Connor's mother, Regina, shielded her daughter's privacy with a ferocity rare, but by no means unwelcome, among guardians of literary flames.

Whatever the explanation for A.'s insistence on anonymity, it remains that O'Connor's letters to her explore and explain her Catholicism as does little else written by or about her. In her very first letter to A., O'Connor made the "bald statement" that "I write the way I do because (not though) I am a Catholic," and she expanded on that theme in letter after letter: "For me a dogma is only a gateway to contemplation and is an instrument of freedom and not of restriction," and (to another correspondent), "I feel that if I were not a Catholic, I would have no reason to write, no reason to see, no reason ever to feel horrified or even to enjoy anything," and, describing a literary evening to A.:

> Well, toward morning the conversation turned on the Eucharist, which I, being the Catholic, was obviously supposed to defend. [Mary McCarthy] said when she was a child and received the Host, she thought of it as the Holy Ghost, He being the "most portable" person of the Trinity; now she thought of it as a symbol and implied that it was a pretty good one. I then said, in a very shaky voice, "Well, if it's a symbol, to hell with it." That was all the defense I was capable of but I realize now that this is all I will ever be able to say about it, outside of a story, except that it is the center of existence for me; all the rest of life is expendable.

If there is, among the other major figures of American literature, one with religious faith as deep and heartfelt as O'Connor's, that person does not leap to mind; American writers (and other artists) are more likely to be skeptical about religion than committed to it. Yet religion never descended into religiosity with O'Connor, and it certainly did nothing to ameliorate a sharp sense of humor or tart literary opinions. When A. pressed a book by Nelson Algren on her, O'Connor ruefully opined that his was "a talent wasted by sentimentalism and a certain over-indulgence in the writing." She recommended William Faulkner's *Light in August* to A. but acknowledged that "I keep clear of Faulkner so my own little boat won't get swamped." (Later, in an essay, she memorably reworked the imagery: "Nobody wants his mule and wagon stalled on the same track the Dixie Limited is roaring down.") Carson McCullers's *Clock Without Hands* was, O'Connor said, "the worst book I have ever read," but then she disliked "intensely" McCullers's work, period. As for her fellow Catholic Graham Greene:

> . . . there is a difference of fictions certainly and probably a difference of theological emphasis as well. If Greene created an old lady, she would be sour through and through and if you dropped her, she would break, but if you dropped my old lady, she'd bounce back at you, screaming "Jesus loves me!" I think the basis of the way I see is comic regardless of what I do with it; Greene's is something else.

Her letters, like her fiction, are suffused with comedy. She preferred typewriter to pen: "On the basis of the fact that you use ten fingers to work a typewriter and only three to push a pen, I hold the typewriter to be the more personal instrument. Also on the basis of that you can read what comes off it." She loved birds, and kept swans and peacocks at the place in Milledgeville (a photo of one of her peacocks adorns the jacket of *Mystery and Manners*), but she was no more sentimental about them than she was about any of her human characters:

> I came back from my trip with enough money to order me another pair of swans. They are on their way from Miami and Mr. Hood, the incumbent swan, little suspects that he is going to have to share his feed dish. He eats out of a vase, as a matter of fact, and has a private dining room. Since his wife died, he has been in love with the bird bath. Typical Southern sense of reality.

On the central Southern reality of her day, O'Connor was ambivalent. Unlike her approximate contemporary Eudora Welty, she embraced the civil rights cause slowly and skeptically, though eventually she grasped its essential justice.

O'Connor cared about people, not categories and races, and she treated her black characters with as much love and compassion as her white ones. Rereading her letters reminds me, with a force I had not anticipated, that she is one of the essential writers of my life, and that it is time to return to the rest of her work.

THE DEATH OF THE HEART
by Elizabeth Bowen

Elizabeth Bowen turned painful childhood experience into one of the great novels of the twentieth century. Born in Ireland in 1899 to a respectable family of the Anglo-Irish gentry, she suffered childhood losses that eventually led her to two powerful convictions: Innocence inevitably must confront and be vanquished by experience, and physical objects, things, provide stability and continuity amid the uncertainties and disruptions of life.

Bowen returned to these themes over and over again in the many splendid books she wrote during her subsequent literary career, almost always with interesting and affecting results, but never with greater success than in what is widely regarded as her masterpiece. *The Death of the Heart,* published in 1938, was received at once with near-universal enthusiasm bordering on awe. Its reputation has not faded over three-quarters of a century: *The Death of the Heart* will be found on almost any required-reading list of 20th-century fiction, and anecdotal evidence suggests that it is a popular choice of reading-club members.

I first read it in the 1950s, when I was a teenager, far too young and callow to appreciate it, much less understand it. I read it because it was one of my mother's favorite books, and my mother shaped my reading tastes more than anyone then or since. She had a great love of 19th-century British fiction, which she passed on to me, and she was receptive to twentieth-century fiction and poetry of almost any stripe; it was from her that I learned to love the fiction of Eudora Welty and John Cheever, the poetry of e.e. cummings (her favorite) and Ogden Nash. But with *The Death of the Heart* she lost me; Bowen's leisurely, measured, Jamesian prose was too dense for me, her irony and wit were too subtle. I was out of my depth.

Rereading the novel now, five full decades later, is like entering a new and wholly unexpected place, full of wonders and surprises. *The Death of the Heart,* like so much of Bowen's fiction, is about a child, but it is a book for adults. A certain measure of experience, of exposure to life's cruelties and compromises, is necessary for a full grasp of it. The destination for sixteen-year-old Portia Quayne is inevitable from the beginning, yet the path along which Bowen leads her to it is full of unexpected nuances and pleasures. It is a book to be read slowly, to be savored, skills only rarely bestowed upon teenaged readers. I realized only a few pages into this second reading that, like the innumerable people who complain about being force-fed Faulkner in high school or college, when they simply weren't ready for him, for me in the 1950s, *The Death of the Heart* was too much, too soon.

Undoubtedly the novel was shaped to a significant degree by people and events of Bowen's own youth, though one should always be skeptical about looking for autobiography in fiction when it is just part of the story. She was the only child of Henry and Florence Bowen, and grew up at Bowen's Court, the handsome if somewhat down-at-the-heels family mansion in the Irish countryside. Her family was of the gentry but scarcely wealthy. Her father, a lawyer, had to work, and when a mysterious mental illness forced him into an institution, six-year-old Bitha and her mother came upon hard times. Eventually he recovered, but just as he did, in 1912, Florence Bowen died of cancer, leaving her devoted daughter utterly bereft. She was thirteen years old.

She was strong, though, and soldiered on. By the age of

twenty she was writing, by twenty-five she was married to Alan Cameron and had published her first book of stories, *Encounters*. She had, according to Victoria Glendinning's fine biography, *Elizabeth Bowen* (1978), an "almost vulgar gypsy romanticism which was just as much a part of her as her perfect, ladylike demeanor and beautiful manners," a romanticism that is especially strong in her early work. Her marriage, which lasted until Cameron's death in 1952, was happy and mutually fulfilling but apparently passionless; from time to time she found lovers, but "she was a writer before she was a woman." A contemporary of Evelyn Waugh and Cyril Connolly, a friend of Virginia Wolff, she led a lively social life but sought solitude. Her personal characteristics included "stylishness, vanity, discipline, energy, lack of cant, independence, courage," which enabled her to struggle against the financial difficulties that bedeviled her right up to her death from lung cancer (like most in literary circles of her day, she was a heavy smoker) in 1973.

The sense of being orphaned that Bowen surely felt after her mother's death clearly informs *The Death of the Heart*. Portia has lost first her father and now her mother, with whom she had moved rather merrily through a succession of cut-rate European hotels. Bereft and lost, she is shipped off to the handsome house on Regent's Park in London of her half brother and his wife, Anna. Thomas Quayne, two decades older than she, the child of their father's first marriage, is a successful advertising man whom Bowen captures perfectly in just a few words:

> His head and forehead were rather grandly constructed, but at thirty-six his amiable, mobile face hung already loosish over the bony frame. His mouth and eyes expressed something, but not the whole, of him; they seemed to be cut off from the central part of himself. He had the cloudy, at some moments imperious look of someone fulfilling his destiny imperfectly; he looked not unlike one of the lesser Emperors.

The house in which Thomas and Anna live is indeed hand-some, but it is "all mirrors and polish," offering "no place where shadows lodged, no point where feeling could thicken." It is a house where "people said what they did not mean, and did not say what they meant." Thomas is vaguely well-inten-tioned, but distracted and distant. Anna is beautiful but cold and devious. Soon it becomes the house where Portia "has learnt to be lonely," her only friend the housekeeper Matchett, reticent and terse but kindly inclined.

Then into the house comes Eddie, twenty-three years old, "a bright little cracker that, pulled hard enough, goes off with a loud bang." My old Avon paperback copy of the novel calls him "an astonishing cad," but sleek opportunist is more to the point: "He took an underlyingly practical view of life, and had no time for relations that came to nothing or for indefinitely polite play." He pays court on Anna, who humors him but does not succumb to him, and turns his attentions on Portia, who falls wildly, hopelessly in love with him. He strings her along, and when she's sent to the seacoast while Thomas and Anna go to Europe, he comes for a weekend that turns into a disaster. The precise reason for the devastation she feels will seem tame to many of today's readers, but the devastation itself is utterly real and believable. It is here that she learns the lesson so cher-ished by Bowen:

> After inside upheavals, it is important to fix on imperturbable things. Their imperturbableness, their air that nothing has hap-pened renews our guarantee. Pictures would not be hung plumb over the centers of fireplaces or wallpapers pasted on with such precision that their seams make no break in the pattern if life were really not possible to adjudicate for. These things are what we mean when we speak of civilization: they remind us how exceedingly seldom the unseemly or unforeseeable rears its head. In this sense, the destruction of buildings and furniture is more palpably dreadful to the spirit than the destruction of human life.

Eddie has come close to destroying her, and when, back in London, she comes to his room in a foolish, self-abasing attempt to win him over he repudiates her. She realizes, finally, that, as she tells him, "You like despising more than you like loving. You pretend you're frightened of Anna: you're frightened of me." What he fears is the innocent, unconditional love she offers him, and the possibility of returning it in kind. So she retreats to the hotel room of the decent, feckless Major Brutt—"Makes of men date, like makes of cars; Major Brutt was a 1914-18 model: there was now no market for that make"—from which she issues her defiant challenge to Thomas and Anna.

The book's final pages are breathtaking, stunning, yet Bowen proceeds through them as deliberately and steadily as she has brought the reader to them. Ultimately her subject is betrayal, and her final words on it are definitive: "One's sentiments—call them that—one's fidelities are so instinctive that one hardly knows they exist: only when they are betrayed or, worse still, when one betrays them does one realize their power." Portia's only hope is to go forward, but at the novel's final page we cannot know how, or if, she will do so. Instead we are left to marvel at the intricacy with which Bowen has woven this exquisite tapestry, at the wisdom with which she explores the human heart and the places humans inhabit, at the majestic pace of her prose. To call *The Death of the Heart* a masterpiece is simply to speak the truth.

Satchmo: My Life in New Orleans
by Louis Armstrong

Sometime around 1918, after a night on the town, a seventeen-year-old boy in New Orleans was brought home to his mother "dead drunk." She gave him "a good physic"—patent medicine—and a few days later took him to a few neighborhood honky-tonks so that "I can show you how to really enjoy good liquor." Her aim was to teach him how to drink properly, but as they made their rounds the mother got a good deal drunker than the son, to the point that when they got to Henry Ponce's saloon, "she fell flat on her face." Gabe, one of the boy's several honorary stepfathers—men with whom his mother had enjoyed occasional relations—came by to help out:

> He stopped to shake hands with Ponce and tell him what a swell gentleman he was. He thanked him for giving me the chance to play [in the saloon's band] when an older musician would have given better service. Ponce told Gabe that an older musician did not have what this youngster had—sincerity and a kind of creative power which the world would eventually recognize. Gabe did not understand all those big words, but he thanked Ponce and went out supporting both mother and me with his strong arms.

By now you have figured out—I certainly hope you have—that the youngster was Louis Armstrong and that Henry Ponce should have been awarded the gold medal for prognostication. Even then Armstrong was known as Satchelmouth, or Dippermouth, and was playing cornet around New Orleans, but his hometown wasn't big enough for him. Already he had played with the biggest names in New Orleans music, most notably Joe "King" Oliver and Kid Ory, and he'd been in Fate Marable's band on a Mississippi riverboat. He was soon to meet "a fine young white boy named Jack Teagarden" and "the almighty Bix Beiderbecke, the great cornet genius," and before long he was on a train headed for Chicago, to join King Oliver's Creole Jazz Band at the Lincoln Gardens.

That was in 1922, and it is here that Armstrong ends his story in *Satchmo: My Life in New Orleans,* but, of course, this was only the beginning. By 1925 Armstrong was recording with his own small groups, first the Hot Five and then the Hot Seven, and in 1928 he made the recording that changed jazz forever, "West End Blues." The first four notes of his piercing introductory phrases, with their clarity, power and originality, are simply—to this day—astonishing. As Gunther Schuller has written, they "are as instructive a lesson in what constitutes swing as jazz has to offer." During the more than four decades between that historic moment and his death in 1971, Armstrong was what he remains to this day: the most celebrated, beloved and influential of all American musicians.

Armstrong wasn't just a musician of incandescent gifts and accomplishment, he was a remarkably talented writer. A lovely photograph in Gary Giddins's exemplary study of the man and his music, also called *Satchmo* (1988), shows him at a cluttered dressing-room table, eyeglasses perched on his nose, a serious expression on his face, pecking away at the typewriter that was always with him. Giddins writes:

> Of Armstrong's many accomplishments, the least recognized is his prolificacy as a writer of autobiographical prose. He was by far the most expansive musician-writer jazz has ever known. . . . He was unschooled in spelling and grammar, but he had an ear for language and could express himself with enviable clarity in trim, speechlike cadences. Tallulah Bankhead wrote in 1952, "He uses words like he strings notes together, artistically and vividly." She

was referring to his conversation, which was peppered with an inventive brand of slang, but the observation holds for his prose as well. Usually, he typed single-space and fast. Sometimes he would write dozens of pages at a clip in an always legible and authoritative hand. He favored yellow typing paper and pens with green ink.

Two books were published by Armstrong during his lifetime. *Swing That Music* (1936) is, as Giddins puts it, "so heavily ghosted as to be spurious." *Satchmo* (1954) is his own work, though fiddled with here and there—nothing really serious—by a priggish editor. In 1999 a wonderful compilation of his unpublished autobiographical writings, *Louis Armstrong, in His Own Words,* was published, adding much to our understanding of his post-New Orleans days, but *Satchmo* remains the definitive work, not merely splendid in its own right but one of the essential American memoirs.

My parents gave me a copy at Christmas 1954; probably I asked for it, as my father turned up his nose at jazz and wouldn't have chosen it himself, though my mother liked "Fats" Waller and the big bands. I was fifteen and had fallen in love with jazz about four years earlier. Somehow I'd gotten my hands on a 45-rpm extended-play "album"—remember those?—with four tracks by Jelly Roll Morton and His Red Hot Peppers, and from there it was a short step to Armstrong and his monumental recordings of the 1920s. A love affair had begun for me that will end only when I do, and though I subsequently came to love jazz in almost all forms, the music of its early years remains for me—as for jazz itself—the foundation upon which everything else rests.

It's the American music, and Armstrong was its most transcendently American figure. For years legend had it (legend aided and abetted by Armstrong himself) that he was born on the Fourth of July 1900, but that's too good to be true and it isn't; Giddins conclusively proves that he was born on August fourth, 1901, in what Armstrong describes as "the crowded section of

New Orleans known as Back o' Town . . . the very heart of what is called The Battlefield because the toughest characters in town used to live there, and would shoot and fight so much." The neighborhood was black and poor, and New Orleans was rigidly segregated, yet there's not a scintilla of bitterness in *Satchmo*. This isn't because Armstrong was an Uncle Tom—he was anything but—but because he always rolled with life's punches, as on a Mississippi journey with the Fate Marable Band:

> We were the first colored band to play most of the towns at which we stopped, particularly the smaller ones. The ofays [whites] were not used to seeing colored boys blowing horns and making fine music for them to dance by. At first we ran into some ugly experiences while we were on the bandstand, and we had to listen to plenty of nasty remarks. But most of us were from the South anyway. We were used to that kind of jive, and we would just keep on swinging as though nothing had happened. Before the evening was over they loved us. We couldn't turn for them singing our praises and begging us to hurry back.

Armstrong was tolerant and patient. He was also tough. Even as a fairly small boy, Armstrong "was pretty wise to things." He "had been brought up around the honky-tonks on Liberty and Perdido where life was just about the same as it was in Storyville [the famous red-light district and jazz hotbed] except that the chippies were cheaper." He was "spellbound" by the likes of "Black Benny, Cocaine Buddy, Nicodemus, Slippers, Red Cornelius, Aaron Harris and George Bo'hog," street characters all of whom were "as tough as they come" yet all of whom "liked good music" and encouraged him as he mastered first the bugle, then the cornet.

The bugle was put into his hands at the Colored Waifs Home for Boys, to which he was sent in 1913 after a boyish prank. He dreaded going there, but learned so much about music by playing in its band that upon his release at the age of fourteen he was "proud of the days I spent" there, as he remained for the rest of his life. Back in the city, he continued with his music—older musicians seem to have recognized him as a prodigy—but he was "the sole support" of his mother, sister and his own adopted son (the boy's mother, Armstrong's cousin, was dead), so he took whatever jobs he could find. These included working on a junk wagon and helping on a milk wagon, but mainly he hauled coal for the place where Stepfather Gabe worked. On the day World War I ended he "put about three more shovels of coal into the wheelbarrow," then thought: "The war is over. And here I am monkeyin' around with this mule. Huh!" He dropped everything, said, "So long, my dear. I don't think I'll ever see you again" to the mule, and got on with the rest of his life.

It was, as no one needs to be told, an extraordinary life. Armstrong had no more than a fifth-grade education, but "with my good sense and mother-wit, and knowing how to treat and respect the feelings of other people, that's all I've needed through life." He led small bands and big ones (the small ones were best), recorded abundantly, traveled all over the world. It was my good fortune to hear him everywhere from clubs in New York to auditoriums in North Carolina to the Newport Jazz Festival, but there was nothing unusual about that: Everybody heard him. Among his many nicknames was "Ambassador Satch," because during the Cold War he toured the world on behalf of his country and came to embody, at a time when the world still loved America, this country at its best, not to mention its most swinging.

Satchmo: My Life in New Orleans is a quintessentially American story, and one of the best books ever written about New Orleans, which is saying something. Armstrong loved New Orleans more than any place on earth, and would have been shattered by Hurricane Katrina. One can only hope that his spirit is guiding those who labor to bring it back to life.

THE AUTOBIOGRAPHY OF BENJAMIN FRANKLIN

In recent years Americans have become fascinated with their country's early history, though it's exceedingly difficult to say precisely why. This is almost entirely at odds with the national character, which tends to view all history as bunk, to look to the future rather than the past; yet David McCullough's *1776,* a vivid account of the first year of the American Revolution, was on the bestseller lists in 2005, just as previously were Joseph Ellis's *Founding Brothers* and Walter Isaacson's *Benjamin Franklin.* Other books on the Colonial and Revolutionary periods by the likes of Gordon S. Wood, Bernard Bailyn, Edmund S. Morgan and H.W. Brands have sold respectably, and the film *The Patriot* (2000), starring Mel Gibson, did well.

All of which is nice, though it's hard to tell whether it reflects genuine interest in the country's origins or merely passing fancy. In any case, people who have read one or more of the many current books about Benjamin Franklin really ought to direct their attention to the man himself, specifically to *The Autobiography of Benjamin Franklin.* It is, as Edmund Morgan writes in his foreword to the Yale University Press edition, "the most widely read autobiography ever written by an American," a book to which countless readers have turned "for what it tells us about Franklin's view of himself, for its embodiment of American values, for its homely admonitions, its deceptively simple style." Its "posthumous publication and popularity have made [Franklin] an American founding father in a more intimate fatherly way than the others who earned that title."

It is the first great American book. Other books of note—particularly the tales of Washington Irving—appeared well before 1867, when the complete text finally came out, but the *Autobiography* was written before 1790, when Franklin died. My first reading of it was in the late 1960s, during an academic sabbatical from my career in journalism. I sat in on a course in biography taught by a biographer of considerable eminence who included Franklin, as best I can recall, in some measure to mock him and his book, in particular the passages in which he describes his "bold and arduous Project of arriving at moral Perfection." In the atmosphere of the late 1960s it was easy to make sport of Franklin's earnest moralizing and his flattering self-portrait. Franklin set himself up as an exemplar for his fellow Americans, and in so doing made himself a fetching target for ridicule.

Still, even that teacher had to acknowledge—and to his credit readily did—that though Franklin doubtless twisted some of the facts of his life to his advantage, his *Autobiography* is an extraordinary document. It struck me so then, and it strikes me so even more strongly now. For one thing, it is the ultimate Horatio Alger story—which is to say the American success story—in this case about a Boston soapmaker's son, "the youngest Child but two" among 17, who "emerg'd from the Poverty and Obscurity in which I was born and bred, to a State of Affluence and some Degree of Reputation in the World," the stuff of Dickens as well as Alger. For another, it is plainly yet vividly written, its eighteenth-century prose still accessible to ordinary readers more than two centuries later. For yet another, it portrays Colonial and Revolutionary America—the former most particularly—with an immediacy unmatched in almost any other document.

The first and best part of the *Autobiography*, which takes up about a third of its total length, is written, as the introduction to the Yale edition puts it, "in the form of a long letter to his son William (the royal governor of New Jersey), but actually addressed to all his 'Posterity.'" This section was begun during a visit to England in 1771, though whether it was completed then is not known, nor is it known for certain whether Franklin at that point intended it for publication. The three final sections, which "deal almost exclusively with Franklin's external, rather than his internal, life," surely were meant for a wider readership. As the Yale editors say, the private Franklin almost completely disappears from them, replaced by the revolutionary and the scientist and the statesman.

As recent studies of Franklin have emphasized, he was a reluctant revolutionary, and in the *Autobiography* we can see him looking with admiration and longing to England. He was a loyal subject of the crown and wanted nothing so much as to keep the American colonies under what he regarded as its benevolent protection, but when the choice had to be made, he chose his native America, and became its most effective and articulate representative, first in England—where an arrogant Parliament turned aside his eloquent pleas for leniency toward the colonies—and then in France, which he cajoled into crucial support for the Revolution.

Franklin is often referred to as "the first American," or words to that effect, and the self-portrait he paints in the *Autobiography* is rich in qualities that have come to be associated with the American character; he is ambitious, pragmatic, common sensical, inventive, self-made, earthily humorous. Here, for example, is a passage in which he describes himself as a young man in Philadelphia, shaping himself and making his way:

> I now open'd a little Stationer's Shop. . . . In order to secure my Credit and Character as a Tradesman, I took care not only to be in Reality Industrious and Frugal, but to avoid all Appearances of the Contrary. I drest plainly; I was seen at no Places of idle Diversion; I never went out a-fishing or shooting; a Book, indeed,

sometimes debauch'd me from my Work; but that was seldom, snug, and gave no Scandal; and to show that I was not above my Business, I sometimes brought home the Paper I purchased at the Stores, thro' the Streets on a Wheelbarrow. Thus being esteemed an industrious thriving young Man, and paying duly for what I bought, the Merchants who imported Stationary solicited my Custom, others propos'd supplying me with Books, and I went on swimmingly.

Indeed he did. He was the personification and embodiment of the American belief in reinvention and in self-actualization. To call him the linear precursor of George Babbitt no doubt is unfair, but his desire to advance himself by pleasing others, by putting on the best possible face, and by making every effort not merely to be "Industrious and Frugal," but to present the appearance of same, reminds us that not merely was he the first American, he was also the first Rotarian.

Yet hard though he labored to achieve flawlessness in every possible way, he retained his sense of humor and self-awareness. Alas, he had to admit that, regarding the list of thirteen "Virtues with their Precepts" that he attempted to perfect, he "never arrived at the Perfection I had been so ambitious of obtaining, but fell far short of it." Still, "I was by the Endeavour a better and a happier Man than I otherwise should have been, if I had not attempted it." He was fully capable of laughing at himself, as when he recalls how, as a youth, he had undertaken a "Resolution of not eating animal Food," but then found himself becalmed at sea among people cooking cod:

> I had formerly been a great Lover of Fish, and when this came hot out of the Frying Pan, it smelt admirably well. I balanc'd some time between Principle and Inclination: till I recollected, that when the Fish were opened, I saw smaller Fish taken out of their Stomachs: Then thought I, if you eat one another, I don't see why we mayn't eat you. So I din'd upon Cod very heartily and continu'd to eat with other People, returning only now and than

occasionally to a vegetable Diet. So convenient a thing it is to be
a reasonable Creature, since it enables one to find or make a
Reason for every thing one has a mind to do.

Certainly his tongue seems to have been in his cheek as he
wrote that, but he was a preternaturally wise man whose
famous aphorisms were most notably published, of course, in
Poor Richard's Almanack, which he began in 1732 and issued
for about a quarter-century; much of his folk wisdom is also to
be found in the *Autobiography*. After recounting at some length
his efforts to keep city streets free of dust, he acknowledges that
"some may think these trifling Matters not worth minding or
relating," then continues: ". . . tho' Dust blown into the eyes of
a single Person, or into a single Shop on a windy Day, is but of
small Importance, yet the great Number of the Instances in a
populous City, and its frequent Repetitions give it Weight and
Consequence. . . . Human Felicity is produc'd not so much by
great Pieces of good Fortune that seldom happen, as by little
Advantages that occur every day."

Small wonder that millions here and overseas have taken this
book as a vade mecum for life itself. The world in which we live
today is very different, but Franklin's wisdom is for the ages,
our own as much as his. So read the *Autobiography,* and—
among the many editions available—read Yale's. Its text is the
most reliable (the Franklin papers are at Yale) and its supple-
mentary material is uniformly useful. Even this Chapel Hill man
has to admit that this time Yale gets things exactly right.

LOOK AT ME
by Anita Brookner

In the closing paragraphs of *The Great Gatsby,* F. Scott Fitzgerald passes final judgment on Tom and Daisy Buchanan, those spoiled, willful rich people who leave a string of deaths in their wake. "It was all very careless and confused," Fitzgerald writes. "They were careless people, Tom and Daisy—they smashed up things and creatures and then retreated into their vast carelessness, or whatever it was that kept them together, and let other people clean up the mess they had made."

Since those are among the more notable lines of twentieth-century literature, obviously it is possible that Anita Brookner had them in mind when, in the early 1980s, she wrote her third novel, *Look at Me.* Certainly they could serve as an epigraph for the novel, which tells in chilling detail how Nick and Alix Fraser—who could just as well be Tom and Daisy's British cousins—casually break the heart of Frances Hinton, a "well-behaved and rather observant" young woman who works "in the reference library of a medical research laboratory dedicated to the study of problems of human behaviour" and who yearns, in her quiet way, for love.

I first read *Look at Me* in 1985. By then Brookner had published four novels, the most recent of which, *Hotel du Lac,* had won the Booker Prize the previous year. I had not read her work but wanted to review her forthcoming *Family and Friends,* so I read two or three of her previous books in preparation. Precisely where *Look at Me* (1983) fell in this process I do not recall, but

I remember with utter clarity that I was stunned by it. Personal experience gives me no particular affinity for the recurrent motif in this and many of her other novels—intelligent but lonely women disappointed in love—but it seemed to me that she had taken the theme of "careless people" and had wrought her own distinct, powerfully moving changes on it.

In the years since, I have read and occasionally reviewed most of Brookner's other novels—there are about two dozen—and have taken a certain satisfaction in seeing her broaden her canvas, as in, for example, *Dolly, Incidents in the Rue Laugier* and *Making Things Better,* but I have always harked back to *Look at Me* as the one that most deeply impressed me, as, indeed, one of the best novels I'd read over the past quarter-century. So it was with a certain trepidation that I turned to it for a second reading: Was my memory playing tricks on me? Was it really as good—even half as good—as I remembered it?

The answer? It is, if anything, even better. Most of the books that have been reconsidered in this series have held up well, but few have actually grown—in my own mind if nowhere else— even larger. *Look at Me* most certainly has. Like all of Brookner's novels, it is short—under 200 pages—but for that matter so is *The Great Gatsby.* In measuring literary accomplishment, size is irrelevant. *Look at Me* takes on large themes and deals with them subtly, sensitively and astutely.

It is, though such matters in the end are utterly unimportant, a novel with roots—perhaps deep ones—in Brookner's own experience. Like Frances Hinton, she has spent much of her adult life in intellectual cloisters. Born in 1928, she was trained in art history, was the first woman to be awarded the Slade Professorship at Cambridge University, and has a long association with the Courtauld Institute of Art in London. In addition to her novels, she has published several well-regarded works of art criticism. She has never married. She once told an interviewer that her success as a novelist and art historian was not what she really wanted: "Those two activities . . . are out-side the natural order. I only ever wanted children, six sons."

There are words in *Look at Me* that echo those so precisely as to border on heartbreaking. Frances Hinton has been dis-appointed in love—"I knew about love and its traps. . . . I never speak of it"—and has turned to writing as a form of ther-apy and escape, as a way to reorder her world. She does it well, and manages to sell a story to a prestigious magazine in America, but she views it harshly:

> I saw the business of writing for what it truly was and is to me. It is your penance for not being lucky. It is an attempt to reach oth-ers and to make them love you. It is your instinctive protest, when you find you have no voice at the world's tribunals, and that no one will speak for you. I would give my entire output of words, past, present, and to come, in exchange for easier access to the world, for permission to state "I hurt" or "I hate" or "I want." Or, indeed, "Look at me." And I do not go back on this. For once a thing is known it can never be unknown. It can only be forgotten. And writing is the enemy of forgetfulness, of thoughtlessness. For the writer there is no oblivion. Only endless memory.

That passage, which seems to me very close to a summation of Brookner's most essential themes, occurs at a point in the novel at which Frances has had "the happiest night of my life" with James Anstey, one of the doctors at the laboratory. Something started that night—"Beginnings are so beautiful"—and though she insists that "I was not falling in love," the pos-sibility beckons in the near distance: "The worst thing that a man can do to a woman is to make her feel unimportant. James never did that. That whole late autumn, which was exception-ally cold and exceptionally dry, favouring our walks, was for me a time of assurance and comfort and anticipation. There were no images in my head. I did not write. I was happy."

But there are snakes in the grass: the handsome Nick Fraser and his beautiful wife, Alix. He, too, is a doctor at the lab, "tall and fair, an athlete, a socialite, well-connected, good-looking, charming: everything you could wish for in a man." Alix is "one of those fortunate women who create circles of friends wherever she goes, so that being with her is like belonging to a club." Their marriage is, or appears to be, sublimely happy—"Of course, the spectacle of two people's happiness is always something of a magnet for the unclaimed"—so Frances is enchanted, and seduced, when they welcome her into their circle:

> What interested me . . . was their intimacy as a married couple. I sensed that it was in this respect that they found my company necessary: they exhibited their marriage to me, while sharing it only with each other. I soon learned to keep a pleasant noncommittal smile on my face when they looked into each other's eyes, or even caressed each other; I felt lonely and excited. I was there because some element in that perfect marriage was deficient, because ritual demonstrations were needed to maintain a level of arousal which they were too complacent, perhaps too spoilt, even too lazy, to supply for themselves, out of their own imaginations. I was the beggar at their feast, reassuring them by my very presence that they were richer than I was. Or indeed could ever hope to be.

She is in thrall to them. She understands that "extremely handsome men and extremely beautiful women exercise a power over others," and she succumbs to it even as she sees it with a measure of clarity: "I recognize that they might have no intrinsic merit, and yet I will find myself trying to please them, to attract their attention. 'Look at me,' I want to say. 'Look at me.'" The web, though, is a trap. As matters develop with James, Frances comes to understand that she is not a friend to Nick and Alix but a puppet: "I had wanted the company of my friends to sustain my golden enjoyment and my new future, but those friends had turned into spectators, demanding their money's worth, urging their right to be entertained." Soon enough even that no longer interests them. Alix is bored. At last, having paid a terrible price, Frances realizes that "those people were innocent of everything except greed, that, like children or animals, they simply took what they wanted. That this was the law."

For a while Frances had thought that Nick and Alix offered her a ticket into the real world, but at the end she is left in her lonely apartment with pen and paper for company. She remembers that "something had happened"—something terrible— and she realizes that her task must be to write about it: "The details escaped me, although I knew that they were all stored somewhere, and could, at some future date, be retrieved, intact. It would be my wearisome task to retrieve them with gusto, to make my readers smile wryly at the accuracy of my detail. No mercy given, none received. And the purpose of it all distinctly questionable. Perhaps to lighten the burden of things unsaid. For those who put pen to paper do so because they rarely trust their own voices, and, indeed, in society, have very little to say. They are, as I now knew, the least entertaining of guests."

As these several quotations from *Look at Me* make plain, Brookner persistently and (I suspect) deliberately violates one of fiction's allegedly inviolable rules: Show, don't tell. It is, generally, a rule I prefer to see enforced: Let character and theme emerge from plot and event rather than from exposition. Yet Brookner's style of narrative—reflective, measured, expository—is, in her hands, exactly right; her prose alone is, quite simply, exquisite. I cherish her novels almost without reservation, and I cherish *Look at Me* above all.

BEAT TO QUARTERS
by C.S. Forester

One year, for its annual holiday issue, the *Washington Post* Book World asked several literary eminentos "what book they would recommend to a friend craving a little escape from the world's cares." I wasn't among those asked, but my answer would have been ridiculously easy: any of the eleven *Hornblower* novels by C.S. Forester, most particularly the first in the series, *Beat to Quarters*.

For nearly six decades I have escaped into the *Hornblower* novels as often as time and occasion have permitted. I was introduced to them as a middle-schooler in the early 1950s by my father, who adored them. The first that I read, *Mr. Midshipman Hornblower* (1950), doubtless was given to me because my father knew I would identify with the mere boy who was its protagonist, but over the years the three novels about Horatio Hornblower when he was in his thirties and held the rank of captain—*Beat to Quarters, Ship of the Line* and *Flying Colours,* all of them, incredibly, published in 1938—have been my favorites, and they remain so to this day.

It seems most unlikely that many readers now need to be introduced to Horatio Hornblower. All the novels chronicling his long career are very much in print and, if sales rankings at Amazon.com are any guide, continue to sell remarkably well. The 1951 film *Captain Horatio Hornblower,* directed by Raoul Walsh and starring Gregory Peck in the title role—my father and I drove across the state of Virginia to see it—was well received and remained popular for years. More recently, the

BBC made a *Hornblower* series with Ioan Gruffudd perfectly cast as Hornblower; eight episodes are available on DVD, and all are terrific, completely faithful to the original and considerably grittier than the 1951 movie.

Forester is now known almost entirely for *Hornblower,* but when he began to write *Beat to Quarters* in the mid-1930s at age thirty-eight, he was a well-established, successful author of highly literate, carefully researched novels of adventure and suspense, most notably *Payment Deferred* and *The African Queen.* He had published over twenty books and had been lured to Hollywood, which he found not to his taste. He fled back to England aboard a Swedish freighter, a leisurely voyage during which he thought through the personality and character of his flawed but heroic protagonist, a British naval officer serving during the Napoleonic Wars. Forester decided to name him Horatio, "not because of Nelson but because of Hamlet," from which "it seemed a natural and easy step to Hornblower."

That is how Forester put it in *The Hornblower Companion,* published two years before his death in 1966. This book, with its detailed maps of all of Hornblower's naval engagements and its candid, instructive account of how Forester wrote fiction, is a useful supplement to the novels, but reading it really isn't necessary because Forester's descriptive powers are so keen that every location and battle comes vividly alive in the reader's imagination. Although he wasn't in love with the movie industry, he obviously had a highly cinematic mind and animated scenes with clarity and immediacy.

In writing the *Hornblower* series, Forester paid no attention to the King's storytelling advice in *Alice in Wonderland*: "Begin at the beginning and go on till you come to the end: then stop." Forester began in the middle, moved to the end, then went to the beginning before filling in some miscellaneous blanks. Whether it is best to read the novels in chronological order has been debated endlessly by those who love them, but a good case can be made for doing so. Following Hornblower's steady advance from midshipman to lieutenant to captain to commodore to admiral and to lord is a way to become totally engaged with the life of one of fiction's greatest characters, and I recommend it without reservation.

Still, for those who haven't time to read the entire series, or merely want a taste of it, *Beat to Quarters* is the place to go. Here Forester establishes Hornblower's character once and for all, places him in command of the frigate Lydia in two astonishing engagements off the Pacific Coast of Central America, and introduces him to the woman who will become the most important person in his life. All the pleasures of the series are to be found in this one novel, which is the real core of the *Hornblower* saga.

As *Beat to Quarters* opens, in June 1808, the Lydia is sailing toward its destination, known only to Hornblower and the Admiralty back in London. The ship has been "seven months at sea without once touching land." This has "given an admirable opportunity for training the gang of jailbirds and pressed men into seamen, but it was too long without distraction," and supplies are perilously low. So when the Lydia pulls into the Gulf of Fonseca in Guatemala, Hornblower welcomes the chance to give his men some shore time while replenishing everything from fresh water to fruit to beef and pork.

England is at war with Spain. Hornblower's orders are to ally with Don Julian Alvarado, "a large landowner with estates along the western shore of the bay," and to supply him with munitions for his intended rebellion against Spanish rule. Hornblower is "to do everything which his discretion dictated to ensure the success of the rebellion." Soon enough it becomes clear that "everything" embraces a lot more than Hornblower had bargained for, since Alvarado turns out to be a monomaniac who fancies himself "El Supremo" and since nearby is a Spanish warship, the Natividad, with fifty guns on two decks. Lydia has thirty-six guns on a single deck, which is to say Hornblower is strictly the underdog in the fight to come.

But Hornblower is no ordinary man and no ordinary captain. As a seaman he is an accomplished navigator and a resourceful strategist, and as a leader of men he is stern and disciplined but also fair and, when the occasion demands it, merciful. But the gruff face he presents to his crew, his enemies and the world disguises a far more complex and far less confident man. He is ceaselessly self-critical, it being his nature "to find no pleasure in achieving things he could do; his ambition was always yearning after the impossible, to appear a strong silent capable man, unmoved by emotion," and for all the suppleness and flexibility of his mind, he can be stubborn: "Risk and danger lured him even while he knew he was a fool to expose himself to them, and he knew that no risk would deter him once he had embarked on a course of action." He is deeply sensitive to real or imagined mockery ("Hornblower dreaded the thought of being a figure of fun"), not least because he "had always been a poor man."

This is of little moment when he is at sea, but he is a class-conscious Englishman and a resentful one as well: "He disliked the aristocracy—it hurt him nowadays to remember that as the doctor's son he had had to touch his cap to the squire. He felt unhappy and awkward in the presence of the self-confident arrogance of blue blood and wealth." This becomes a matter of some urgency when a highly placed member of the aristocracy—Lady Barbara Wellesley, sister to two men high in government and the military, one being Arthur Wellesley, duke of Wellington, who eventually trounces Napoleon at Waterloo—sends a note requesting that she be given passage back to England, since "owing to an outbreak of yellow fever [in Panama] she cannot return home the way she would desire."

Hornblower is angry at what he regards as her arrant presumption, dismayed at the prospect of having a woman aboard under any circumstances but especially when he faces a deadly battle against the Natividad. He has no choice: "At thirty-seven he still was not more than one eighth the way up the captains' list—and the goodwill of the Wellesleys could easily keep him in employment until he attained flag rank. There was nothing for it but to swallow his resentment and to do all he could to earn that goodwill, diplomatically wringing advantage from his difficulties."

Those who already have read *Beat to Quarters* know that the stage is now set for many delights, including a brutal engagement with the Natividad that takes place over two endless days and a gradual, reluctant thaw in Hornblower's relationship with his unwelcome passenger. Of the first, suffice it to say that Forester's prowess in writing about warfare at sea is unsurpassed, and his knowledge of the workings of the warships of the Napoleonic era is encyclopedic. As to the second, Lady Barbara in time emerges as every bit Hornblower's match, which makes matters doubly difficult since back in England waits his wife, Maria, "short and tubby, with a tendency to spots in her complexion."

The issue this poses is not resolved in *Beat to Quarters*, which is yet another reason you will want to continue on to *Ship of the Line* and then *Flying Colours* and then on and on until the full story unfolds. Indeed, I aim to continue on myself, as the pleasures of these books have never dimmed for me. I do not feel the same about the novels of Forester's ostensible and now much-celebrated successor, Patrick O'Brian, which are skillfully written and knowledgeable but tend toward the arch and precious. The saga of Horatio Hornblower is presented without pretense, yet it is elegantly written, profoundly intelligent, historically and factually accurate, and deeply humane. It is that rare and precious thing, literature that entertains while it enriches.

THE FATHERS
by Allen Tate

The literature of the Civil War is not merely vast and var-
ied but at the very heart of American literature itself.
Without the Civil War we would not have the work of
William Faulkner, whose every syllable was informed and
inspired by the war. It gave us *The Red Badge of Courage,* the
finest book of Stephen Crane's brief, incandescent career, and
Stark Young's *So Red the Rose,* Shelby Foote's *Shiloh* and, of
course, Margaret Mitchell's *Gone With the Wind.* It gave us the
magisterial memoirs of Gens. Ulysses S. Grant and William
Tecumseh Sherman and much of the poetry of Walt Whitman.
The issues raised by the conflict may have torn the nation asun-
der, but they gave—and still give—our writers rich and fruitful
raw material.

The most famous of these countless books, *Gone With the
Wind,* was published in 1936. Two years later there appeared
another first novel about the war, Allen Tate's *The Fathers.*
Superficially similar in some respects to *Gone With the Wind*—
a protagonist not unlike Rhett Butler, an assortment of jejune
aristocrats, male bonding and bristling rivalry—it enjoyed none
of that book's commercial success, though its reviews were
laudatory. Thanks to the good offices of the Swallow Press it
remains in print, but it almost certainly is little read outside university courses in Southern literature and even goes unmen-
tioned in the brief overview of Civil War literature in the usually reliable *Oxford Companion to American Literature.*

This is not especially surprising, given that the American

market for serious works of literature is not exactly robust, but it certainly is an injustice, for *The Fathers* is a work of genuine consequence. It is not, as the late Arthur Mizener quite foolishly says in the beginning of his introduction to the Swallow Press edition, "the novel *Gone With the Wind* ought to have been," since that is pitting an apple against an orange, but it most certainly is an intelligent, vivid, multi-layered and historically accurate novel, one that treats the antebellum South not without sympathy but with far more irony and distance than Margaret Mitchell was capable of mustering.

At the time *The Fathers* was published Tate was in his late thirties and already had achieved a considerable reputation within the literary and scholarly communities. Born in 1899 in Kentucky, he was the child of an impecunious, unhappy marriage. Tate did not begin to find himself until he entered Vanderbilt University in 1918, where he found personally and intellectually congenial company, fellow students with whom he established a magazine called *The Fugitive*. It became the house organ of a group of poets and scholars, the Agrarians, who detested the modern industrial world and looked back with longing to the Old South—not to slavery, but to the Southern countryside and farms and even plantations. The Agrarians romanticized Ol' Dixie every bit as much in their own way as did the Daughters of the Confederacy in theirs, but they wrote out of a deep belief in farms rather than factories.

In 1930 Tate and several others published *I'll Take My Stand*, an Agrarian manifesto that provoked great debate about the South and its future. Tate himself had gained renown with the publication in 1928 of *Ode to the Confederate Dead,* which to this day remains his most famous poem, as well as with brief biographies of Stonewall Jackson and Jefferson Davis. As this suggests, he was haunted by if not obsessed with the antebellum and Civil War South. His biographer, Thomas A. Underwood, traces this to Tate's mother, who fancied herself a member of the Virginia aristocracy and clung to romantic illusions about it and the Old South. Underwood argues that Tate "learned to think of himself as a member of the genteel class" and "compensated for the shame he felt over his parents' financial condition by carrying himself as something of a Southern aristocrat."

It was as part of his struggle to locate his place in Southern history and tradition, Underwood says, that Tate wrote *The Fathers.* He saw himself, in Underwood's words, as "an orphan of the South" and started writing this book as a history of his mother's Virginia ancestors, presumably in the hope of proving them to be every bit as distinguished as she had represented. Gradually, though, Tate's search for fact turned into the creation of fiction, a novel that simultaneously mourns the passing of a world that Tate cherished yet that exposes, with utter clarity and lack of sentimentality, the self-inflicted wounds that made its demise inevitable.

My own first encounter with the novel came during a fairly systematic study of Southern literature that included a rereading of *Gone With the Wind* and then *The Fathers,* which a professor suggested as an antidote to it. As one who has always found things to admire as well as dislike about *Gone With the Wind* I was unsure that an antidote was needed, but I quickly realized that *The Fathers* was fiction of a different, and far higher, order with robust prose and exceptionally believable characters.

A second reading leaves me even more strongly convinced of this. Taking place over a period of about a year beginning in April 1860, it uses "domestic trials" to illuminate and humanize the "public crisis" then taking place. Set in rural Virginia, Alexandria and Washington, it tells of two white families—the Buchans, members of "that unique order of society known latterly as the Virginia aristocracy," and the Poseys, who, "like children playing a game . . . had their fingers perpetually crossed—which permitted them to do what they pleased." The novel is not told in a linear fashion but through an exploration of the ties and tensions between the two families, and how these reflect what is happening to America as its terrible war begins.

The narrator is Lacy Gore Buchan, sixty-five years old, "an unmarried old man [who], having nothing else to do, with a competence saved from the practice of medicine, thinks he has a story to tell." He continues: "Is it not something to tell, when a score of people whom I knew and loved, people beyond whose lives I could imagine no other life, either out of violence in themselves or the times, or out of some misery or shame, scattered into the new life of the modern age where they cannot even find themselves? Why cannot life change without tangling the lives of innocent persons? Why do innocent persons cease their innocence and become violent and evil in themselves that such great changes may take place?"

Lacy is looking back to events of half a century before, when he was fifteen and mourning the death of his mother. The funeral takes place at Pleasant Hill, the family place in the countryside, and his recollection of that day's events sets him off on a seemingly discursive but tightly controlled (by Tate, that is) excursion into the past. "I was suspended nowhere, in a world without time," he says at one point, and this is true of the novel itself, which moves back and forth within time much as do the most complex novels of Faulkner.

Yet *The Fathers,* though carefully and intricately constructed, is not at all difficult to read. Its prose is leisurely and at times somewhat dense, which requires one to read slowly and attentively (a demand most certainly not placed by *Gone With the Wind*), but one also reads eagerly as the individual characters and the society they inhabit move toward their unhappy ends.

The story that Lacy Buchan tells is not his own, though he figures in it. It is instead the story of George Posey, "the handsomest, most affable young man I had ever seen"; his wife, Susan, Lacy's sister; their father, Lewis Buchan, and his manservant, Coriolanus; a mulatto slave named Yellow Jim; and a great many other characters, white and black, Buchans or Poseys or neighbors or friends. Dominating all of them, though, is George, "Brother George" as Lacy calls him, a charismatic, compelling man who inhabits a universe entirely his own. Lacy, who as a boy idolized him, finds him an endless mystery. At a crucial moment in the novel, Lacy's dead grandfather appears to him as in a dream and discusses George:

> It is never, my son, his intention to do any evil but he does evil because he has not the will to do good. The only expectancy that he shares with humanity is the pursuing grave, and the thought of extinction overwhelms him because he is entirely alone. My son, in my day we were never alone, as your brother-in-law is alone. He is alone like a tornado. His one purpose is to whirl and he brushes aside the obstacles in his way.

Impulsive and oddly innocent, George commits foolish and dangerous acts with no apparent thought for their terrible consequences. He is an individualist, a man of the new world, in stark contrast to Lacy's father and others who went before: "Men of honor and dignity—where are they now? . . . They did a great deal of injustice but they always knew where they stood because they thought more of their code than they did of themselves." Eventually, though, that old order became ingrown and stultified, and withered away. Allen Tate, who admired its codes and standards even as he lamented the injustice of slavery, gives it a crisp and clear-eyed salute in this estimable novel.

SULA
by Toni Morrison

Thirty-three years ago, Toni Morrison labored in relative obscurity: She was the author of one novel, *The Bluest Eye* (1970), an editor at Random House, an associate professor of English at the State University of New York in Purchase. She was in her early forties, the divorced mother of two boys, slowly gaining respect in the scholarly and literary worlds but almost entirely unknown to the general public.

Certainly, she was unknown to me. I was a relatively young man, doing freelance reviewing for various publications, one of which was the *Washington Post*'s Book World. When in 1973 its editor, William McPherson, invited me to review a new novel titled *Sula*, I had absolutely no idea what I was in for but accepted the assignment because I trusted Bill's judgment.

The rest of the story—Morrison's, not mine—is history. *Sula* was enthusiastically reviewed (with, on my own part, certain reservations), found a decent number of readers and was nominated for the National Book Award for Fiction. Thereafter, Morrison's career took off. *Song of Solomon* (1977), *Tar Baby* (1981) and *Beloved* (1987) made Morrison a best-selling author and the winner of numerous prizes: a National Book Critics Circle Award, a Pulitzer Prize and, most important, the 1993 Nobel Prize for Literature. She became this country's most famous literary novelist—not least because of occasional appearances on the television show of Oprah Winfrey, her most sedulous booster—and an international figure as well. Now in her seventies, Morrison has left the prestigious chair she occupied for two decades at Princeton but shows no sign of reducing her literary activity.

In choosing to revisit *Sula* for this series, I had a couple of things in mind. My memories of the novel were admiring and fond but vague; I wanted to see how it had held up over more than three decades. I also had been troubled by Morrison's work since *Beloved,* which upon publication I praised for the power and grace of its prose but lamented that "it is a novel in which themes are more important than people, with the predictable consequence that the people never really come to life." I had been especially vexed by *Love* (2003), which I found "clotted, tedious, uninviting . . . oracular and ponderous." I wondered whether Morrison's penchant for Delphic pronouncements was something I had overlooked in *Sula* or whether it was a consequence of subsequent fame and the bully pulpit it offered her.

The answer appears to fall somewhere in between. There are, indeed, oracular touches in *Sula* that I missed back in the 1970s, and in her foreword to the 2004 Vintage International edition, Morrison goes out of her way to defend herself—and, by extension, *Sula*—as deeply political. Yet, now as in 1973, *Sula* seems most remarkable for its humor, its dialogue, its deftly realized title character and, in particular, its portrait of "the Bottom," the black community of an Ohio town called Medallion where the novel is set. In other words, *Sula* can—and in my view should—be read not as a political tract but as a "mere" novel, a human story, a statement that cannot so easily be made about Morrison's later work.

In that foreword to the 2004 edition, Morrison quite disarmingly describes the circumstances of her life as she began writing the book:

> I was living in Queens while I wrote *Sula,* commuting to Manhattan to an office job, leaving my children to child-minders and the public school in the fall and winter, to my parents in the summer, and was so strapped for money that the condition moved from debili-

tating stress to hilarity. Every rent payment was an event; every shopping trip a triumph of caution over the reckless purchase of a staple. The best news was that this was the condition of every other single/separated female parent I knew. The things we traded! Time, food, money, clothes, laughter, memory—and daring. . . . We were being encouraged to think of ourselves as our own salvation, to be our own best friends. What could that mean in 1969 that it had not meant in the 1920s? The image of the woman who was both envied and cautioned against came to mind.

This image in Morrison's mind metamorphosed into the character of Sula Peace: granddaughter of Eva Peace, daughter of Hannah Peace, closest friend of Nel Wright. They all live in the Bottom, the ironic name given to the "hilly land" above the "rich valley floor in that little river town," leaving blacks only "small consolation in the fact that every day they could literally look down on the white folks." Here, as in all her fiction, Morrison writes with affection for the tight black communities of the past, and toward the end of the novel, as this particular community begins to disintegrate, she chants what amounts to a dirge for it:

> The black people, for all their new look, seemed anxious to get to the valley, or leave town, and abandon the hills to whoever was interested. It was sad, because the Bottom had been a real place. These young ones kept talking about the community, but they left the hills to the poor, the old, the stubborn—and the rich white folks. Maybe it hadn't been a community, but it had been a place. Now there weren't any places left, just separate houses with separate televisions and separate telephones and less and less dropping by.

That is in 1965. In the 1920s, when all but a few pages of *Sula* are set, the Bottom is full of life—shaped, to be sure, in great measure by white bigotry and discrimination, but also by its own culture and sustained by its own institutions. As I wrote in 1973, "The most fully realized character in the novel . . . is the community of the Bottom. Toni Morrison is not a

Southern writer, but she has located place and community with the skill of a Flannery O'Connor or Eudora Welty." There is no reason to alter that judgment today; Morrison's portrait of the Bottom remains superb.

The lives of all four of the women mentioned above are contained within the Bottom. The themes that Morrison explores through them, she describes as follows: "What is friendship between women when unmediated by men? What choices are available to black women outside their own society's approval? What are the risks of individualism in a determinedly individualistic, yet racially uniform and socially static, community?" All four women confront these issues in one way or another, but it is in Sula that they are most forcefully brought home.

As a girl Sula is "heavy brown with quiet eyes, one of which featured a birthmark that . . . gave her otherwise plain face a broken excitement and blue-blade threat." Nel by contrast is "the color of wet sandpaper" and in other ways is Sula's opposite, yet from the age of twelve "their friendship was as intense as it was sudden. They found relief in each other's personality. Although both were unshaped, formless things, Nel seemed stronger and more consistent than Sula, who could hardly be counted on to sustain any emotion for more than three minutes." Sula is sassy and independent, Nel cautious and conventional, yet "they never quarreled, those two, the way some girlfriends did over boys, or competed against each other for them."

About the time she turns twenty, Nel is courted by and marries Jude, a decent man who "needed some of his appetites filled, some posture of adulthood recognized, but mostly he wanted someone to care about his hurt, to care very deeply." Flattered, and encouraged by what she interprets as Sula's support, she accepts Jude's proposal. While they have children, form a happy family and lead quiet lives, Sula leaves town for adventures unknown but generally assumed to be of a scandalous nature. When she suddenly returns ten years later, Nel springs to life: "It was like getting the use of an eye back, having a cataract removed." As to the rest of the Bottom, it quickly accords Sula the status of pariah:

> Their conviction of Sula's evil changed them in accountable yet mysterious ways. Once the source of their personal misfortune was identified, they had leave to protect and love one another. They began to cherish their husbands and wives, protect their children, repair their homes and in general band together against the devil in their midst. In their world, aberrations were as much a part of nature as grace.

The people of the Bottom may not know it, but Sula's misbehavior—which, when she turns it against Nel, seems unspeakably cruel and gratuitous—is as essential to their being as the verities they claim to worship. Sula is an outlaw, and, Morrison seems to argue, the community defines itself as much by the outlaw as by the paragon. Beyond that, the question is whether the friendship of two women—who in this case also, importantly, happen to be black—can survive the pressures that the outlaw's behavior places upon it.

Morrison's answer to that question, as offered in the closing pages of *Sula*, is interesting and convincing. This, though, seems to me of less moment than the novel's success as fiction, pure and not so simple. *Sula* is Toni Morrison before she became grand, before she garbed herself in the robes of spokeswoman, before she became more interested in politics than in people. It is also—different strokes for different folks—the Toni Morrison I much prefer.

THE REVOLT OF MAMIE STOVER
by William Bradford Huie

In December 1953, an unknown journalist named Hugh
Hefner published the first issue of a magazine called
Playboy with a nude Marilyn Monroe as Sweetheart of the
Month; it gave no hint of the seismic changes soon to follow.
The lid was still tightly clamped. When, a few months later, a
far better known journalist named William Bradford Huie
published a novel about prostitution called *The Revolt of
Mamie Stover,* he clearly felt that there were limits to what he
could write, and he observed them with care.

There was a very mildly graphic sex scene in the opening
pages of the novel, but after that, the tone was more reportorial
than arousing. Still, to the fourteen-year-old me in 1954, and to
many thousands of others, the adventures in Honolulu of this
blonde from Mississippi seemed pretty hot. The book enjoyed
lively sales, and two years later was made into a movie, with the
pneumatic Jane Russell in the title role. Today, the only way
you'll see the movie is on late-night television, and an Internet
search for the book turned up only a couple of dozen copies,
one from a bookseller who described it as "pulp fiction."

Sic transit gloria mundi. In his day, which lasted from the
publication of his first novel, *Mud on the Stars,* in 1942 until his
death in 1986, Huie was one of the most successful writers in
this country, and one of the most interesting. Born in Alabama
in 1910, Huie attended the University of Alabama, worked as a
journalist until joining the Navy in 1942, and—so it certainly
seems—at war's end had fire in his eyes. He was a crusader, and

the South in the postwar years was about as inviting a target as this country ever has offered. During the years of the civil rights movement, he did freelance magazine work and published several books, most notably *Three Lives for Mississippi* (1965), about the civil rights workers murdered in 1964. He was vilified by innumerable Southern whites, but he stuck to his guns.

All in all he published twenty-one books, about evenly divided between fiction and nonfiction, that sold more than twenty-eight million copies. Only two are still in print—*The Execution of Private Slovik* (1954) and *He Slew the Dreamer: My Search With James Earl Ray for the Truth about the Murder of Martin Luther King* (1970)—but others live on in movies, though people who watch them may have no idea of Huie's pivotal role: *The Americanization of Emily, The Outsider, Wild River.* He was an amazing guy: tough, passionate, opinionated, fearless, principled, courageous. He was compassionate, but he was no sentimentalist. The narrator of *Mamie Stover,* a Southern journalist named James Monroe Madison, doubtless speaks for Huie himself:

> I have little patience with the generality that all mankind is tragic; that men-in-the-mass are important or valuable. I believe that each individual must prove himself valuable. I believe that mankind is composed of individuals who are valuable and individuals who are worthless. I believe there are individuals whose souls can be nourished and developed, and there are others whose souls are desiccated and dead. . . . I believe that there is an aristocracy among men—an aristocracy of will, work, intelligence, and character. I believe that these aristocrats, these valuable individuals of the world are important, worthy to be free, and worthy of opportunity and aid, but that others are relatively unimportant.

So: A man who believed in equal opportunity for everybody long before that became the social and political received wisdom, but also a man who believed that only a part of humankind—a small part, in all likelihood—is capable of seizing that opportunity and making the most of it. Huie was a democrat, but he was also a meritocrat. The first part of that equation sits well today, but the second isn't exactly popular in a Mr. Rogers' Neighborhood culture where everyone is taught to have "self-esteem" even if there is nothing estimable about him or her.

One person Huie clearly regarded as among the world's "valuable women" was Mamie Stover. It is not clear to what extent she emerged full-blown from his imagination and to what extent she was based on a prostitute whom he knew in Hawaii during the war, but he clearly liked and respected her. Jim Madison meets her in 1939 "on a freighter out of Los Angeles bound for Honolulu." He is returning to his home after a period of hard, satisfying work. Her story is less happy. As a teenager she won a beauty contest in the Mississippi Delta, which led to Hollywood, which led to a producer who slept with her, beat her, had his thugs slice her cheek open, and shipped her off to Honolulu to work for the city's leading madam, Bertha Parchman. Mamie is twenty-two years old, tall, leggy, with "extraordinary . . . golden-blonde" hair, a staggering figure, yet "a discarded bundle of despair and hate, with an ugly scar on her face."

Aboard the freighter, she and Jim have a fling, though he senses it has less to do with any particular appeal of his own than with her need "to use me as a barrier against loneliness; she wanted to use me to help her in the Islands." This turns him off, yet he likes her; he discovers "a certain native niceness about her," and he admits "that, physically, she had been almost perfectly assembled for the satisfaction of vigorous lust." Recognizing that there's something of worth here, he offers to pay for her passage back to the mainland and for surgery to remove her scar; he doesn't want her to fall into prostitution, and hopes she'll be able to have a normal life.

Thanks a lot but no thanks, she says. "Why shouldn't I have just as much as any other woman in the world?" she asks. "If

I've lost my chance to get mine in Hollywood, then I'll get it in Honolulu. If I can't get it from one man I'll get it from a thousand. If I've got just one thing left to sell, then, by God, I'll sell it faster than it's ever been sold before!" Which is pretty much what she does. She goes to work for Bertha and becomes the number one girl in her stable. She starts salting away money, and asks Jim to help her take care of it. More than that, she asks him to invest it for her surreptitiously, because Honolulu's whores are under the thumb of "what was known as the Thirteen Articles," one of them being that "no girl may own real estate or maintain a residence outside the brothel."

She and Bertha become friends—Bertha respects Mamie's earning power, Mamie respects Bertha's business acumen—and eventually Bertha turns her brothel over to Mamie. Meantime, the Japanese attack Pearl Harbor, and suddenly Honolulu is under the control of the Army. Whereas the old Honolulu establishment had reviled the prostitutes and demanded strict obedience to the Thirteen Articles, the Army knows that fighting men need R&R, and that well-equipped, sanitary whorehouses supply plenty of it.

Mamie is just the girl for them. She sets up a four-bed Bull Ring that permits her to service men at an astonishing rate: ". . . she judged her efficiency by the length of time required to make a complete circuit. Ten minutes was par, though quite often she made it in eight. She was never longer than twenty minutes, for if any customer attempted to monopolize her services beyond five minutes he found himself jerked to attention by two alert M.P.s." The money rolls in almost faster than she can count it. Through an attorney whom Jim finds for her, she begins buying up real estate. By late in the war she's worth $600,000 or more—at least ten times that in today's dollars—and she's in close cahoots with the military, to some of whom she extends her favors as just that—favors—and with almost all of whom she strikes a firm alliance against the old order.

Her revolt first occurs when, emboldened by her military connections, she sunbathes at Waikiki, forbidden to prostitutes under the Thirteen Articles; then she buys a car, also forbidden, and "one by one, with the aid of the military, Mamie Stover defied each of the Thirteen Articles." Then she does two things absolutely forbidden: She marries a soldier—a major, no less—and she buys "a $40,000 home on Pacific Heights." She has it made, just like all the others who profited from the Second World War.

Of whom there were many, making "financial killings" while ordinary soldiers fought and died. If the central subject of *The Revolt of Mamie Stover* is prostitution and the degradation of women, war profiteering is almost equally important. Mamie herself is a war profiteer, one whom Huie likes anyway. The rest he holds in contempt, "the American people—the humble along with the arrogant—who spurned sacrifice and insisted upon enriching themselves while the nation bled."

That theme, needless to say, remains pertinent today, as does Huie's portrait of a strong woman who makes it on her own. If a half-century ago I read *The Revolt of Mamie Stover* in hopes of titillation, a second time through I find it smart, provocative and funny. The N-word pops up with a frequency that will unnerve today's reader, but that's the way people talked back then. It's not a great book, but it's not pulp fiction either. How nice it would be to have it back in print, and to find a new generation of readers for an American writer who scarcely deserves the neglect into which he has fallen.

THE ROBBER BRIDEGROOM
by Eudora Welty

Eudora Welty started out fast. Her first book, a collection of short stories called *A Curtain of Green,* was published in 1941, when she was thirty-two. It included an admiring introduction, "A Note on the Author and Her Work," by Katherine Anne Porter, whose reputation was then at its height. Reviewers and readers shared Porter's admiration for this unknown young writer's fiction. Small wonder, when one considers that among the book's seventeen stories were "Petrified Man," "Why I Live at the P.O.," "Death of a Traveling Salesman" and "A Worn Path"—every one of them instantly recognizable as an American classic.

A year later her second book was published, a novella called *The Robber Bridegroom.* It too was received with much enthusiasm, but it was a very different piece of work. Though written with the same grace and humor as the short stories, it was wildly fantastic, part fairy tale and part folk ballad, set along the Natchez Trace in the antebellum South and containing a cast of characters virtually all of whom were larger—far larger—than life. As Welty's career unfolded, it became clear that *The Robber Bridegroom* was unique among all her works, a startling and winning departure for a writer whose fiction mostly is deeply rooted in the realities of twentieth-century small-town Southern life.

No doubt the critical and popular esteem that Welty now enjoys is largely attributable to the short stories and the major novels—*Delta Wedding* (1946), *Losing Battles* (1970) and *The*

Optimist's Daughter (1972)—but for me *The Robber Bridegroom* occupies a place in her work, and in American literature, that is all its own and that has grown, rather than shrunk, over the decades. I read it many years ago as a young man and was enchanted by its humor, its magic and its romance. Now, after my umpteenth reading of it, I remain under the spell of all those attributes, but it is Welty's prose that draws me in most powerfully and leaves the most lasting impressions. Consider, by way of example:

> New Orleans was the most marvelous city in the Spanish country or anywhere else on the river. Beauty and vice and every delight possible to the soul and body stood hospitably, and usually together, in every doorway and beneath every palmetto by day and lighted torch by night. A shutter opened, and a flower bloomed. The very atmosphere was nothing but aerial spice, the very walls were sugar cane, the very clouds hung as golden as bananas in the sky. But Clement Musgrove was a man who could have walked the streets of Baghdad without sending a second glance overhead at the Magic Carpet, or heard the tambourines of the angels in Paradise without dancing a step, or had his choice of the fruits of the Garden of Eden without making up his mind. For he was an innocent of the wilderness, and a planter of Rodney's Landing, and this was his good.

The language of that paragraph is exquisite, and so too is the delicate balance between the exotic settings so precisely evoked and the ordinary, decent, plodding innocence of the planter Clement Musgrove. He is in search of his beautiful daughter, Rosamond, whom he believes to have been kidnapped by a bandit. What he does not know is that she has gone to her gentleman bandit of her own free will, lured by love and passion even though she does not even know his name, which is Jamie Lockhart. She lives with him and the bandits in the deep woods, and another extraordinary passage leaves no doubt why she freely and gladly does so:

The trees were golden under the sky. The grass was as soft as a dream and the wind blew like the long rising and falling breath of Summer when she has just fallen asleep. One day Jamie did not ride away with the others, and then the night was day and the woods were the roof over their heads. The tender flames of the myrtle trees and the green smoke of the cedars were the fires of their hearth. In the radiant noon they found the shade, and ate the grapes from the muscadine vines. The spice-dreams rising from the fallen brown pine needles floated through their heads when they stretched their limbs and slept in the woods. The stream lay still in the golden ravine, the water glowing darkly, the colors of fruits and nuts.

It is difficult to imagine a more deeply, ardently erotic passage than that, yet its eroticism is almost wholly within the imagery of nature and the woods. It reminds us that Welty, who never married and whose own amatory life remains an apparently unsolvable (and essentially unimportant) mystery, wrote often about sexual passion and desire, and though she did so with the utmost discretion and taste, one also senses her own longings not far beneath the surface. It is a characteristic she shares with Anita Brookner, who in almost all other respects is utterly unlike her but conveys the same impression of deep but perhaps unfulfilled yearning.

Certainly there can be no question that sexual matters are at the very core of *The Robber Bridegroom*. The story begins with Clement Musgrove arriving at Rodney's Landing on his way back from New Orleans with the sack of gold he has been paid for his tobacco. He puts up at an inn and immediately is thrown in with two rowdy fellows, one of whom is the legendary Mike Fink, "champion of all the flatboat bullies on the Mississippi River," the other a "yellow-haired stranger" who, after saving Clement from a cruel scheme of Fink's, identifies himself as Jamie Lockhart. Clement overflows with gratitude for his kindness and promises him an introduction "to my daughter Rosamond, who is so beautiful that she keeps the memory of my first wife alive and evergreen in my heart."

Echoes of Cinderella, for Rosamond has a stepmother, Salome, "as ugly as the night" and as jealous as she can be—the wicked stepmother to end all wicked stepmothers. She aims to kill off Rosamond with the help of a lout named Goat, but instead she drives Rosamond into the forest, where a bandit with a face stained berry-red—Jamie Lockhart in disguise— merrily orders her to remove all her clothes, then sends her home "as naked as a jay bird." Later he finds her in the woods, swoops her onto his horse Orion, and takes her away in "the fastest kidnapping that had ever been in that part of the country." Then:

> . . . the red horse stood stock-still, and Jamie Lockhart lifted Rosamond down. The wild plum trees were like rolling smoke between him and the river, but he broke the branches and the plums rained down as he carried her under. He stopped and laid her on the ground, where, straight below, the river flowed as slow as sand, and robbed her of that which he had left her the day before.

She does not know that her robber/lover is Jamie Lockhart; he does not know that she is Clement's cherished daughter Rosamond: "Sometimes she would wake up out of her first sleep and study his sleeping face, but she did not know the language it was written in. . . . The only thing that divided his life from hers was the raiding and the robbing that he did, but that was like his other life, that she could not see, and so she contented herself with loving all that was visible and present of him as much as she was able."

Still, curiosity eventually gets the best of her, and she is able to see him without the stain that disguises him. He is furious. "Good-by," he says. "For you did not trust me, and did not love me, for you wanted only to know who I am." Soon enough she learns his name, but she also learns "that names were nothing and untied no knots." Her lover has gone, and she is left to reassemble the pieces of her life; though if she ever again sees him she has, thanks to all that happy activity on "grass soft as a dream," good news to impart to him.

Well. *The Robber Bridegroom* is a fairy tale, and fairy tales usually have happy endings. This one is no exception, which is as it should be. There can be no question that Welty wrote the tale in high spirits, and she certainly wasn't about to punish these two handsome young people whom she had so lovingly brought to life by keeping them apart from each other. Still, she puts them through a few adventures and disappointments before reuniting them, and she permits them—and us—to meet some of the Mississippi River's more outlandish characters in the process.

The Mississippi and the Natchez Trace, "that old buffalo trail where travelers passed along and were set upon by the bandits and the Indians and torn apart by the wild animals," are as vividly brought to life in this novella as are any of its characters. Place was of central, abiding importance to Welty, and she loved no place on Earth more than the Mississippi landscape she inhabited and the great river that ran through it. This is evident in much of her other writing—*Delta Wedding* and *Losing Battles* most particularly—but nowhere does she convey her affinity for it with more sureness and intimacy than in this lovely miniature. *The Robber Bridegroom* probably is not Welty's best book—that distinction must be bestowed on *A Curtain of Green*—but it is the one that I love most.

FANNY HILL
by John Cleland

In the long, complicated history of literary censorship in the
United States, no one event or period can be singled out as
indisputably pivotal, but a case can be made that in 1963 a
decisive change took place. That was the year in which Grove
Press published a five-volume unexpurgated edition of Frank
Harris's highly fictionalized erotic memoir, *My Life and Loves*,
and in which Putnam brought out the first trade American edition in more than two centuries of John Cleland's *Memoirs of a
Woman of Pleasure*, more commonly known as *Fanny Hill*.

Both books remain in print in various editions from various
publishers, and their widespread acceptance as works of legiti-
mate literary interest undoubtedly has contributed to the high
degree of tolerance now accorded to the treatment of sexual
subjects in books (and everything else) in this country. They are
indeed candid about sex, but the similarities pretty much end
there. Originally published in the 1920s, *My Life and Loves* is
fiction masquerading as fact, filled with chest-thumping by an
egomaniacal albeit influential British editor and writer. *Memoirs
of a Woman of Pleasure,* which first appeared in London in 1748
and 1749, is something else altogether, a work of real if limited
literary merit, a fascinating depiction of the demimonde in
Georgian England, and an exceedingly amusing book that may,
or may not, have been written as a spoof.

Its origins are just about as mysterious as the life of its
author. Cleland (1710-1789) worked for a while for the East
India Company as a young man and enjoyed temporary success

in Bombay, but by the early 1740s he was back in England and working, according to Peter Wagner's introduction to the Penguin Classics edition of *Fanny Hill*, as "a literary hack, Grub Street writer, and journalist." He seems to have been perpetually short of funds and spent some time in debtors' prison. Apparently it was during one of these jail terms that he completed the manuscript of *Fanny Hill*, which at times over the years has been seen as a satire of Samuel Richardson's *Pamela* (1740-41), beloved by readers for its moralizing but ridiculed by the literati as priggish humbug. Henry Fielding satirized it brutally in *Shamela* (1741) and Cleland may well have had similar intentions, though so little is known about him that one can only guess.

The novel appeared off and on in this country, mostly in bowdlerized editions or in bits and pieces. No doubt Putnam was encouraged to bring it out in 1963, in a six dollar hard-cover edition, because of a legal decision four years earlier that permitted publication in the States of D.H. Lawrence's *Lady Chatterley's Lover*, as well as by the many legal actions in 1961 and thereafter on behalf of Henry Miller's *Tropic of Cancer*. New York authorities immediately sought to ban *Fanny Hill* as obscene, but publication was upheld in New York's Supreme Court by Justice Arthur G. Klein, who wrote: "While the saga of Fanny Hill will undoubtedly never replace 'Little Red Riding Hood' as a popular bedtime story, it is quite possible that were Fanny to be transposed from her mid-eighteenth-century Georgian surroundings to our present day society, she might conceivably encounter many things which would cause her to blush."

Exactly. Justice Klein understood what the novel's critics too often have not, that it is in its own fashion a morality tale and that Fanny herself is in some respects as innocent as she is worldly. Whether I was smart enough to grasp that when I first read it, I do not recall, but probably not. I glommed onto the ninety-five-cent paperback that Putnam rushed out on the heels of Klein's decision, and no doubt I was vastly more interested in the exquisitely detailed accounts of her amorous adventures than in Fanny's concluding apologia: "if I have painted vice in all its gayest colours, if I have decked it with flowers, it has been solely in order to make the worthier, the solemner, sacrifice of it to virtue."

This is true. Fanny ends her tale "in the bosom of virtue," happily married to Charles, with whom several years before she had fallen in love—"He was the universe to me, and all that was not him was nothing to me"—but who had been lost to her for several years due to circumstances beyond their control. Charles's absence, though, does not prevent her from going about discovering the delights "of a pleasure merely animal" with other men and then setting herself up as a woman of pleasure. As she nicely puts it, while succumbing to the advances of a gentleman to whom she is introduced shortly after Charles's disappearance:

> Had anyone, but a few instants before, told me that I should have ever known any man but Charles, I would have spat in his face, or had I been offered infinitely a greater sum of money than that I saw paid for me, I had spurned the proposal in cold blood. But our virtues and our vices depend too much on our circumstances. . . . I considered myself as so much in his power that I endured his kisses and embraces without affecting struggles or anger; not that they as yet gave me any pleasure, or prevailed over the aversion of my soul to give myself up to any sensation of that sort; what I suffered, I suffered out of a kind of gratitude, and as a matter of course after what had passed.

Fanny, in other words, is something of a situational ethicist, and this situation soon leads her to become "a kept mistress in form, well lodged, with a very sufficient allowance and lighted up with all the lustre of dress." This lasts until she accidentally discovers "Mr. H...." (the only name by which we know him) in flagrante with the maid. Her pride hurt, she takes revenge by coupling with "a very handsome young lad, scarce turned of nineteen, fresh as a rose, well shaped and clever-limbed: in short, a very good excuse for any woman's liking," and has a splendid time for which she pays a pretty price: She's tossed off the payroll and out of the house.

But this self-described "artless inexperienced country maid" picks herself up, dusts herself off, and starts all over again. Mrs. Cole, "a middle-aged discreet sort of woman, . . . came to offer her cordial advice and service to me," and Fanny's world continues to expand, "because keeping a house of conveniency, there were no lengths in lewdness she would not advise me to go" and, for that matter, just about none that Fanny herself is unwilling to go. Rather than a rapacious madam, Mrs. Cole is a good-hearted gentlewoman who just happened to fall into a spot of bad luck, and before long it becomes plain that Mrs. Cole's loss is Fanny's gain—and Mrs. Cole's, too.

In no time Fanny is off and running, though that's not precisely the right verb. At this point writing about *Memoirs of a Woman of Pleasure* in a family newspaper becomes tricky, for what Fanny is up to, or down to, can scarcely be described as vividly there as it is in Cleland's spirited prose. Suffice it to say that gentlemen of a sporting inclination are serviced regularly and to the enjoyment of all—Fanny herself most emphatically included—and that some of these fellows sport equipment that leaves Fanny on the edge of speechlessness; okay, I'll mention that one of them presents himself complete with "a maypole" and leave it at that. There's a most amusing scene in which an unattractive man—"gentleman" won't do for this one—pays extravagantly for the privilege of separating Fanny from her maidenhead; having long since surrendered it elsewhere, she, with Mrs. Cole's help, devises an ingenious strategy for fooling him into thinking himself a success.

Along the way Fanny is invariably cheerful, and enters into

every—well, almost every—new encounter with boundless enthusiasm. To say that she's a woman of pleasure is complete understatement: She is the original Happy Hooker. Her heart may belong to Charles, but the rest of her belongs to anyone who can pay the rent. Many can, and do, and no one has more fun than Fanny. She also learns a few things about men, and women, and life:

> [I]f I may judge from my own experience, none are better paid or better treated during their reign than the mistresses of those who, enervated by nature, debaucheries, or age, have the least employment for the sex: sensible that a woman must be satisfied some way, they ply her with a thousand little tender attentions, presents, caresses, confidences, and exhaust their invention in means and devices to make up for the capital deficiency . . . But here is their misfortune, that, when by a course of teasing, worrying, handling, wanton postures, lascivious motions, they have at length accomplished a flashy enervated enjoyment, they have at the same time lighted up a flame in the object of their passion that, not having the means themselves to quench, drives her for relief into the next person's arms, who can finish their work.

Hard-earned wisdom, but wisdom all the same. *Fanny Hill* is more than two hundred years old, and at times its language is a trifle dated, but in matters of the human heart and body it is as up to date as anything you'll find in *The Playboy Advisor*, and a whole lot more fun. Fanny's story tells us that morality is a far more slippery business than most moralists would have us believe, and that the road to happiness and virtue is not necessarily either straight or narrow. No, *Fanny Hill* will never supplant *Little Red Riding Hood*, but it's a splendid bedtime story for grown-ups.

POETS IN THEIR YOUTH
by Eileen Simpson

In 1982 Eileen Simpson, a little-known but thoughtful and graceful writer, drew upon William Wordsworth's autobiographical poem "Resolution and Independence" for the epigraph and title of her third book: "We poets in our youth begin in gladness; / But thereof comes in the end despondency and madness." That book, *Poets in Their Youth,* illustrates Wordsworth's point with clarity, sympathy and an utter lack of sentimentality. It is as powerful and knowing an account of the literary muse and its effects as one could hope to read, and the neglect into which it seems to be sliding is a genuine injustice.

On New Year's Day 1941, Simpson, then in her early twenties and living and working in New York, met a young lecturer at Harvard who had a quick mind and an "irresistible grin." He went by the name of John Berryman, though he had been born John Allyn Smith; his father had committed suicide when he was a boy, and he readily permitted his new stepfather to adopt him and give him his own surname, a decision he subsequently—and obsessively—came to regard as rank and contemptible disloyalty. He was, in any event, a young man of great charm and she, having been orphaned at the age of seven, probably yearned for what she must have believed to be the stability and security of marriage.

So in October 1942, in the Lady Chapel of St. Patrick's Cathedral on Fifth Avenue, Eileen Mulligan and John Berryman were married, with his former teacher and mentor

Mark Van Doren as best man, and they moved after the briefest of honeymoons into a chilly apartment in Boston's Beacon Hill, in which there was little except their love to keep them warm. It was the beginning of just over a decade of marriage, of much happiness punctuated by her ever more frequent awareness of her husband's "need to live in turbulence—if it wasn't drinking and women, it was the way he worked." The marriage ended with her decision, in 1953, to leave him, not for someone else but for herself and, in a way, for him:

> John's life had become a high-wire act. He was flirting with his subtle foe [suicide] in the certainty that there was an invisible net, held by me, which would catch him should he lose his footing. The job of net-holder had exhausted me. More important, I realized that by making myself available in this way I had been encouraging him to be more and more incautious, less vigilant against the current that was threatening to suck him under.

Simpson knew that leaving him would cause "anguish" for both of them, though she was surprised after it happened that "the emotions I had expected to feel on separation, the predictable anger and bitterness at the failure of a marriage, were smothered under a blanket of grief." She recovered, moving along to a successful career as psychotherapist and a happy second marriage to Robert Simpson, a diplomat and authority on the Middle East; she published a couple more books before her death in 2002. Berryman recovered, too, in his fashion, publishing poetry to ever greater acclaim, winning a Pulitzer Prize in 1965, marrying twice more—but then, perhaps inevitably, killing himself in Minneapolis in 1972 by doing "what he had been rehearsing at least as far back as the night of our engagement party: He jumped from a railing, this time of a bridge, with no net and the frozen Mississippi River below." He was fifty-seven years old.

But that is the end of the story. What Simpson tells in *Poets in Their Youth* is its beginning, those days of promise and excitement before its heartbreaking end made itself clear. They were days of intense friendships with Delmore Schwartz, R.P. Blackmur, Robert Lowell, Randall Jarrell, Allen Tate, Theodore Roethke—the successors to Robert Frost, T.S. Eliot (who makes an engaging cameo appearance in this book), E.E. Cummings, Hart Crane and Wallace Stevens, and perhaps the last generation of American poets whose voices could be heard outside the narrow circle in which they themselves moved.

From almost the moment they met, Berryman talked to Simpson of little else except poetry, "the writing of which, he said, quoting Delmore, was 'a vocation.' It demanded, and should have, a poet's whole attention. . . . He must be engaged in it with his whole being. But how could he, John, be so engaged when he had to earn a living?" The dilemma haunted him throughout his marriage to Simpson and was never really resolved until the publication of his long poem "Homage to Mistress Bradstreet" in 1956 brought modestly remunerative opportunities for readings and lectures, and his Pulitzer a decade later for "Dream Songs" established him as a major literary figure.

The early years, though, were unremittingly hard. He lectured for a while at Harvard, then at Princeton, but such assignments came irregularly, paid poorly and were distracting: "He liked teaching, was good at it, also liked the boys. But the important thing, the real thing, the *only* thing was to write poetry. All else was wasted time." Marriage was a distraction, too: "Responsibility toward marriage vs. responsibility toward art became a serious conflict for one who was almost as ambitious to be a good husband as a good poet." Simpson loved her husband deeply, and almost three decades after leaving him, as she wrote this book, that love still colored her view of him and his work, but his "psychological instability," often manifested as threats of suicide, taught her that "no amount of love and care could protect him from external circumstances, and that these could bring him to the edge of madness."

Whether Berryman was manic-depressive is not clear—his beloved friend Delmore Schwartz most certainly was, and there were plenty of signs of it elsewhere in their tight poetic circle—but his moods swung swiftly and sometimes violently. When he was happy he was irresistible, and surely it was the memory of such times that kept Simpson by his side even as it became ever more apparent that she had to leave him, but when he was unhappy he dragged as many people down with him as he could. One year during the war—he was rejected by the armed services because of poor vision—he was happy, and admitted it to his wife: "He was touched to hear me say what he already knew, that I too had never been happier. 'What the hell is happiness?' he asked with a happy laugh. And, more uneasily, 'Should a poet seek it?'"

This, Simpson subsequently realized, was their last prolonged period of happiness. One short-lived academic post or literary chore followed another, putting a bit of food on the table—the various jobs that Simpson found for herself supplied the rest of their support—but leaving Berryman to wonder: "What price did one pay for teaching creative writing?" Eventually he decided that "he did not want to climb the academic ladder," and stayed as far outside the system as he could, but in the postwar years the system was changing, drawing poets and other writers onto the campuses and turning literary writing into a hothouse flower. The academic circuit paid Berryman's bills for most of his adult life, as it did for his friends and fellow poets.

They were a remarkable group, and one of the great strengths of *Poets in Their Youth* is the group portrait that Simpson paints. She loved and cared about them all, and their wives—among whom were Jean Stafford and Caroline Gordon—and delighted in their company. A long chapter about two weeks in Maine with

Lowell and Stafford gives us that notable couple in all the joy and misery they inflicted on each other; Simpson's picture of the sublimely gifted but tormented Schwartz is especially loving and, in the end, despairing. Many of them had come from unhappy childhoods with quarreling parents. They seemed to seek in their poems and their friendship the warmth they had not known as boys, and the orphaned Simpson was drawn to this, as well as to their loyalty to each other:

> One hears so much talk about the competitiveness of poets that I've often wondered: Are they any more competitive than astronauts, art collectors, assistant professors, jockeys, hostesses, ballet dancers, professional beauties? I doubt it. In the years during which John and his contemporaries were making their reputations, what impressed me was the generosity with which they offered one another advice, praise and encouragement. . . . As those of their generation neared the finish line and saw how few there were left in the race, they kept a close eye on one another's positions, of course, and rivalry undoubtedly became as keen with them as with any other finalists. With only a few prizes worth having, how could it not be so?

The cleareyed compassion of that passage is characteristic of *Poets in Their Youth*, which never sensationalizes these brilliant but wildly erratic young men, only seeks to understand them. So, too, is Simpson's final judgment on her former husband's death: "The litany of suicides among poets is long. After a while I began to feel that I'd missed the obvious. It was the poetry that had kept him alive." This struck me as uncommonly wise when first I read the book in 1982, inspired to do so by a review I no longer remember, and it strikes me as even more so now. *Poets in Their Youth* has more to tell us about the minds and lives of poets than anything else I've read—except, of course, the poems themselves.

THE DAMNATION OF THERON WARE
by Harold Frederic

I arrived on Harvard's campus in the fall of 1968 to begin a
year long fellowship. I was expecting to study ethical issues
in American life but found myself in rapt attendance at a
seminar on the works of William Faulkner. While my fellow
journalists immersed themselves in public affairs and other
weighty matters, I went on to study literary biography and, just
because the course was there, American fiction of the late nineteenth and early twentieth centuries.

One never knows, do one? The course that I stumbled into
turned out to be a turning point. We read books I'd never
heard of—Kate Chopin's *The Awakening*, Hamlin Garland's
Main-Travelled Roads, Jack London's *Martin Eden*—and books
I'd heard of but never read: Theodore Dreiser's *Sister Carrie*,
Frank Norris's *The Pit*, Stephen Crane's *Maggie: A Girl of the
Streets*. We also read a novel that came from far, far out in the
blue and that knocked me for a loop: *The Damnation of Theron
Ware*, by Harold Frederic. Since then, like *The Awakening*,
Frederic's novel has been rescued from obscurity by academia
and can be found in college curricula, as well as in two paper-
back editions, but then it was little more than a literary curiosity that almost no one had read.

These novels introduced me to a period in American literature that my own undergraduate education had scanted. In the
1950s and 1960s courses in our literature tended to begin with
Hawthorne and Melville et al., then to leap half a century or
more to Henry James, Willa Cather and the novelists of the

1920s. Little attention was paid to those who thrived in the period between them, except perhaps for William Dean Howells and, of course, Mark Twain, who fit into nobody's category and who tended to be regarded as a special case because he committed the most unliterary sin of being funny.

The novels and stories of the period roughly from 1880 to 1920 for the most part do not have the literary flair of those that preceded and followed them, but they established the realist tradition—the accumulation of mundane but revealing detail, the rejection of romanticism and idealism, the determination to see things as they really are—that remains an important strain in our literature, albeit now more in popular and genre novels than in "serious" fiction. *The Damnation of Theron Ware* is a minor classic of realism, yet it rarely is ranked with the works of Dreiser, Norris, Crane and the rest, perhaps because it is Harold Frederic's only genuinely notable work of fiction, his career having been devoted largely to journalism.

Frederic was born in 1856 in Upstate New York, and before reaching the age of twenty had made a beeline for the *Utica Observer*. His upward trajectory was sharp: editor of the *Observer* a few years later—in his early twenties!—then editor of the *Albany Evening Journal*, then London correspondent of the *New York Times*. He began publishing fiction while he was in England, but not until the appearance of *Theron Ware* in 1896 was he taken seriously as a novelist. Unfortunately his private life was exceedingly sloppy. He had a wife and five children, to whom he added a mistress and three more children. His mistress was a Christian Scientist who tried faith healing when he suffered a stroke in 1898. It didn't work, and he died that October. She was tried on charges of manslaughter, and acquitted.

In this as in other respects, he defied convention, which in the late nineteenth century was a lot more rigid and intolerant than it is now. In his early journalistic career he was a passionate reformer who ran into trouble with the Albany newspaper when he defied the dominant Republican machine, and much of that spirit is evident in *Theron Ware*. Its protagonist is a young Methodist minister who is appointed to serve the parish in a dreary Upstate town called Octavius. He is genial and handsome, "with the broad white brow, thoughtful eyes, and features moulded into that regularity of strength which used to characterize the American Senatorial type in those far-away days of clean-shaven faces and moderate incomes before the [Civil] War," but he is also ambitious beyond his limited abilities, foolish, spineless and self-deluding. From the moment he reaches Octavius, he sets himself on the path to self-destruction.

Soon after his arrival he is visited at the modest manse by the church's three trustees, who inform him that "no new-fangled notions can go down here" and that his wife, Alice, had best stop wearing bright flowers in her bonnet at church. This command is "a source of bitter humiliation to him," and worse for Alice, who loathes both the command and her husband's pliant acquiescence in it. Their marriage, which had been joyful, starts to turn sour, and at the same time Theron's eyes begin wandering in the direction of Celia Madden, the glamorous daughter of the richest man in town and a practicing Roman Catholic who is a close friend of the local priest.

"Celia Madden," I'm told, is an anagram for "Alice Damned." Whether Frederic intended that cannot be known, but it certainly points in the right direction: Theron's infatuation with Celia is poison to his marriage. Celia, apparently amused by his utter innocence, toys with him, inviting him to a secret room in her family's mansion where she plays Chopin on the piano, driving him to fits of ecstasy that lead to no consummation but persuade him in the baseless conviction that she loves him and that he must offer himself to her.

Significant parts of her allure for him are her Irishness and her Catholicism, though he came to Octavius with conventional late-nineteenth-century Protestant "race and religious aversion," which Frederic sums up in a stingingly satirical passage:

> Pigs wallowed in the mire before [Catholicism's] base, and burrowing into this base were a myriad of narrow doors, each bearing the hateful sign of a saloon, and giving forth from its recesses of night the sounds of screams and curses. Above were sculptured rows of lowering ape-like faces . . . and out of these sprang into the vague upper gloom, on the one side, lamp-posts from which negroes hung by the neck, and on the other gibbets for dynamiters and Molly Maguires; and between the two glowed a spectral picture of some black-robed, tonsured men, with leering satanic masks, making a bonfire of the Bible in the public schools.

Now, though, Theron meets Father Forbes, and becomes almost as infatuated with him as with Celia. The priest is cynical, world-weary and, in Theron's eyes, the acme of intellect and sophistication. He talks with Forbes and the equally cynical, world-weary Dr. Ledsmar, and comes away from the evening convinced "that his meeting with the priest and the doctor was the turning-point in his career." The curtains part and the light shines forth: "Evidently there was an intellectual world, a world of culture and grace, of lofty thoughts and the inspiring communion of real knowledge, where creeds were not of importance, and where men asked one another, not 'Is your soul saved?' but 'Is your mind well furnished?'"

Armed with what he imagines to be this life-changing knowledge, Theron goes right around the bend. He becomes sarcastic about his own religion and convinces himself that the once-reviled Catholics in fact have achieved the ideal blend of faith and worldliness; he imagines that Alice is in love with—perhaps even having an affair with—a lawyer who has taken a kindly interest in her; he pursues Celia ever more inanely, all the while fantasizing that her friendship with Father Forbes is far more than platonic. He is "entirely deceived about yourself," Celia's brother tells him, and finally Celia herself confronts him with the brutal truth:

> We were disposed to like you very much when we first knew you. . . . You impressed us as an innocent, simple, genuine young character, full of mother's milk. . . . Instead we found you inflating yourself with all sorts of egotisms and vanities. We found you presuming upon the friendships which had been mistakenly extended to you. . . . Your whole mind became an unpleasant thing to contemplate. You thought it would amuse and impress us to hear you ridiculing and reviling the people of your church, whose money supports you, and making a mock of the things they believe in, and which you for your life wouldn't dare let them know you didn't believe in. You talked to us slightingly about your wife. What were you thinking of, not to comprehend that that would disgust us?

Theron Ware's story will remind today's reader of the one told three decades later by Dreiser in *An American Tragedy*: a young man married to a woman of his own modest class becomes infatuated with a woman beyond his reach and pays terrible consequences for it. Dreiser's novel is the more famous, but Frederic's is the better. It gives us America at a watershed moment in its history, with science advancing and orthodox religion retreating, with the old Anglo oligarchy challenged by new immigrants, with sexuality slowly moving beyond closed doors and shadows, with ambition becoming more rank and unashamed, with early stirrings of what we now know as feminism. More than a century after its publication it remains vivid and pertinent. Frederic's occasional lapses into sarcasm and melodramatic language may seem excessive, but they were characteristic of his time and should be accepted as such. *The Damnation of Theron Ware*, according to the editor of my old hardcover copy, is "a minor masterpiece," and I say he's right.

A MOVEABLE FEAST
by Ernest Hemingway

S ometime in 1960 Ernest Hemingway completed a memoir of his years in Paris from 1921 to 1926. "If the reader prefers," he wrote in a three-paragraph preface, "this book may be regarded as fiction. But there is always the chance that such a book of fiction may throw some light on what has been written as fact." He did not submit the manuscript for publication, and the next year he was dead, a suicide at the age of sixty-one at his place in Idaho.

Three years later the manuscript was published as *A Moveable Feast*. The title apparently was chosen by Hemingway's widow, Mary, who recalled words he had written to a friend in 1950: "If you are lucky enough to have lived in Paris as a young man, then wherever you go for the rest of your life, it stays with you, for Paris is a moveable feast." Hemingway himself may have wanted to delay its publication so long as people mentioned in it were still alive (though such a kindness would have been uncharacteristic of him), but the essentially finished condition of the manuscript and the tone of the preface suggest that he wanted it brought out sooner or later.

It was the first of many posthumous publications that Mary Hemingway permitted—or, more accurately, actively encouraged—almost none of which did anything to enhance her husband's reputation, though presumably they enhanced the Hemingway estate's exchequer. *A Moveable Feast* is the one notable exception. Reviewers recognized it immediately as a valuable addition to its author's literary legacy, and readers gobbled it up. They still do; it enjoys steady sales and is often taught in high school and college.

I remember very well its publication in 1964, first in *Life* magazine—which still did things like that in those lost days—and then as a book. I was in my mid-twenties. I had begun to have second thoughts about most of Hemingway's novels and deep reservations about his strutting literary persona, but the best of his short stories still seemed to me small masterpieces, and like virtually every young American at that time I was in thrall to Hemingway's famous prose style. Even though I made no effort to emulate it, I knew it was unique in American literature and believed that it was uniquely important.

To say that my judgments changed in the ensuing four decades is understatement. I came to regard Hemingway's style as more self-conscious and mannered than pure, declarative and spare; I realized that in almost all of his writing, he had little of interest to say; and I came to loathe his worst traits of personality and character—meanness that often turned into cruelty; self-centeredness; bluster and braggadocio; exaggerated, showy machismo. Rereading *A Moveable Feast* in the late 1960s and again in the 1970s, I understood that in certain passages—those dealing with Gertrude Stein, Ford Madox Ford and, most particularly, F. Scott Fitzgerald—it is unforgivably vicious. I also came to understand that Morley Callaghan's *That Summer in Paris* (1963) is a better book about the same time and place, not least because Callaghan was a better man than Hemingway, more tolerant of and amused by other people's shortcomings.

Yet *A Moveable Feast* retained a certain irresistible charm. It was a privilege to be able to read about that time in Paris in the words of one of the most important literary expatriates, and it remains so to this day. Reading *A Moveable Feast* for the fourth (and probably not the last) time, I was struck by how much of it is still agreeable to me. It is actually possible to like Hemingway as he plays with his little son and his cat, fondly nicknamed Bumby and F. Puss, as he talks and travels with Hadley, the first of his four wives and the only one whom he may have loved, as he swaps gossip and stories with friends and rivals while knocking back impressive amounts of alcohol in the cafes and (when he could afford them) restaurants of Paris.

It was a famous time, by now deeply embedded in legend, and much of the legend probably is fiction embroidered by nostalgia: the nostalgia of those few who were there, the nostalgia of those of us who wish we had been. In Hemingway's specific case, it was the nostalgia he felt for the days when he was writing at his peak. In the last years of his life, his creative gifts entirely deserted him—those posthumous novels are uniformly dreadful, embarrassments that he almost certainly would have refused to publish and should have burned—and he missed those gifts badly. Thus we find him writing here with pride and fondness about years in which he had very little money but a great deal of energy and determination:

> It was wonderful to walk down the long flights of stairs knowing that I'd had good luck working. I always worked until I had something done and I always stopped when I knew what was going to happen next. That way I could be sure of going on the next day. But sometimes when I was starting a new story and I could not get it going, I would sit in front of the fire and squeeze the peel of the little oranges into the edge of the flame and watch the sputter of blue that they made. I would stand and look out over the roofs of Paris and think, "Do not worry. You have always written before and you will write now. All you have to do is write one true sentence. Write the truest sentence that you know." So finally I would write one true sentence, and then go on from there. . . . If I started to write elaborately . . . I found that I could cut that scrollwork or ornament out and throw it away and start with the first true simple declarative sentence I had written. Up in that room I decided that I would write one story about each thing that I knew about. I was trying to do this all the time I was writing, and it was good and severe discipline.

Obviously Hemingway is sentimentalizing himself in this well-known passage, and the "one true sentence" shtick has become tiresome over the years, but what Hemingway describes is essentially true. However one may feel about the literary style that emerged from this protracted period of self-discipline and self-denial, there can be no disputing the seriousness of Hemingway's purpose or the dedication he brought to the task. This apprenticeship was undoubtedly hard. "I knew the stories were good and someone would publish them finally at home," he writes. "When I stopped doing newspaper work I was sure the stories were going to be published. But every one I sent out came back."

Too often the little family went hungry. In his fifties Hemingway tended to romanticize this—"When you are twenty-five and are a natural heavyweight, missing a meal makes you very hungry. But it also sharpens all of your perceptions"—but it was entirely real and it must have been exceedingly difficult for Hadley, who seems to have had bottomless patience and good cheer. Whether Hemingway could have done what he did without her is at the very least open to question, and one senses from this book that he knew this better than anyone.

The gratitude that he expresses toward her is not often echoed elsewhere. One of Hemingway's least attractive traits was that he turned against just about everyone who helped him, the exceptions in *A Moveable Feast* being Hadley and Sylvia Beach, the generous proprietor of the famous Left Bank bookshop Shakespeare and Company. Ford, who helped him achieve early publication, is dismissed as a "heavy, wheezing, ignoble presence." He writes favorably about Stein at first— she, too, had encouraged him in his apprenticeship—but turns on her sharply when an overheard conversation underscores her lesbianism: "She got to look like a Roman emperor and that was fine if you liked your women to look like Roman emperors."

Homosexuality scared Hemingway, probably because he feared it in himself, and he used it as a real or imagined weapon against others, none to crueler effect than Scott Fitzgerald, who had been extraordinarily munificent to him, shouting his praises to his own editor, the celebrated Maxwell Perkins, who soon took Hemingway on. But when the two writers met in Paris, Hemingway saw Fitzgerald as "a man then who looked like a boy with a face between handsome and pretty . . . and a delicate long-lipped Irish mouth that, on a girl, would have been the mouth of a beauty." Then he slips in the dagger: "The mouth worried you until you knew him and then it worried you more." And: "he was cynical and funny and very jolly and charming and endearing, even if you were careful about anyone becoming endearing."

It gets worse, in two famous scenes: one in which a drunken Fitzgerald persuades Hemingway to help him recover an abandoned automobile, a second in which a nervous Fitzgerald asks Hemingway to confirm that his apparatus is large enough to satisfy a woman. In both scenes Hemingway's disdain for and condescension toward Fitzgerald are palpable, and deeply unattractive. Yes, over the years he did some very good writing—the Nick Adams stories, "The Short Happy Life of Francis McComber," "The Snows of Kilimanjaro," "A Clean, Well-Lighted Place"—and there is much of it in "A Moveable Feast." It reminds us, though, of how spiteful he could be, and disloyal, and just plain heartless.

THE GREAT GATSBY
by F. Scott Fitzgerald

F. Scott Fitzgerald and Ernest Hemingway met for the first time in 1925 in Paris, just as Fitzgerald's third novel, *The Great Gatsby*, was being published in the United States. As recounted in the previous Second Reading, Hemingway was not a kind man and was especially unkind to Fitzgerald in *A Moveable Feast*, but when Fitzgerald gave him a copy of *Gatsby*, Hemingway had to draw in his horns. With characteristic self-importance, he said it was now his duty to "try to be a good friend" to Fitzgerald because, he acknowledged, "If he could write a book as fine as *The Great Gatsby* I was sure that he could write an even better one."

He never did. He took a bold shot at it a decade later with *Tender Is the Night*, a thinly veiled account of the wealthy expatriates Gerald and Sara Murphy and their circle, and at his death in 1940 he had written a significant part of a novel about Hollywood, *The Love of the Last Tycoon*, published the next year in its uncompleted form, but *Gatsby* was, and remains, the monumental achievement of Fitzgerald's career. Reading it now for the seventh or eighth time, I am more convinced than ever not merely that it is Fitzgerald's masterwork but that it is the American masterwork, the finest work of fiction by any of this country's writers.

To say this is not to call *The Great Gatsby* the Great American Novel. That was a self-serving conceit drummed up by certain ambitious writers of the postwar era, most notoriously Norman Mailer, who fancied themselves in the boxing ring with Hemingway, delivering a succession of literary body blows to Papa and other writers of his celebrated generation. A few great American novels have been written, several of them by William Faulkner, but no single book knocks everything else out of the ring. It's mildly amusing to make lists and do rankings, but they aren't to be taken seriously. Hemingway and Mailer to the contrary, writers don't compete against each other, and neither do their books; each must be measured on its own merits.

It seems to me, though, that no American novel comes closer than *Gatsby* to surpassing literary artistry, and none tells us more about ourselves. In an extraordinarily compressed space—the novel is barely 50,000 words long—Fitzgerald gives us a meditation on some of this country's most central ideas, themes, yearnings and preoccupations: the quest for a new life, the preoccupation with class, the hunger for riches and "the last and greatest of all human dreams; for a transitory enchanted moment man must have held his breath in the presence of this continent, compelled into an aesthetic contemplation he neither understood nor desired, face to face for the last time in history with something commensurate to his capacity for wonder."

That famous passage—every passage in *Gatsby* is famous—is on the novel's final page, near the end of six pages of prose so incandescent as, in my case quite literally, to send shivers down the spine. Precisely because the book is so well known, there is little point in retracing in detail the novel's familiar ground. All of this has been done to a much-overcooked turn by academics (a few of them genuine scholars) and practitioners of lit crit. People have spent their entire adult lives in the study of Fitzgerald generally and *Gatsby* specifically, in some cases to considerable financial profit. Though most of the work of theirs that I have read is pedestrian and essentially irrelevant, the cumulative effect of it has been to leave *Gatsby*, like *The Adventures of Huckleberry Finn*, totally strip-mined.

Coming to it now for an umpteenth reading, I tried to imagine myself a reader in 1925, opening the book for the first time. I would have known Fitzgerald as the author of two previous novels, *This Side of Paradise* (1920) and *The Beautiful and Damned* (1922), as well as numerous short stories, the most famous being "The Ice Palace," "Bernice Bobs Her Hair" and "The Diamond as Big as the Ritz," many of them published in the Saturday Evening Post. Probably I would have thought of Fitzgerald as a skillful "popular" writer rather than a literary one, though even in his most commercial fiction—of which there was a good deal—the grace and beauty of his prose were obvious. I also would have been well aware of him as what we now call a celebrity: jumping into the fountain at the Plaza with his glamorous wife, Zelda, hanging out with the great names of what he had christened the Jazz Age, startling readers (and non-readers) with his cinematic good looks.

Within just a few pages I surely would have been hooked. Nick Carraway, the twenty-nine-year-old narrator, introduces himself forthrightly but modestly, describing how he had left a comfortable existence in the Midwest "to go east and learn the bond business" in New York. He rents a "weather beaten cardboard bungalow" in a town on Long Island called West Egg, and soon meets up with Daisy Buchanan, "my second cousin once removed," and her husband, Tom, whom Fitzgerald nails in just a few words. He "had been one of the most powerful ends that ever played football at New Haven—a national figure in a way, one of those men who reach such an acute limited excellence at twenty-one that everything afterward savors of anti-climax. . . . Now he was a sturdy straw haired man of thirty with a rather hard mouth and a supercilious manner."

As for the beautiful Daisy, "her face was sad and lovely with bright things in it, bright eyes and a bright passionate mouth— but there was an excitement in her voice that men who had cared for her found difficult to forget." There is something else in her voice that Jay Gatsby identifies as he begins to realize that he will never fulfill his dream of having her for his own. "Her voice," he says, "is full of money." She and Tom are two of the most memorable and readily identifiable characters in American fiction, and when at last they have done all their terrible damage, Fitzgerald pronounces his immortal verdict on them: "They were careless people, Tom and Daisy—they smashed up things and creatures and then retreated back into their money or their vast carelessness or whatever it was that kept them together, and let other people clean up the mess they had made."

That passage, like the whole of *Gatsby*, should make conclusively clear that Fitzgerald's preoccupation with money and those who have it was a far more complicated business than is often understood. He once said that "the rich are different from the rest of us," but if as is widely believed Hemingway said in rejoinder, "Yes, they have more money," then he missed the point. Fitzgerald understood that the rich live in a bubble the rest of us cannot enter, as the upwardly mobile Gatsby eventually understands to his painful regret.

Ah yes, Gatsby. What, in 1925, would I have thought of him? If he remains to this day one of American fiction's most enigmatic characters, how must he have seemed at first encounter? Over the course of the novel it becomes apparent, though it is never conclusively stated, that his fortune has dishonorable roots, planted by Meyer Wolfsheim, "the man who fixed the World's Series back in 1919," who played "with the faith of fifty million people—with the single-mindedness of a burglar blowing a safe." Would I have focused on the corruption that enabled Gatsby to have his vast house on Long Island Sound, or would I have understood that Fitzgerald saw him as much more than that: a man "who represented everything for which I have an unaffected scorn," yet who has "something gorgeous about him, some heightened sensitivity to the promises of life, as if he were related to one of those intricate machines that register earthquakes ten thousand miles away."

As that lovely passage suggests, Fitzgerald writes with extraordinary subtlety in *Gatsby*, and sustains that tone throughout. He describes, for example, Tom Buchanan reading a racist tract: "Something was making him nibble at the edge of stale ideas as if his sturdy physical egotism no longer nourished his peremptory heart." Or: "Americans, while occasionally willing to be serfs, have always been obstinate about being peasantry." In 1925, perhaps I would have said to myself that this Saturday Evening Post writer turns out to have a sophisticated wit and a keen eye. Perhaps at the end I would have called him a poet:

> One of my most vivid memories is of coming back west from prep school and later from college at Christmas time. . . . When we pulled out into the winter night and the real snow, our snow, began to stretch out beside us and twinkle against the windows, and the dim lights of small Wisconsin stations moved by, a sharp wild brace came suddenly into the air. We drew in deep breaths of it as we walked back from dinner through the cold vestibules, unutterably aware of our identity with this country for one strange hour, before we melted indistinguishably into it again.

If in 1925 I didn't gasp at that, there would have been something seriously wrong with me. Those words, and the few hundred others that follow as the novel reaches its end, seem to me now—eight decades after that imagined first reading— the most beautiful, compelling and true in all of American literature. Each reading of them is a revelation and a gift. If from all of our country's books I could have only one, *The Great Gatsby* would be it.

My Life and Hard Times
by James Thurber

When James Thurber died in November 1961, I had just turned twenty-two years old, and I felt as if a large part of my world had gone with him. Probably it's difficult for readers today to understand just how much Thurber meant to readers then, even though many of his books are still in print and enjoy respectable sales. Thurber in my youth wasn't something you went to the bookstore for—though of course you could—but something that came in the mail almost every week, as regular and reliable as the clocks of Columbus, Ohio, which he wrote about in the pages of the *New Yorker*.

Today the *New Yorker* still comes in the mail, but it isn't the same magazine. It's less a writer's magazine now than a reporter's, and except for its cartoons and an occasional light piece, it isn't a humor magazine anymore. The humorous touch brought to it by Thurber and his fellow immortal E.B. White—not to mention S.J. Perelman and Wolcott Gibbs and Dorothy Parker and Ogden Nash and Robert Benchley and Phyllis McGinley and . . . well, how much time have you got?—hasn't entirely vanished, but it's no longer the magazine's chief characteristic.

For the first quarter-century of its existence—it was founded in 1925—the *New Yorker*'s editor was Harold Ross, but Thurber and White were its public face. No one could imagine it without them. In time we'll get to White in this series of reconsiderations, but today it's Thurber's turn, and what a pleasure that is. Picking one of his books at first didn't seem exactly easy—how could I omit *Lanterns and Lances*, or *Thurber's Dogs*, or *Thurber Country*, or *My World—and Welcome to It*, or *The Owl in the Attic?*—but actually it was easy indeed. If you can have only one book by James Thurber, then it has to be *My Life and Hard Times*, the memoir of his youth in Columbus that is, as Russell Baker writes in a column reprinted as an afterword to my Harper Perennial edition, "possibly the shortest and most elegant autobiography ever written."

My Life and Hard Times was published in book form in 1933, when Thurber was one year shy of his fortieth birthday. He had firmly established himself as a writer "of light pieces running from a thousand to two thousand words," and firmly denied that "such persons are gay of heart and carefree." No, he said: "They sit on the edge of the chair of Literature. In the house of Life they have the feeling that they have never taken off their overcoats. Afraid of losing themselves in the larger flight of the two-volume novel, or even the one-volume novel, they stick to short accounts of their misadventures because they never get so deep into them but that they feel they can get out."

Thurber then proceeded to disprove every syllable of that by writing a book that, though barely over 20,000 words, comes far closer to Literature and Life than all but a handful of other American memoirs, and into the bargain has something that no other memoirist can offer: drawings, in abundance, by James Thurber. He still had limited eyesight when he wrote this book—he went blind in 1951, the same year that Harold Ross died—and was at the peak of his idiosyncratic but uniquely effective drawing style. The drawings of citizens of Columbus "in full flight" from an imagined dam break, or of the Thurber family in "a tremendous to-do" when it was learned that grandfather had taken the car out for a spin, or of Thurber's botany professor at Ohio State "beginning to quiver all over like Lionel Barrymore"—they alone are worth the very modest price of admission, yet they're merely lagniappe.

One does indeed turn to Thurber for the drawings, but the great glory is his prose. Whether he was the funniest of all American writers can be debated to the end of time, but he was much more than funny. Like his friend White he was wise, and there was a soft spot to him. As John K. Hutchens writes in his introduction to this book: "He loathes cruelty. His sympathy for the out-of-luck man is as intense as his contempt for the pretentious and stupid one. He sees that children, being closer to the natural world than their elders are, have more true wisdom than adults. He finds the family life of dogs to be more rational than that of humans, and their courage and loyalty generally superior."

Certainly there was precious little rationality to the family life of the Thurbers of Columbus. They were forever caught up in "those bewildering involvements for which my family had, I am afraid, a kind of unhappy genius." In the Thurber household things went bump in the night as a matter of routine, always—at least as revised and re-imagined by Thurber as an adult—to hilarious effect. With the very first paragraph of the famous first chapter, he sets the tone:

> I suppose that the high-water mark of my youth in Columbus, Ohio, was the night the bed fell on my father. It makes a better recitation (unless, as some friends of mine have said, one has heard it five or six times) than it does a piece of writing, for it is almost necessary to throw furniture around, shake doors, and bark like a dog, to lend the proper atmosphere and verisimilitude to what is admittedly a somewhat incredible tale. Still, it did take place.

Well, it did and it didn't. The night that father retreated to the old bed in the attic, the bed never actually fell on him. Instead the teenaged James, sleeping on a rickety Army cot, found himself suddenly under the cot when it took a flip. The noise woke his mother, "who came to the immediate conclusion that her worst dread was realized: the big wooden bed upstairs had fallen on father. She therefore screamed, 'Let's go to your poor father!'" This set off a chaotic chain reaction involving James, his brother Roy, their dog Rex and "a nervous first cousin of mine named Briggs Beall, who believed that he was likely to cease breathing when he was asleep."

If you're reading this, chances aren't bad that you already know by heart *The Night the Bed Fell*. It is an American classic. I have no recollection of when I first read it, but it may well have been read to me by one of my parents, who adored Thurber and passed that passion along to me. Over the years I have read it dozens of times, heard it read onstage by Tom Ewell in the early 1960s on Broadway in *The Thurber Carnival*, and listened to it dozens of times on the wonderful recording of that show.

But splendid though *The Night the Bed Fell* most certainly is, it is but one among the nine brief chapters of *My Life and Hard Times*, each of which is a gem. Some have to do with alarms at night (the phrase, in fact, is the title of one), which seem to have befallen the Thurbers with remarkable frequency. There was the night the ghost got into the house, which "caused my mother to throw a shoe through a window of the house next door and ended up with my grandfather shooting a patrolman." There was the time when Thurber himself had been trying for hours to think of the name Perth Amboy:

> I fell to repeating the word "Jersey" over and over again, until it became idiotic and meaningless. If you have ever lain awake at night and repeated one word over and over, thousands and millions and hundreds of thousands of millions of time, you know the disturbing mental state you can get into. I got to thinking that there was nobody else in the world but me, and various other wild imaginings of that nature. Eventually, lying there thinking these outlandish thoughts, I grew slightly alarmed. I began to suspect that one might lose one's mind over some such trivial mental tic as a futile search for terra firma Piggly Wiggly Gorgonzola Prester John Arc de Triomphe Holy Moses Lares and Penates. I began to feel the imperative necessity of human contact.

*

So he got out of bed and woke his father, and said: "Don't bother about dressing. Just name some towns in New Jersey." The elder Thurber, thinking his son had gone round the bend, got out of the room and called out to the rest of the household, which in a jiffy was in precisely the sort of turmoil in which it specialized.

It was a family of eccentrics to whom eccentric things happened. Thurber's boyhood in the early years of the twentieth century was close enough to the Civil War so that people still remembered it—his grandfather occasionally complained "that the federal Union was run by a passel of blockheads and that the Army of the Potomac didn't have any more chance than a fiddler's bitch"—and coincided with the arrival of the automobile. Both proximities inspired some of the funniest stories Thurber tells.

But *My Life and Hard Times* is more than a collection of laughs. It is also a book about the ties of family, about the connections between people and places ("Columbus is a town in which almost anything is likely to happen and in which almost everything has"), about the ways in which dogs insinuate themselves into families, even Muggs, "the worst of all my dogs." Though Thurber does not dwell on it, the mood of the book is thoroughly Midwestern, i.e., bedrock American. Thurber never got over his love of Ohio and the Midwest, the points of his compass that directed his entire life. He's as genuinely American a writer as any we have, and a true national treasure.

THE WOMAN WARRIOR
by Maxine Hong Kingston

Three decades ago the memoir was a relatively minor genre in American literature. Of the few acknowledged classics—*Personal Memoirs of Ulysses S. Grant*, *The Education of Henry Adams*, Edith Wharton's *A Backward Glance*, Richard Wright's *Black Boy*—all but the last were the work of people who had reached sufficient maturity to be able to look back on long lives. Though memoirs by three younger men (Frank Conroy's *Stop-Time*, Willie Morris's *North Toward Home* and Frederick Exley's *A Fan's Notes*) had been published in the late 1960s, the received wisdom was that memoir was an older person's—an older man's—genre.

Precisely when and why this began to change—not to mention whether the change was for the better—is open to debate, but a strong case can be made that the decisive moment came in 1976 with the publication of *The Woman Warrior*, by Maxine Hong Kingston. It is, as was immediately recognized at the time, a work of considerable literary distinction, but it was also very much a book of its moment. In the mid-seventies two movements were gaining strength and public attention: feminism and multiculturalism. Though not written as a political tract, *The Woman Warrior* spoke to both causes with remarkable immediacy. It gained a following that seems, if anything, to have increased over the years.

Thus, for example, Bill Moyers has reported that *The Woman Warrior* and Kingston's second memoir, *China Men* (1980), are the most widely taught books by a living American author on college campuses today, which echoes a claim made by the Modern Language Association. This rather astonishing information no doubt reflects the various categories of political and cultural opinion to which Kingston's work appeals, but it also means that *The Woman Warrior* is probably one of the most influential books now in print in this country—and certainly one of the most influential books with a valid claim to literary recognition.

It is a sign of how far the country has come that this distinction is enjoyed by a woman whose parents were immigrants from China, who was born Maxine Ting Ting Hong in 1940, who worked in her parents' laundry as a girl, yet who managed to win admission to the University of California at Berkeley. She married Earll Kingston in 1962, taught in California public schools, then moved to Hawaii and continued to teach. There she wrote *The Woman Warrior*, which was given a National Book Critics Circle Award. She now is professor emeritus of writing at Berkeley.

I was one of the many people who first read *The Woman Warrior* soon after its publication. One good thing about reading it three decades ago was that one could do so free of all the baggage the book subsequently accumulated, much of it having to do with politically correct attitudes fashionable in academic and literary circles. In 1976 it was simply a very good book—smart, tough, witty, simultaneously self-deprecating and self-assertive, a missive from a part of America about which most of us knew nothing—and it could be read as such with great pleasure, which is exactly what I did.

Books' subtitles often are unimportant or gratuitous, but this one matters: *Memoirs of a Girlhood Among Ghosts*. Kingston's are both conventional ghosts—the memory of her dead aunt, for example, the "No Name Woman" of the book's deservedly celebrated opening section—and more fanciful ones. Americans are ghosts: "Taxi Ghosts, Bus Ghosts, Police Ghosts,

Fire Ghosts, Meter Reader Ghosts, Tree Trimming Ghosts, Five-and-Dime Ghosts. Once upon a time the world was so thick with ghosts, I could hardly breathe; I could hardly walk, limping my way around the White Ghosts and their cars. There were Black Ghosts too, but they were open eyed and full of laughter, more distinct than White Ghosts."

Ghosts, then, are creatures of imagination and memory, many of them introduced to her by her mother, who "would talk-story until we [children] fell asleep." As a girl "I couldn't tell where the stories left off and the dreams began," which is a useful clue to a book that is as much dream as story, that crosses the line between fact and fiction so frequently and blithely that it is pointless to try to distinguish between the two. What matters is that Kingston is trying, through what she remembers and what she imagines, to explore her central subjects: the place of women in Chinese society (whether in China itself or in immigrant communities elsewhere), the relationship of mothers and daughters, the experience of immigration.

A case in point is the story of her aunt, who committed suicide just before the men of her family sailed for America, "the Gold Mountain," in the mid-1920s. She was unmarried and pregnant, and the people of her village persecuted her mercilessly; finally, after giving birth, she threw herself and her infant into the family well. Young Maxine is told this story—or at least the bare details of it—by her mother:

> Whenever she had to warn us about life, my mother told stories that ran like this one, a story to grow up on. She tested our strength to establish realities. Those in the emigrant generations who could not reassert brute survival died young and far from home. Those of us in the first American generations have had to figure out how the invisible world the emigrants built around our childhoods fits in solid America. . . . Chinese-Americans, when you try to understand what things in you are Chinese, how do you

separate what is peculiar to childhood, to poverty, insanities, one family, your mother who marked your growing with stories, from what is Chinese? What is Chinese tradition and what is the movies?

Coming to a new country isn't easy for anyone. Coming to the United States from China has been especially hard because the two cultures are so dissimilar. Kingston doesn't bother to dwell on the discrimination the Chinese have faced here; that's a given. Instead she zooms in on the differences: "It is the way Chinese sounds, chingchong ugly, to American ears, not beautiful like Japanese sayonara words with the consonants and vowels as regular as Italian. We make guttural peasant noise and have Ton Duc Thang names you can't remember. And the Chinese can't hear Americans at all; the language is too soft and western music unhearable. I've watched a Chinese audience laugh, visit, talk-story, and holler during a piano recital, as if the musician could not hear them." More, perhaps, than most immigrants to this country, Chinese remain resolutely Chinese even as they become Chinese American, a subject Kingston explores without passing judgment.

She does pass judgment, on the other hand, against the discrimination inflicted upon Chinese women within their own culture, which barely acknowledges, as she says, that if a society wants to have boys, it has to have girls as well. When she was in college she "would have liked to bring myself back as a boy for my parents to welcome with chickens and pigs," and if her mother called her "Bad girl," "sometimes that made me gloat rather than cry" because, "Isn't a bad girl almost a boy?" In "White Tigers," the chapter in which she imagines her instruction as "a warrior woman," she fantasizes about "the men I would have to execute," and though this is only (one assumes!) a dream of revenge, doubtless the bitterness is real. She was, after all, born into a culture that believed, as her father told her: "Chinese smeared bad daughters-in-law with honey and tied them naked on top of ant nests. A husband may kill a wife who disobeys him. Confucius said that."

Her mother is the heroic figure in this book. The two women obviously had many confrontations over the years, but her mother's resourcefulness and strength are evident. In the 1930s, while Kingston's father worked in America, her mother studied at the Hackett Medical College for Women in Canton for two years, receiving a diploma certifying her proficiency in midwifery, pediatrics, gynecology and other practices. She was "brilliant, a natural scholar who could glance at a book and know it," and she was self-confident enough to keep her maiden name, Brave Orchid, even after coming to the United States in 1940, "adding no American name nor holding one in reserve for American emergencies."

All of which makes abundantly clear why *The Woman Warrior* is treasured by feminists and people of minority cultures. I have it on good authority that many women were inspired by it to write their own stories of immigrant life in this country, that it convinced them that they, too, had stories to tell, that American literature is not solely the property of white males. As a result our literature is constantly being enriched these days by people whose voices were not heard as recently as a generation ago. That is reason enough to esteem *The Women Warrior*. But what matters, and in the end is the only thing that really matters, is that it is a book of unusual originality and power. If what it tells us seems familiar now that is because Maxine Hong Kingston made it so.

MR. BLANDINGS BUILDS HIS DREAM HOUSE
by Eric Hodgins

In the late 1930s, an executive at what was then still called Time Incorporated decided that his considerable success—he was the publisher of *Fortune*, the highly regarded business magazine—required that he abandon his cramped quarters in Manhattan and find a place in the country suitable to his exalted position. It was, he thought, The Thing to Do for one thus blessed. So he and his wife ventured out to northwest Connecticut and began to poke around:

> They had begun a search for land and an old house in the country in a manner that was not only halfhearted but shamefaced; they were doing something because it seemed to be expected of them, not because they felt any true inner urge. Then, suddenly, the land fever had seized them; they knew, in a flash, what had been wrong with them all those years: the peace and security that only the fair land itself could provide they had left out of their lives altogether.

His name was Eric Hodgins. In 1939 he and his wife bought a piece of land at New Milford—a classic New England small town—and began construction of a house suitable for them and their two children. As Patricia Grandjean reported fifteen years ago in the *New York Times*, he "anticipated a budget of $11,000 for his dream house. But the completed project ultimately escalated to a total of $56,000 . . . a sum so inflated by his misconceptions that it nearly drove him into bankruptcy. He was forced to sell the house two years later."

Soon after World War II, though, the house paid handsome dividends. In 1946, Hodgins resigned his job in order to write a book that, as he recalled later, "wrote itself." Ostensibly a work of fiction, it was his own story thinly disguised. It was about a New York advertising man who "had been lucky enough to hit upon a three-word slogan for a laxative account that had broken four successive agency vice-presidents" and quickly became a cash cow. He and his wife buy an old house in Connecticut, tear it down and build a new one. They budget $20,000 for land and house but end up shelling out $56,263.97.

By now you may have guessed that the novel Hodgins wrote is *Mr. Blandings Builds His Dream House*. Published in 1946, it immediately became a huge bestseller. Within two years, 540,000 copies had been sold, and movie rights earned him $200,000 in addition to royalties on book sales. The film of the same title, released two years later, starred Cary Grant and Myrna Loy and was itself a great hit, with good reason, as it is in equal measures funny and smart. A very loose remake, *The Money Pit*, starring Tom Hanks and Shelley Long, was released in 1986. Both films are available on DVD. As for Hodgins, he published a sequel to *Mr. Blandings*, *Blandings' Way* (1950), retired from Time in 1958 and died in 1971.

Probably most people today know Mr. Blandings's story from one of the movies. That certainly was true of me. I probably saw it during the 1950s, when I was a teenager. What I do remember is that I absolutely loved it—just as I loved other classic Cary Grant comedies such as *His Girl Friday*, *Bringing Up Baby*, *I Was a Male War Bride* and *Monkey Business*—and that I went immediately to the book. It was different, of course, as books always are, but even in callow youth I was taken by its wit, its author's engaging self-deprecation and the universality of its story.

Yes, universality. The Blandings may be prosperous WASPs and the house they build may end up costing vastly more than most of us can afford, but almost all of us can identify with the rest of the tale: yearning for a "dream house," being taken to the cleaners by contractors and others, worrying about money, squabbling about curtains and paint and appliances and everything else. Rereading *Mr. Blandings Builds His Dream House* for the first time in half a century, I'm struck not merely by how well it reads but how up-to-date it is. Except for the money—try multiplying by ten to get the Blandings' figures closer to current dollars—just about everything in the book could have been written today, including Hodgins's smooth, ironic prose.

From the minute the Blandings make their first foray into Connecticut, these city rubes are taken to the cleaners by country slickers. The fifty-acre spread turns out to be thirty-five acres in the sales contract, and thirty-one and a half acres when it's surveyed. The real-estate agent is a smooth con man and the old hick who owns the land and house, Ephemus W. Hackett, is "shrewd, vague and incisive," playing their self-evident longing for the house into an $11,000 deal, maybe twice what he'd get from a local buyer. As for the Revolutionary-era house, it has gone untouched by "self-conscious restoration" or "museum hand." It's also a wreck, and the Blandings shell out more good money to tear it down.

So they engage an architect and tell him what they want: "a two-story house in quiet, modern, good taste; frame and brick-veneer construction; something to blend with the older architectural examples that dotted the countryside around them, but no slavish imitation of times past. It would be, in effect, a bringing up to date of the Old House, with obvious modifications dictated by the difference between the eighteenth and twentieth centuries and by the difference between the profession of farming, for which the Old House had been constructed, and advertising, which should somehow be exemplified in the New."

Between what they want and what they get lie "one demented decision [after] another." Mr. Blandings wonders if he is "becoming an utter, vacuous fool, with a simian knack of writing advertising copy for a tonnage laxative, and no other use or capacities whatever." He talks to himself: "He was being cheated, he was being bilked, he was being made a fool of, but he could not find the villain, because everyone was a villain . . . all, all had made him the butt and victim of a huge conspiracy, clever and cruel." He wonders "whether everybody else's life was such a succession of roller-coaster plunges from elation to despair and swoops back to elation, or whether, as his closest friends and office mates insisted, he was a sufferer from severe emotional instability."

There is, for example, the quest for water. John Tesander, well driller, appears on the scene. Mr. Blandings finds him "one of those skilled workmen who restored a man's faith in his kind," but as he cheerfully drills away "one circumstance remained always the same: in his methodical progress through the earth's crust, he was encountering everything in an omnipotent God's creation except water." Not until he drills down 297 feet (at four dollars and fifty cents a foot, for a total of $1,336.50—make that somewhere around $15,000 today) does he hit a sufficient supply.

That's only the beginning. Literally. With water out of the way, the architect informs the Blandings "in a sepulchral voice" that it is "time to ask for bids." When they arrive and the manila folder is opened, Mr. Blandings leaps up "as from a bayonet thrust through the chair bottom" and lets fly an inventive curse. They end up at $26,991.17—after whittling away many of the most cherished parts of the architect's design—and find themselves wondering how, exactly, they had managed to get so far beyond the $20,000 grand total they had once so foolishly decided upon.

On top of everything else, it begins to dawn upon Mr.

Blandings that "in the midst of the bucolic loveliness where he had wanted to live in peace and harmony with nature and his fellows, he was disliked. . . . It was just that he was an outlander. He could wear overhalls, or dress in mail-order clothes, or part his hair down the middle, until kingdom come, and it would make no difference. He could live in a cow barn until all the perfumes of Araby were powerless to lighten the smell of wet leaves and manure, but the natives of Lansdale County would still know him for an alien, forever." It is the old story of town come to country, as any Manhattanite resident among the potato farmers of eastern Long Island (if any are left) could ruefully attest.

Gamely, though, Mr. Blandings presses on. So does Mrs. Blandings. She sees four unused pieces of flagstone and asks the contractor to "give me a nice stone floor" in her flower room, for which the contractor, by the time he's pulled everything apart in order to satisfy her, weighs in with another $1,247 in charges. Then she turns her attention to the color scheme, writing out detailed instructions for the painters. The dining room is to be yellow: "Ask one of your workmen to get a pound of the A&P's best butter and match it exactly." Bathrooms? "In the master bath, the color should suggest apple blossoms just before they fall."

Et cetera. *Mr. Blandings Builds His Dream House* is a comedy, of course, and a very funny one at that, but it is also a cautionary tale with which many of us can connect. Few of us get to build our own houses, but all of us live in places that someone built and all of us have to contend with the vicissitudes of our residences and the people whom we pay to keep them functioning. There are any number of morals to be drawn from Eric Hodgins's lovely little book, but the two main ones are as old as the hills: Never want anything so much that you'll pay anything to have it, and caveat emptor.

MORTE D'URBAN
by J.F. Powers

T he business of America is business, as Calvin Coolidge
so succinctly (and accurately) put it, so it's surprising
and disappointing that business is the subject of so little serious American fiction. Boardroom drama and similar
high-level high jinks are often to be found in popular fiction,
but by and large our ostensibly literary writers have looked
down their noses at workaday life, apparently finding it unwor-
thy of their finely-tuned sensibilities.

Thus it's both revealing and ironic that one of the few genuinely good American novels about business isn't about "business" at all, but about the Roman Catholic Church. J.F. Powers's
Morte d'Urban, first published in 1962 (it won the National
Book Award the following year), can be read in any number of
ways, but reading it now for the fourth time I am struck more
sharply than ever before by how Powers turns this story of a go-
getter priest into a metaphor for the world of business. It's a
much better novel than Sinclair Lewis's far more famous *Babbitt*,
subtler, wittier and much more elegantly written.

I read *Morte d'Urban* not long after it won the NBA; in those
years that prize still occasionally went to books that deserved
it—Ralph Ellison's *Invisible Man,* Walker Percy's *The
Moviegoer*, Saul Bellow's *The Adventures of Augie March*,
Bernard Malamud's *The Magic Barrel*—and I completely agreed
with the judges' decision. I read it again a few years later for a
discussion group I led on religious issues in contemporary fiction, then a third time purely for pleasure. Now, four and a half

decades after that first reading, I'm as convinced as ever that the oblivion into which it seems to have sunk is inexplicable and wholly undeserved.

Oblivion, though, was a condition all too familiar to Powers during his lifetime. Between his birth in Illinois in 1917 and his death eighty-one years later, he published only four other books: three collections of short stories and a second novel, *Wheat That Springeth Green* (1988). His short stories appeared in various places, from the *Catholic Worker* to the *New Yorker*, and, though widely admired by the literati, found him relatively few readers. He spent much of his time in Ireland and frequently taught at St. John's University in Minnesota, the state that is the setting of *Morte d'Urban* and much of his other work. In a wry, admiring tribute to Powers after his death in 1999, published in the *New Criterion*, John Derbyshire called him "the patron saint of slow writers," and quoted his daughter Katherine: "He had powers of procrastination that went far beyond the merely amateur."

Powers wrote about many subjects, but the Catholic Church was his chief one. His interest in it may well have been more psychological and sociological—"Though religious by instinct," Derbyshire wrote, "Powers does not seem to have been deeply pious"—and the affection with which he viewed the church always was sharpened by the satirist's edge. Certainly he was by no stretch of the imagination a "Catholic writer" in the sense that Flannery O'Connor or Graham Greene was; though matters of theology crop up from time in *Morte d'Urban*, they are scarcely the novel's principal concern.

Its protagonist, Father Urban of the Order of St. Clement, is a hustler, "an operator," but unlike George Babbitt he is also a complex and deeply sympathetic human being. He is fifty-four years old, "tall and handsome but a trifle loose in the jowls and red of eye." As the novel opens he is working out of the Clementines' decidedly modest office in Chicago, traveling the rubber-chicken circuit to boost the order. Audiences love him for his forceful speeches and infectious glad-handing, but this doesn't translate into much for the Clementines, who exist under "a cloak of incompetence." Powers writes:

> It seemed to him that the Order of St. Clement labored under the curse of mediocrity, and had done so almost from the beginning. In Europe, the Clementines hadn't (it was always said) recovered from the French Revolution. It was certain that they hadn't ever really got going in the New World. Their history revealed little to brag about—one saint (the Holy Founder) and a few bishops of missionary sees, no theologians worthy of the name, no original thinkers, not even a scientist. The Clementines were unique in that they were noted for nothing at all. They were in bad shape all over the world.

Apart from his traveling and lecturing, Father Urban's main contribution to the order has been to reel in a big fish named Billy Cosgrove, a Chicago businessman with a taste for golf, sailing and whiskey who decides that Urban is a regular guy in a turned-around collar and by way of rewarding him for this becomes the order's biggest benefactor. This does not sit well with some higher in the order, notably Father Boniface, the head of the Chicago office, who sees Urban as a rival and, in a classic office-politics maneuver, exiles him to "the newest white elephant, the new foundation . . . near Duesterhaus, Minnesota," so far from Billy Cosgrove and the good life as to be on another planet.

Urban is appalled, but he is also a good priest: He does what he is told to do. So he packs off and moves to Duesterhaus, "a one-stoplight town" where "the main street was a state highway" and "the drugstore was the bus station." There he falls in with two hapless priests—the rector, Father Wilfrid, and Father John—as well as the novitiate, Brother Harold, and almost immediately finds that priestly duties are low on Father

Wilfrid's list of priorities. What he wants to do is to get the tat-
terdemalion main building into shape so that it can be used as
a retreat for priests and laymen, perhaps with profitable results.
So Urban is put to work "as a common laborer." Why, Urban
soon asks himself, "had he been cast into outer darkness,
thrown among fools and failures?"

Then a bit of a break comes his way. The priest at a nearby
church—a real church, with a real congregation—goes off for
a while and Urban is asked to stand in for him. With the amiable but indecisive Father Phil out of the way, Urban has room
to operate, and, "Suddenly St. Monica's was a busy, happy rec-
tory." He's there for about a month and a half, and though he
doesn't exactly work miracles, he gives the church a big boost,
and he gets one himself: "the deep satisfaction there was in
doing the work of a parish priest—his daily Mass meant even
more to him at St. Monica's." Yes, he's guilty as charged of
being "something of a showboat," but he's also a priest to the
core, and the showboating is almost always done in the service
of the priesthood.

He returns to Duesterhaus recharged and full of plans. An
attractive spread of farmland next door comes on the market,
and Urban makes his move. This involves Billy Cosgrove once
again, as well as a meddlesome, domineering bishop who is the
church's local CEO. For those who do not yet know the rest of
the tale, and whom I hope to lure into reading it, I will keep
the rest of it in confidence, but suffice it to say that Urban is
awarded a great triumph that, when he finally receives it, is
emptier than he could have imagined, and he learns that ven-
turing out into the real world can have painful consequences.

All of this is most rewardingly seen as a microcosm of
American business, with its suffocating layers of bureaucracy
and its bitter, silly rivalries. Observing the Clementines at
work, "For the life of him, Father Urban couldn't see how the
Catholic Church (among large corporations) could be rated

second only to Standard Oil in efficiency, as *Time* had reported a few years back." Laboring away with Father Wilfrid, Urban sees things for what they are:

> A good part of his working day was spent in wandering back and forth between the lavatory and the job. Yes, he knew what he was, a disgruntled employee blowing himself to a bit of company time, but he didn't care, and he didn't give the boss quite enough cause to complain. However, it got so that the employee knew what to expect if, in his journeys to and from the lavatory, he paused too long at a window for a look at the outside world. He knew that the boss would soon come along and offer him a cigarette—there was no use trying to smoke a cigar if you did the kind of work they did—and then a light. There they'd be, then, just a couple of average guys such as they saw in the evening on television, taking their well-earned break.

In the end then, *Morte d'Urban* isn't just about a Catholic priest and the Catholic Church, it's about the American workplace. If there's a better novel about that subject, I don't know what it is; certainly Joseph Heller's ambitious but numbing *Something Happened* falls far short of it. That *Morte d'Urban* is still in print is thanks to New York Review Books Classics, which also has in print *Wheat That Springeth Green* and *The Stories of J.F. Powers*. These are books that matter, and keeping them alive—in the face of general indifference to Powers's work—is a genuine service to American literature.

I Was Dancing
by *Edwin O'Connor*

Waltzing Daniel Considine is up there with Robert Penn Warren's Willie Stark, Edith Wharton's Lily Bart, Theodore Dreiser's Frank Cowperwood among our great literary characters, so it's too bad that so few readers have met him. He is the protagonist of *I Was Dancing*, a short and wildly funny novel by Edwin O'Connor that originally appeared in 1964, made a small splash that lasted only a couple of years, and now seems pretty much to have disappeared.

It's often said in these Second Readings that it is a "pity" or an "injustice" that such-and-such a book is out of print or ignored or unknown or whatever. Well, there have been ninety-seven of these reconsiderations, and I'd be hard-pressed to say that any book discussed therein is more undeservedly neglected than this one. Precisely why it has met this fate is difficult to determine, though it is worth noting that today not even O'Connor's more famous novels—*The Last Hurrah* (1956), *The Edge of Sadness* (1961) and *All in the Family* (1966)—are easily found in bookstores.

Perhaps this is a lesson in the evanescence of fame. For about a dozen years, from 1956 to his sudden death from a stroke at the age of forty-nine in 1968, O'Connor was one of the country's most popular and respected writers. He put a phrase in the language with the title of *The Last Hurrah*, the story of a scurrilous but lovable mayor of Boston closely modeled on James Michael Curley; the movie adaptation of it star-

ring Spencer Tracy was hugely successful; O'Connor won a
Pulitzer Prize in 1962 for *The Edge of Sadness*; his books routinely were chosen as major book-club selections at a time
when the Book-of-the-Month Club, the Literary Guild and
others still packed enormous clout. He enjoyed impressive
sales and literary respect, yet now he's just about vanished, lost
in the mists that enshroud John P. Marquand, James Gould
Cozzens, Jean Stafford and other once-popular writers who
certainly don't belong there. Go figure.

I was a teenager when *The Last Hurrah* was published—I
gobbled it up right away, loved it, loved the movie, too—and
when *I Was Dancing* appeared, I was a twenty-four-year-old
journalist apprentice whose first published book review was
still more than a year away. I clearly recall that I read *I Was
Dancing* because the *New York Review of Books*, a journal not
normally hospitable to popular, upper-middlebrow fiction,
praised it lavishly as "his best book." My 1965 Bantam paperback (seventy-five cents!) has notes scribbled inside the back
cover in what can only be my own illegible handwriting, but I
very much doubt that I reviewed the paperback edition; maybe
I taught it in a class, as in those days I was occasionally bitten
by the teaching bug.

Whatever the case, I thought *I Was Dancing* was wonderful
then and now I admire it even more. The passage of more than
four decades has added a touch of maturity to my critical faculties (so at least I hope) and I am better able now to appreciate
the skill and grace with which O'Connor moves from uproari-
ous comedy to fierce confrontation and then to pathos. Perhaps
I'm also better able to appreciate the snap, crackle and pop of
O'Connor's dialogue, especially Daniel Considine's exchanges
with his friends Billy Ryan, Father Feeley and Al Gottlieb.

These take place in a bedroom of Daniel's son Tom's house
in a city that probably bears more than passing resemblance to
Providence, Rhode Island, where O'Connor was born in 1918

and where he grew up before moving along to Boston after World War II. Daniel is seventy-eight years old, a veteran of half a century on the vaudeville circuit as "the best damn comedy dance act in the business." Now vaudeville is dead. A year ago Daniel showed up wholly unannounced at his forty-three-year-old son's doorstep in the middle of the night, declared that he just wanted to come in "for a minute"—this after twenty years of total absence from Tom's life—and he's been there ever since.

At first Tom and his wife, Ellen, enjoyed his presence, his stories of globetrotting and vaudeville ("Orville Stamm the Strong Boy and Thelma De Onzo the World's Greatest Candlestick Jumper," et al.), his not inconsiderable charm. But gradually it became clear to Ellen "that the entertaining transient was in fact a self-centered and determined old man who had decided to make what was hers his own." Tom agreed, so he gave his father an ultimatum: After a month he will move to Saint Vincent's Smiling Valley for Senior Citizens.

Now it is the day of his departure, but Daniel isn't about to go. "Good God Almighty!" he shouts to Billy Ryan. "Old as I am, I damn near knocked him down! Waltzing Daniel Considine in an Old Man's Home!" For a month he has been in "upstairs isolation," his door closed, refusing to speak to Tom or Ellen, plotting his strategy. His only visitors are the three aforementioned friends and, less frequently, his unbearable sister Delia, with whom he has stupendous arguments, a quartet that leads Tom to conclude "that nearly everyone he had met or talked to in connection with his father had been very close to certifiable."

They're quite a bunch. Billy Ryan is a self-appointed "Free Lancer of Medicine" who turns up his nose at "the Official Doctors that have gone through medical schools and have diplomas and all that nonsense." Al Gottlieb was once Daniel's biggest fan—"There wasn't a vaudeville show came to town he didn't see. He loved vaudeville. And if I played any place within a hundred miles of here, Gottlieb would be right there in the front row"—but now has been reduced to "an air of almost radiant dejection" by his wife's and son's perfidies. As for Father Feeley, he really wanted to be a jockey yet ended up in the priesthood, but that doesn't prevent him from complaining that the world is "a roaring farce" and "we're all two steps from the zoo!" He's tough and funny:

> I never liked vaudeville. By and large it seemed to me a collection of absurd people: middle-aged idiots with dyed hair singing love songs, Chinese laundrymen throwing Indian clubs at each other, malformed women doing indecent gymnastics. Farcical nonentities, all of them. You were an exception, Daniel. It always seemed to me that your performance was a marvelous burlesque of your co-workers. Consciously or unconsciously, you were indicating contempt for the whole imbecilic milieu. It was the kind of performance a sane man could enjoy.

They're all old men, and they look with suspicion on the young, especially Tom, who "had begun to realize that old age was a strange and usually hostile world, whose ways and weapons he did not understand at all." The irascible Delia puts it straight to Daniel: "Use the brains God gave you and start packing your bags. . . . The young don't want old people around: haven't you even learned that yet? We're too slow for them, we mix up their lives, we get in the way. That goes double for someone like you, someone that they hardly even know. So pack up, Daniel, because you've got until tonight. Then out you go!"

Gottlieb agrees—"today young people want to say only one thing to their old folks: Goodbye Charlie!"—but Daniel doesn't believe he's going anywhere. He has an elaborate (and hilarious) strategy for shaming Tom into changing his mind. All his life he's gone his own way, gotten what he wants, and he has no reason to think it's going to be any different now. It goes without saying that he's a dreadfully selfish old man, totally uninterested in anything except his only two loves. As Tom tells him in the novel's brutally frank climactic confrontation: "I was almost going to say you never gave a damn about anyone or anything, but then I remembered that wasn't true. You actually did have two great loves in your life, Dad: Vaudeville, and You. Well, Vaudeville's dead—but you've still got You. So keep the old love affair going, but don't expect any help from me."

And yet . . . and yet it's impossible not to love Waltzing Daniel Considine. It's a measure of the depth and skill of O'Connor's portrait that even as you want to wring his neck—not to mention kick him out of the house—you want to hug him. He's been a terrible father to his only son—not to mention a terrible husband to the wife, now dead, whom he left behind—yet "he had the touch of the transient," and probably was fated to do what he did. The clash between father and son toward which the book leads is inevitable, too, and is rich in all the doubts and qualms with which even healthy father-son relationships are loaded, but it is between two distinctly human men who have equal claims on the reader's sympathy and affection.

It's a lovely little book: funny, sad, absolutely true. Rereading it again after all these years I am reminded of what a fine writer O'Connor was, and how keenly he understood the lives of Irish-Americans. Much good fiction and nonfiction has been written about them, but no one has done it better than he. His old publisher, Little, Brown and Company, now has a fine paperback line called Back Bay Books in which it has rescued John P. Marquand and C.S. Forester, among others. Isn't it about time to get Edwin O'Connor back in the bookstores?

ONLY YESTERDAY
by Frederick Lewis Allen

I t is scarcely uncommon among middle-class Americans of
my generation, but as a teenager in the 1950s and a young
adult in the 1960s, I was utterly, obsessively, terminally fascinated by the 1920s. I listened avidly to the early recordings
of Louis Armstrong and Duke Ellington, the musical comedies
of George Gershwin, the album of Edward R. Murrow's "I
Can Hear It Now" series that covered the decade. I fixated on
Charlie Chaplin, Mary Pickford, Douglas Fairbanks and
Theda Bara. Compulsively, endlessly, I read the novels and
stories of F. Scott Fitzgerald, the biography *The Far Side of
Paradise* by Arthur Mizener, Morley Callaghan's memoir *That
Summer in Paris*, and when Ernest Hemingway's *A Moveable
Feast* was published in 1964 I went bananas.

Being hooked on the Lost Generation, bathtub gin and
mah-jongg was totally romantic and equally harmless, but it
cloaked the 1920s in a nostalgic glow that bore only passing
resemblance to historical reality. For that I finally turned, sometime in the 1960s, to that extraordinary book *Only Yesterday:
An Informal History of the 1920's*, by Frederick Lewis Allen.
Published, astonishingly, almost exactly two years after the
stock market crash of October 1929 that wrote a conclusive
finis to the decade, the book immediately proved at once a
useful antidote to twenties romanticism and proof positive
that this was indeed a remarkable and unique period in U.S.
history.

Unlike that other famous and mythologized American

decade of the twentieth century, the sixties, much of which actually took place in the seventies, the twenties really were a self-contained decade. Yes, they began with the end of World War I in 1918 and the beginning of Prohibition in 1919, but these were preludes, just as the slide into nationwide Depression in 1930-31 was an afterword. Allen had the prescience to understand this immediately, and the skill to synthesize an immense amount of discrete material, to interpret it with intelligence and without sentimentality, and to write about it with grace, fluidity and wit.

Upon its publication in late 1931, *Only Yesterday* became an immense bestseller, with a half-million copies in print by the end of 1932—this, mind you, in the Depression—as well as a critical success. This must have been heady stuff for Allen, who was forty-one when the book appeared, but he seems to have been a gracious, modest man who kept fame under control. He was the son of an old WASP family, not rich but financially secure. He graduated from Groton and Harvard, then worked as a freelance journalist and magazine editor. According to the biographical note in the Harper Perennial edition of *Only Yesterday*, his daughter and then his wife died in 1928 and 1930, and "to get through the grief of these personal tragedies, Allen worked on the manuscript for the book that would become *Only Yesterday*."

In 1932 Allen remarried, to Agnes Rogers, who also worked at *Harper's*, of which he became editor in chief in 1941, a position he held until 1952. His editorship was fruitful and distinguished, as was his own writing career. In 1940 he published *Since Yesterday: The 1930s in America,* which did just about as well as *Only Yesterday*. He and his wife published several pictorial histories of various phases of America's past, and in 1952 he ended his career with *The Big Change: America Transforms Itself, 1900-1950*. He died of a cerebral hemorrhage in 1954 at the age of sixty-three, and was widely mourned.

It is testimony to both the popularity and the staying power of *Only Yesterday* that for more than three-quarters of a century it has remained steadily in print, and to this day enjoys sales that would please plenty of twenty-first-century writers. Rereading it for the first time in at least four decades, I am struck—in all cases favorably—by several aspects of it: the acuity of Allen's judgments, whether of people or events or larger developments and trends; his ability to discriminate between what is important and what is not; his willingness to present differing points of view fairly: his refusal (at a time when this was all too uncommon among people of his class) to stomach prejudice in any form; and, most of all, the degree to which his book has retained its freshness and pertinence over all these years.

It is nothing less than extraordinary for a work of popular history, written in the heat of the moment, to have faded so little in more than seventy-five years. By way of contrast, consider the books of John Gunther, most famously *Inside U.S.A.* Published in 1947, it too was a great bestseller, as were all the other *Inside* books that followed, but it is the only one still in print and its sales are meager. The reason is that, for all Gunther's diligence and professionalism, his books are creatures of their time, which is to say they are now period pieces. Yet *Only Yesterday* sails serenely on, still the one account of America in the 1920s against which all others must be measured.

The great public events that Allen covers—Woodrow Wilson and the League of Nations, the Red Scare, the Ku Klux Klan, Prohibition, Warren Harding and the Teapot Dome scandal, the Scopes trial, Charles Lindbergh's flight, the Florida boom and bust, the Crash—are so familiar to most readers that retracing them here would be a waste of precious space. Instead let me give you a couple of examples of Allen's prose, so you can see for yourself the insights and delights it offers. Here, for one, he is writing about the Red Scare:

Big-navy men, believers in compulsory military service, drys, anti-cigarette campaigners, anti-evolution Fundamentalists, defenders of the moral order, book censors, Jew-haters, Negro-haters, landlords, manufacturers, utility executives, upholders of every sort of cause, good, bad, and indifferent, all wrapped themselves in Old Glory and the mantle of the Founding Fathers and allied their opponents with Lenin. The open shop, for example, became the "American plan." For years a pestilence of speakers and writers continued to afflict the country with tales of "sinister and subversive agitators." Elderly ladies in gilt chairs in ornate drawing rooms heard from executive secretaries that the agents of the government had unearthed new radical conspiracies too fiendish to be divulged before the proper time. Their husbands were told at luncheon clubs that the colleges were honeycombed with Bolshevism. A cloud of suspicion hung in the air, and intolerance became an American virtue.

That's lovely stuff, evocative and dead-on. Yes, there's a hint of Mencken in it, but Allen was his own man and resisted the mere apery to which so many tinhorn Menckenites of his day succumbed. Allen was a fair man, as it must be admitted Mencken really was not, and though he had his own sharp opinions, he sought balance and understanding rather than invective. Thus he writes with clarity and no small amount of amusement about the "revolution in manners and morals" of the twenties, touching deftly on everything from "the post-war disillusion, the new status of woman, the Freudian gospel, the automobile, prohibition, the sex and confession magazines, and the movies," and then strikes this sobering note:

A time of revolution . . . is an uneasy time to live in. It is easier to tear down a code than to put a new one in its place, and meanwhile there is bound to be more or less wear and tear and general unpleasantness. People who have been brought up to think that it is sinful for women to smoke or drink, and scandalous for sex to be discussed across the luncheon table, and unthinkable for a young girl to countenance strictly dishonorable attentions from a man, cannot all at once forget the admonitions of their childhood. It takes longer to hard-boil a man or a woman than an egg.

As both of these passages make plain, the pertinence of *Only Yesterday* scarcely is limited to the 1920s. The cultural, social and political phenomena they discuss have reverberated down the years, from the McCarthy era to Woodstock and Flower Power to the early twenty-first century. In Allen's depiction of the highbrows of the 1920s, it is impossible not to see reflected the highbrows of today:

> They may be roughly and inclusively defined as the men and women who had heard of James Joyce, Proust, Cézanne, Jung, Bertrand Russell, John Dewey, Petronius, Eugene O'Neill, and Eddington; who looked down on the movies but revered Charlie Chaplin as a great artist, could talk about relativity even if they could not understand it, knew a few of the leading complexes by name, collected Early American furniture, had ideas about progressive education, and doubted the divinity of Henry Ford and Calvin Coolidge. Few in numbers though they were, they were highly vocal, and their influence not merely dominated American literature but filtered down to affect by slow degrees the thought of the entire country.

A few pages later Allen argues that "disillusionment (except about business and the physical luxuries and improvements which business would bring) was the keynote of the nineteen-twenties," and certainly disillusionment has been an important American theme ever since, interrupted by occasional bouts of jingoism and hyper-patriotism. The pulse upon which Allen had his finger beat far longer than a mere ten years. To be sure, he doesn't get everything right—he misses jazz entirely, scants the movies as well as the higher arts, founders a bit (as who wouldn't?) in the complexities of Teapot Dome—but mostly he is dead on target. *Only Yesterday* is going to be around for many years to come.

SLOUCHING TOWARDS BETHLEHEM
by Joan Didion

During the winter of 1968-69, I somewhat belatedly got my first taste of the 1960s. In the company of journalists and graduate students I had my first puff of marijuana—it didn't take, my opiate of choice at the time being bourbon—and with my four-year-old son I caught a matinee showing of *Yellow Submarine*, which certainly did take; this lover of jazz became an instant Beatles convert.

I also became a convert to the work of a writer of whom I'd never heard until a graduate student urged that I read her new book. It was a collection of essays called *Slouching Towards Bethlehem*, by Joan Didion. I knew and revered "The Second Coming," the great poem by William Butler Yeats from which she had taken her title—"And what rough beast, its hour come round at last, / Slouches towards Bethlehem to be born?"—but I knew nothing at all about Didion. Soon I learned that she was five years older than I but vastly more accomplished, having published essays and journalistic pieces in many national magazines in addition to a well-received first novel, *Run River*, in 1963.

Precisely why her essays were pressed upon me I do not recall, but I was impressed. There were twenty of them in all, the focus being primarily on California, the author's native state, but also on her own interior landscape and, in virtually all of them, the conviction that, as she put it in the title essay, "the center was not holding." Didion appeared to have been touched by the feminist movement that was gaining currency at the time, but she showed not a scintilla of doctrinal rigidity or orthodoxy. She was a clear-eyed observer who declined to be roped in by fads, publicists or anyone else's expectations. She found the sixties interesting, occasionally amusing, occasionally scary, and she was always a tough sell:

> Joan Baez was a personality before she was entirely a person, and, like anyone to whom that happens, she is in a sense the hapless victim of what others have seen in her, written about her, wanted her to be and not be. The roles assigned to her are various, but variations on a single theme. She is the Madonna of the disaffected. She is the pawn of the protest movement. She is the unhappy analysand. She is the singer who would not train her voice, the rebel who drives the Jaguar too fast, the Rima who hides with the birds and the deer. Above all, she is the girl who "feels" things, who has hung on to the freshness and pain of adolescence, the girl ever wounded, ever young. Now, at an age when the wounds begin to heal whether one wants them to or not, Joan Baez rarely leaves the Carmel Valley.

What I thought when I read that nearly four decades ago was, in a word: Wow. Not merely does that paragraph deftly (yet not wholly unsympathetically) skewer Baez, for whose singing and persona I have not an iota of affection, but it tells us much more: what happens to people when they become "personalities" before they are ready for that, and what uses we make of them to our own ends. Like so many other paragraphs in *Slouching Towards Bethlehem*, it transcends its immediate time and subject; all of these essays can be read with as much pleasure and profit as when they were first published, even if memories of Baez and, say, Haight-Ashbury already have faded.

Reading *Slouching Towards Bethlehem* started me off on what has been a long on-and-off love affair with Didion's work. (I have never met her, though I had a very pleasant e-mail acquaintance with her late husband, John Gregory Dunne.) She has never published a word of nonfiction that I have not liked, and she has almost never published a word of fiction of which I can say the same. Her essays and journalism invariably are smart, witty, iconoclastic and deeply informed—all of them are now collected in a volume from Everyman's Library, *We Tell Ourselves Stories in Order to Live*—but when she turns to fictional storytelling she lapses into unintentional self-parody. Indeed about a quarter-century ago, reviewing her novel *Democracy*, I found her fiction so susceptible to parody that I reviewed it by parodying it, something I'd never done before and probably never will do again, but it was, at the time, a hell of a lot of fun.

Now Didion, who is in her seventies, is generally honored as a major literary figure, almost entirely for her nonfiction. Her brave, heartbreaking account of her husband's death and their grown daughter's descent into terrible illness, *The Year of Magical Thinking*, confirmed and solidified her high position. She maintains an intense interest in matters Californian but still lives in New York, to which she and Dunne moved in 1988.

Though all of her nonfiction stands the test of time—the essays in *Political Fictions*, for example, are to my way of thinking the best and most durable political journalism that has been done in this country in the past quarter-century— *Slouching Towards Bethlehem* even now is, in the minds of many readers, the book of hers that they know best and admire most. This may have something to do with nostalgia for the time in which it was published, but if so, it certainly is false nostalgia, as Didion herself never had a single dewy thought about the sixties. A longer quotation from the book's title essay leaves no doubt about that:

> It was not a country in open revolution. It was not a country under enemy siege. It was the United States of America in the late cold spring of 1967, and the market was steady and the G.N.P. high and a great many articulate people seemed to have a sense of high social purpose and it might have been a spring of brave

hopes and national promise, but it was not, and more and more people had the uneasy apprehension that it was not. All that seemed clear was that at some point we had aborted ourselves and butchered the job, and because nothing else seemed so relevant I decided to go to San Francisco. San Francisco was where the social hemorrhaging was showing up. San Francisco was where the missing children were gathering and calling themselves "hippies."

What follows is a devastating depiction of the aimless lives of the disaffected and incoherent young. Didion is a cool observer but not a hardhearted one, so she treats these people with the sympathy they deserve, but not a teaspoon more:

> They feed back exactly what is given them. Because they do not believe in words—words are for "typeheads," [one guru] tells them, and a thought which needs words is just one more of those ego trips—their only proficient vocabulary is in [their] platitudes. As it happens I am still committed to the idea that the ability to think for one's self depends upon one's mastery of the language, and I am not optimistic about children who will settle for saying, to indicate that their mother and father do not live together, that they come from "a broken home." They are sixteen, fifteen, fourteen years old, younger all the time, an army of children waiting to be given the words.

The ability to dissect the naive and self-indulgent without merely mocking them is rarer than one might think, but it's characteristic of Didion's work. Over and over again, she declines to take the easy way out or to accommodate received opinion. It was fashionable at the time in certain circles to mock John Wayne for any number of reasons, but Didion was honest enough to admit that "when John Wayne rode through my childhood, and perhaps through yours, he determined forever the shape of certain of our dreams," and her portrait of him is, as she subtitles it, "A Love Song." In one sentence, she hits just about all the right notes about Las Vegas, "the most extreme and allegorical of American settlements, bizarre and

beautiful in its venality and in its devotion to immediate gratification, a place the tone of which is set by mobsters and call
girls and ladies' room attendants with amyl nitrite poppers in
their uniform pockets." California? ". . . time past is not
believed to have any bearing on time present or future, out in
the golden land where every day the world is born anew." And:

> California is a place in which a boom mentality and a sense of
> Chekovian loss meet in uneasy suspension; in which the mind is
> troubled by some buried but ineradicable suspicion that things
> had better work here, because here, beneath that immense
> bleached sky, is where we run out of continent.

Didion has had a lifelong love-hate affair with her native
state, as most recently demonstrated by *Where I Was From*, a
superb essay collection published in 2003, but there can be no
question that she understands California as keenly as anyone
ever has. This can be said of only a few other writers—
Nathanael West and Raymond Chandler come immediately to
mind, along with Robert Towne, author of the screenplay for
that masterful movie, *Chinatown*—which is, when one considers the place California has in U.S. history and mythology, no
small distinction in and of itself. What *Slouching Towards
Bethlehem* tells us, though, is that California was only the beginning for Didion. Then as now she had her eyes on the nation
itself, and few people, then or now, have seen it so clearly.

Lie Down in Darkness
by William Styron

The biggest surprise about the Second Reading series was how unsurprised I was by what I found the second time around. A few books that were immensely popular in their day turned out to have weathered the years poorly, but other books that I remembered fondly for literary and other merits revealed themselves, on second reading, to be as good as I remembered them, in some cases even better. I had no significant disappointments.

Until William Styron's *Lie Down in Darkness*. When I first read it in the 1960s I was swept away. Over the ensuing years I read all of Styron's other work, reviewed much of it, and held it in high esteem, especially his celebrated novel *Sophie's Choice* and *Darkness Visible*, his harrowing memoir of depression. Yet through all those years I believed that *Lie Down in Darkness*, his first book, remained his best. I regarded it as a monument of American fiction, cut out of Faulknerian cloth, to be sure, but a monument all the same. Now, though, I realize that the tone of the novel is relentlessly downbeat and that it is far more derivative than I had first understood.

I first read *Lie Down in Darkness* when I was twenty-eight, only a few years older than Peyton Loftis, the beautiful, spoiled and troubled young woman whose suicide is the event at the center of the novel. I remember responding ardently to the devastating scene in which her father, Milton Loftis, wanders drunkenly through a football weekend at the University of Virginia, a "nightmare" that struck me, not so long removed from four years at Chapel Hill, as entirely, breathtakingly real. I thought that the collapse of the Loftis family was tragic, not in the glib American sense but in the profound terms of the ancient Greeks.

I was scarcely the only person to have been captivated by the novel. A few weeks ago a reader of this newspaper, noting that Styron's book was to be discussed in this series, reported that when he was younger he had been "mesmerized" by it. In the late 1970s I had dinner with a young writer who was eager to talk about the novel. From memory, he recited in full the long quotation from Sir Thomas Browne's *Urn Burial* that Styron took as his epigraph, and then went on and on about his passion for the book.

When *Lie Down in Darkness* was published in 1951, most reviewers felt the same. It was treated not merely as a serious and substantial work of literature, but as something of a phenomenon: Styron at the time was a mere twenty-six years old. Himself a Virginian, he had joined the Marines as World War II was ending and returned to enroll at Duke University and study under its legendary teacher of writing, William Blackburn. After college Styron worked as an editor at the New York publishing firm McGraw-Hill, a job he hated with a passion, an experience he describes with great wit in the opening pages of *Sophie's Choice*. After he was fired, he spent three years writing *Lie Down in Darkness*, which was awarded the Prix de Rome by the American Academy in Rome. He was off on a career that included only six other books; he was a slow writer and sometimes was derailed by depression. He won just about all the major prizes except the Nobel and had, in *Sophie's Choice* and *The Confessions of Nat Turner*, two national bestsellers. He died in 2006 at the age of eighty-one.

His first novel still offers much to admire. As readers of *The Confessions of Nat Turner* will recall, Styron had an extraordinary, visceral kinship with Tidewater Virginia, and wrote about its bleak yet beautiful landscape with great power. His prose had not yet achieved in 1951 the suppleness and force of *Sophie's Choice* in 1979, but at moments it achieves real beauty and in a few—too few—wit shines through. Here, for example, the Tidewater gentry reacts to gossip about Milton Loftis and his mistress, Dolly Bonner:

> Hell, they'd say in the country club locker room, you know how Milt's getting his. Everybody knew, bearing testimony to the fact that suburban vice, like a peeling nose, is almost impossible to conceal. It went all over town, this talk, like a swarm of bees, settling down lazily on polite afternoon sun porches to rise once more and settle down again with a busy murmur among cautious ladylike foursomes on the golf course, buzzing pleasurably there amid ladylike whacks of the golf ball and cautious pullings-down of panties which bound too tightly. Everybody knew about their affair and everybody talked about it, and because of some haunting inborn squeamishness it would not have relieved Loftis to know that nobody particularly cared.

Loftis is in his early fifties, married to Helen, with whom he has had two daughters. A lawyer, he has abandoned his youthful political ambitions in favor of the solace of drink. His elder daughter, Maudie, was a cripple who died at the university hospital in Charlottesville, after her father's terrible long weekend there, leaving Helen bereft and bitter. Peyton, who was in her late teens when Maudie died, is stunningly beautiful and obviously intelligent, but her doting father—on his side their relationship has strong sexual undertones, and probably on hers as well—has spoiled her so thoroughly that she expects all of life's pleasures and rewards to come her way without any effort on her part, merely as her due; precisely what anyone sees in her beyond her beauty is never made clear.

The Loftis marriage is a wreck. Early in the novel Milton is caught up in a "surge of anger and futility [that] rose up in his chest—and sudden shame, too, shame at the fact that their life together, which had begun, as most marriages do, with such

jaunty good humor and confidence, had come to this footless-
ness, this confusion," but things only get worse as the story
unfolds. "Sober," Milton "feared Helen; for what seemed ages
he had lived with her not so much in a state of matrimony as
in a state of gentle irritation, together like the negative poles of
a magnet, gradually but firmly repelling each other." In time
"gentle irritation" descends into something very like hatred.
For a while Helen takes her troubles to a kindly, well-inten-
tioned Episcopal minister, who tries to help but finds himself
sucked into a place he'd rather not be:

> . . . He thought briefly about madness, and this family, which had
> succeeded—almost effortlessly, it seemed—in destroying itself,
> and he became so overwhelmed by melancholy that his stomach
> rumbled and his hands and wrists became limp and trembled on
> the steering wheel. He thought of the wild evening after Maudie's
> funeral when, with Peyton absent and Loftis, he supposed, hiding
> upstairs, Helen had told him that everything was finished, there
> was no God, no anything, behold (with a nod upstairs toward
> Loftis, and which included, he gathered, Peyton too) this breed of
> monsters. God, what words she had used! . . . Who was to blame?
> Mad or not, Helen had been beastly. She had granted to Loftis, in
> her peculiarly unremitting way, no forgiveness or understanding,
> and above all she had been beastly to Peyton. Yet Loftis himself
> had been no choice soul; and who finally, lest it be God himself,
> could know where the circle, composed as it was of such tragic
> suspicions and misunderstandings, began, and where it ended?

Unquestionably, that passage has intensity, power and intelligence. No doubt many readers will find it, as I did many years
ago, deeply moving, haunting. Yet now it mainly strikes me as
lugubrious, and so does too much of the rest of the novel. By the
1970s, when he was writing *Sophie's Choice*, Styron had come to
understand that catastrophe and/or tragedy must be alleviated
(and thus in a way illuminated) by humor, but in his mid-twenties he had yet to learn that lesson. The passage quoted above

about the Tidewater gossips is the exception rather than the rule in *Lie Down in Darkness*. Setting out to write the story of a family doomed by its inability to love, he became so bogged down in the agony of it all—as Peyton ruminates, "everywhere I turn I seem to walk deeper and deeper into some terrible despair"— that he ended up writing a 400-page dirge that ultimately is far more stifling than enriching.

The book suffers from other problems. Set as it is in Virginia during and immediately after World War II, it employs the racial language and stereotypes of its time and place, as do other books reconsidered in this series. Today's reader will be startled and probably offended by its frequent use of the most common racial slur, not merely in conversation but as a descriptive adjective. Beyond that, the novel's closing scene, in which the jubilation of black worshipers is clearly meant to provide noble and uplifting contrast with the cynicism and desolation of the Loftis family, is sentimental and patronizing. It does not withstand comparison with the scenes in Faulkner's *The Sound and the Fury* in which the quiet dignity of the black servant Dilsey is juxtaposed against the self-destructiveness of the white Compson family.

Styron always insisted that he was not influenced by Faulkner in writing *Lie Down in Darkness*, but in fact the influence is self-evident: in the closing account of the worshipers, in Peyton's long interior monologue (which also shows much evidence of the Molly Bloom soliloquy in James Joyce's *Ulysses*), in the rich, at times overripe prose, in the story itself, which bears more than passing resemblance to the story of the Compsons.

There's nothing wrong with influence: All writers are touched by it and many profit from it, just as do all other creative artists. But apart from its almost funereal tone, what now strikes me most emphatically about *Lie Down in Darkness* is its sheer derivativeness. That William Styron was, as a young man, a supremely gifted writer, is beyond question, but he had yet to become his own man.

CANNERY ROW
by John Steinbeck

As a teenager, even into my early twenties, there was scarcely a writer dead or alive whose work I treasured more than John Steinbeck's. During the 1950s I devoured his novels—*The Grapes of Wrath*, of course, but also all the rest, including *In Dubious Battle*, *The Long Valley*, *Of Mice and Men*, *The Moon Is Down* and *East of Eden*, which was published when I was twelve—with adolescent passion and utterly without discrimination. My devotion was so blind that, in 1960, I actually let a friend persuade me to trade my crisp new copy of Dwight Macdonald's brilliant *Parodies: An Anthology From Chaucer to Beerbohm—and After* for his review copy of Steinbeck's *Travels With Charley in Search of America*.

Well, time marches on. *Travels With Charley* vanished from my library ages ago, precisely when and where it went I haven't the foggiest idea, and just recently I set things right by purchasing, for not much more than a song, a nice used copy of *Parodies* in its original dust wrapper. Over the years, all of my Steinbeck collection—of which for a time there had been quite a lot—disappeared, *The Grapes of Wrath* being the last to go in the spring of 2006 when, in the process of moving from a large house to a smallish condominium, my wife and I had to make draconian literary judgments to pare down our library.

It's tempting to say that when I was a child I read as a child, and when I became a man I put aside childish books, but that's not fair to Steinbeck or, for that matter, to my own youthful self. In 1994, when I reviewed the first volume of the Library of America's Steinbeck edition, which contains the first five of his books, I was struck, upon rereading, by "the solemnity, the sentimentality, the heavy-handed irony, the humorlessness, the labored colloquialisms, the clumsiness, the political naiveté" that I found in them, but I was also reminded of what had drawn me to him when I was young: "his powerfully sympathetic portraits of American farm workers and . . . the vision of social justice with which his work is imbued." Now, with a number of readers asking whether Steinbeck would be included in these Second Readings, seemed a good time to take another look.

I decided to do so with *Cannery Row*. It was first published in 1945, and I read it no more than six or seven years later. I already had read, and delighted in, Steinbeck's first popular success, *Tortilla Flat* (1935), and was thrilled to discover that *Cannery Row* marked a return to Monterey, the coastal California town whose ordinary people Steinbeck loved and portrayed with sympathy and humor. I remembered that in these two books Steinbeck mostly had set aside the preachiness to which he was susceptible and simply had had fun; he was a long way from a humorist, but I remembered these as good-humored books and wondered if I would find that this quality had not diminished over the years.

The short answer is that the good humor is still there, but the book itself now seems strained, dated and not really very funny. This is disappointing if not surprising, but it leaves unanswered the question about Steinbeck that for years has vexed me and innumerable others: Why is it that the work of this earnest but artless writer continues to enjoy such astonishing popularity? It's not hard to understand why his books are widely assigned in middle and high school English classes; they are easy to read, they are honest in their portrayal of working-class Americans, they passionately support basic American values and principles even when they criticize particulars of

American life. Whatever their literary shortcomings, they have an integrity to which young readers respond.

But why do adults continue to read Steinbeck in such numbers? Four decades after his death, his books are cash cows for his publisher; he is to Viking Penguin what Khalil Gibran is to Knopf, an endless source of revenue, some of which presumably underwrites riskier books of a more literary nature. From *Cup of Gold* (1929) to *America and Americans* (1967), Steinbeck's books remain in print, along with various posthumous volumes of letters, collected miscellany and so forth. My copy of *Cannery Row* is part of a Steinbeck *Centennial Edition* issued by Penguin in 2002. This edition clearly is aimed at adult readers, and clearly it is reaching them; at this writing, its Amazon.com sales rating is far higher than that enjoyed by most recent, well-received books.

Probably the explanation for this will forever be a mystery. It cannot have much to do with the Nobel Prize in Literature that Steinbeck won in 1962; if Nobel Prizes sent American readers into bookstores, they'd still be reading Pearl Buck and Sinclair Lewis. Nor can it have much to do with relevance to the country today, since his books mostly are period pieces. Grace of literary style would send no one to his books, as they have precious little of it.

Why do people still read Steinbeck today while his contemporary William Saroyan (*The Human Comedy*, *My Name Is Aram*, the Pulitzer Prize-winning play *The Time of Your Life*) is almost completely forgotten? The two writers were remarkably similar in their affection for ordinary people, their belief in the United States and their persistent sentimentality, and in their day both were hugely popular, yet now probably no more than one reader in twenty-five would be likely to recognize Saroyan's name. The only reason I can come up with for the high esteem in which Steinbeck is still held is his transparent sincerity. It has long been my pet theory that in the popular marketplace, readers instinctively distinguish between writers whose work draws on genuine feeling and those who rely on art or artifice, and that they reward the former while repudiating the latter. From Jacqueline Susann to Danielle Steel, from James Michener to James Patterson, readers have recognized the sincerity of feeling beneath the utter lack of literary merit, and have rewarded it accordingly.

Steinbeck was scarcely so bad a prose stylist as any of these—though his Nobel Prize is a reminder that literary distinction matters less to the Swedish Academy than leftist political orthodoxy—but his books shine with conviction that comes from the heart. In *Cannery Row*, for example, he gives us an amiable loafer named Mack and his band of friends who settle into an abandoned Monterey building that they christen the Palace Flophouse and Grill. They have "no families, no money, and no ambitions beyond food, drink, and contentment," and the conventional world scorns them as "no-goods, come-to-bad-ends, blots-on-the-town, thieves, rascals, bums," but in Steinbeck's eyes they are "the Beauties, the Virtues, the Graces" because "in the world ruled by tigers with ulcers, rutted by strictured bulls, scavenged by blind jackals, Mack and the boys dine delicately with the tigers, fondle the frantic heifers, and wrap up the crumbs to feed the sea gulls of Cannery Row."

This is sentimentalism pure and simple, if not outright tripe, but Steinbeck's love for these men is transparent and his admiration for their innocent simplicity is utterly sincere. He had a weakness for parable, fantasy and mythology—*Tortilla Flat*, the linear ancestor of *Cannery Row*, is a riff on King Arthur and the knights of the Round Table—and the sweeping thematic generalizations often associated with all of these. He delighted in the antics of Mack and company—the novel's most successful and engaging scene involves their encounter with a henpecked military officer to whom they bring a brief moment of escape and irresponsibility—but he took them very seriously. Doc, a warmhearted marine biologist who is the novel's real hero, speaks for Steinbeck when he says:

> Look at them. There are your true philosophers. I think . . . that Mack and the boys know everything that has ever happened in the world and possibly everything that will happen. I think they survive in this particular world better than other people. In a time when people tear themselves to pieces with ambition and nervousness and covetousness, they are relaxed. All of our so-called successful men are sick men, with bad stomachs, and bad souls, but Mack and the boys are healthy and curiously clean. They can do what they want. They can satisfy their appetites without calling them something else. . . . They could ruin their lives and get money. Mack has qualities of genius. They're all very clever if they want something. They just know the nature of things too well to be caught in that wanting.

This comes perilously close to being a variation on the thoroughly discredited theory of the noble savage, but it speaks to Steinbeck's heartfelt admiration for innocence and selflessness. Himself a complex, difficult and ambitious man who eventually moved to the East and traveled in high-powered circles, he never really lost his connection to the simpler life and values of his native region of early-twentieth-century coastal California. Readers recognized this in his writing and responded to it, as apparently they still do.

For myself, Steinbeck is most comfortably lodged in a past that is now far gone. I no longer can read him—too often, for me, reading his prose is like scraping one's fingernails on a blackboard—but he was important to me once and that should not be forgotten. Not many books of our youth survive unscathed into what passes for our maturity, and many other books await that maturity before we are ready to appreciate and understand them. For me, Steinbeck eventually gave way to William Faulkner and Gabriel García Márquez, but I decline, now, to thumb my nose at my old friend as I bid him farewell.

THE RECTOR OF JUSTIN
by Louis Auchincloss

In the spring of 1954 I was granted one of the most decidedly mixed blessings of a life that has seen many: admission to Groton, the most famous of American prep
schools, and a generous scholarship to ease the way for my parents, who were anything except wealthy. Coming as I did from
a prep school family, I knew this hermetic world all too well
and entered Groton with too many chips on my shoulder. My
three years there were tumultuous and mostly unhappy, with
expulsion an ever-present threat, though I managed to graduate and made a number of friendships that I still treasure.

Congenitally restless in any classroom, I was a lazy, inatten-
tive student who took paltry advantage of Groton's superb faculty, but I learned a great deal, by observation and osmosis,
about this privileged, exclusive, self-contained and surpass-
ingly strange place. I regarded it with equal measures of horror
and fascination, tinged with more than a trace of envy, and thus
unwittingly set myself up as an almost ideally receptive reader
for Louis Auchincloss's masterly novel *The Rector of Justin*,
published in 1964. Himself an alumnus of Groton (Class of
1935), Auchincloss had been inspired to write the novel by his
own experience there—"I was at first abysmally wretched and
later moderately content," he says in his afterword to the 2001
Modern Library edition—and in particular by the example of
its legendary founder, Endicott Peabody.

Auchincloss was one of the most accomplished and distinctive writers this country has known. Born in 1917 into

Manhattanite wealth and position, he was from the end of World War II until his retirement in 1986 a highly successful Wall Street lawyer; it always gave my mother immense pleasure that for many years he held the same partnership at Hawkins, Delafield & Wood that her own father had occupied. From the publication in 1947 of his first novel, *The Indifferent Children*, Auchincloss was almost unimaginably prolific—he published about seventy books, both fiction and nonfiction—and consistently maintained the high standards to which he held himself right up to his death in 2009. He was one of the great American novelists of manners, ranking with Edith Wharton and John P. Marquand, but he was much more, as *The Rector of Justin* makes plain.

I gobbled up the book immediately upon its publication and admired it without reservation, though I realize now this had more to do with reading it as a roman à clef (which in fact it is not) than with its great literary merit. I reread it a quarter-century later while doing research for a book about my parents, primarily for its insights into the prep school culture in which they spent their entire adult lives, and in my book I quoted approvingly Auchincloss's observation about "that curious half paternal, half protective, almost at times half contemptuous, attitude of men of affairs for academics," which perfectly summarized a vexing condition under which my father had labored all his life.

It is not until now, though, with a third reading of *The Rector of Justin*, that I have arrived at a keener appreciation of its extraordinary breadth and depth. *The Rector of Justin* is a "prep school novel" in the same way that *Moby-Dick* is a "whaling novel." It uses the environment of a fictitious Episcopal school for boys, Justin Martyr—"named for the early martyr and scholar who tried to reconcile the thinking of the Greek philosophers with the doctrines of Christ"—to explore grand, universal themes, all of them centered on its protagonist, the

294 · JONATHAN YARDLEY

school's founding father, Francis Prescott. It is, I now realize, a minor masterpiece of twentieth century literature.

The novel begins in September 1939 and ends in April 1947. It is told principally through the diary of Brian Aspinwall, who comes to Justin Martyr at the age of twenty-seven as an instructor in English and soon believes "that I may have a call to keep a record of the life and personality of Francis Prescott," who "is probably the greatest name in New England secondary education." Five other narrators contribute to the portrait: David Griscam, chairman of the trustees, chief architect of the school's wealth; his son, Jules, expelled by Prescott for an act of defiance; Horace Havistock, Prescott's oldest friend, "a remnant of the mauve decade"; Cordelia, Prescott's rebellious daughter; and Charley Strong, one of Prescott's "golden boys, Justin class of 1911 senior prefect and football captain, a kind of American Rupert Brooke," who fled to Paris after World War I and underwent a crisis of identity and faith.

Now nearing eighty, Prescott is still at the head of the school he founded in 1886, but preparing to step aside for a younger man. Readers who are tempted to see Groton's Peabody in him must be dissuaded. Physically they are completely different: Peabody was tall, while Prescott "is short for one that dominating, about five feet six, which is accentuated by the great round shoulders, the bull neck, the noble square head, the thick shock of stiff, wavy grey hair." Auchincloss is at pains to distinguish his school from Peabody's—"Justin Martyr has never had the aura of snobbishness under which Groton and St. Mark's have suffered"—and the men from each other, as he says in his afterword:

> . . . to dramatize the troubled story of the Protestant church school my headmaster would have to be a much more complicated character than Endicott Peabody. He would have to have moments of doubt to balance his faith; he would have to see his school as a mountain of vanity as well as a monastery; he would

have to be intellectual, cultivated, occasionally cynical, sometimes cruel, always clever. If Dr. Peabody had his moments of despair, they didn't show. I wanted my man to be tortured in his brilliant success by constantly having to question its validity, and at times to despise even his own teachers and pupils for their failure to make his ideals seem as shining as he had aspired to make them. I wanted him to be humble and vain, to be St. Francis of Assisi and King Lear on the heath. I wanted him to express the agony of failing ridiculously when he wanted at the very least to fail magnificently, and I wanted him to raise the question—no more than that—if he had failed at all.

All this and more is accomplished in *The Rector of Justin*. Frank Prescott is another of the great characters in American fiction, commanding every page with his presence, yet never becoming a mere Great Man cartoon. He is no saint. Horace Havistock recalls the days of their youth in New York, when Frank worked for the New York Central, before he followed his path to the ministry and Justin Martyr: "Frank all his life had a grudging, half-concealed fascination for big business. He used to say that if you sold out to Mammon, you might as well get a seat in the Inner Temple." When David Griscam proposes raising funds to expand the school—"The idea was not so much to sell Justin Martyr," he says, "as it was to sell Francis Prescott"—Frank responds angrily: "It's hard on the personality to be a headmaster. . . . It's particularly hard on mine. It develops all my tendencies to strut and bully. Here I am, covered with mud from the bottom of my own little puddle, and you want to pitch me into a larger one!"

Here's how he is remembered by Jules Griscam, the prodigal son: "Prescott was surrounded with an atmosphere of almost incredible awe, to which the parents, trustees and faculty all contributed. I do not think that many of the boys liked him, but they respected and feared him, which was much more fun, both for them and for him. . . . They were proud of his fame, excited by the rumble of his leadership and diverted by his wit, his inconsistencies, even by his sermons. As I have said, he was basically a ham actor, and the school was a captured but still admiring audience." It is Jules who, after being apprehended in an act of desecration of school property, calls Prescott on the carpet. Prescott wonders if Jules has been "possessed by the devil," to which Jules replies:

> Well, devils have a way of having the last word, you know . . . particularly with those who are making a peepshow of God's mercy. Who are using God's things as props in vaudeville. And so it was that your beautiful academy, your palace of lies, should have at last a graduate—a moral graduate, shall we say—who carries your act to its ultimate degree and shatters for a gaping multitude the great glass window of your idolatry.

This confrontation is the nadir of Prescott's life, and he never quite recovers from it. On the eve of his farewell tribute he tells David Griscam: "I see that Justin Martyr is like the other schools. Only I, of course, ever thought it was different. Only I failed to see that snobbishness and materialism were intrinsic in its make-up. Only I was naïve enough to think I could play with that kind of fire and not get my hands burnt." There is much honesty in all this, but Brian Aspinwall's judgment, offered after Prescott's death, probably comes closest to the truth:

> He knew his capacity to be petty, vain, tyrannical, vindictive, even cruel. He fully recognized his propensity to self-dramatization and his habit of sacrificing individuals to the imagined good of his school. Yet he also saw at all times and with perfect clarity that his own peculiar genius was for persuading his fellow men that life could be exciting and that God wanted them to find it so.

Too often among the literati it is said of Louis Auchincloss that he was a "mere" novelist of the manners of upper-crust people whose lives are irrelevant to those led by the rest of us.

That anyone could read *The Rector of Justin* and still believe this is all the evidence one needs of the human mind's bottomless capacity for obtuseness. This is fiction set in a small place but on a grand scale, wise, compassionate and utterly unsentimental. It is one of the central books of my life, and I treasure its every word.

THE SHOOTING PARTY
by Isabel Colegate

In the two decades between 1912 and 1933, six English-women were born who went on to become exceptionally gifted and accomplished writers of sophisticated, surpass-ingly civilized novels. Many of their books have been pub-lished in this country, but only Penelope Fitzgerald, Anita Brookner and Penelope Lively are reasonably well known here, and the others—Elizabeth Taylor, Elizabeth Jane Howard and Isabel Colegate—have never found more than modest American readerships.

The loss is ours, for their novels—short stories, too—are distinguished in virtually every regard. Though their styles and subjects vary widely, they have in common keen intelligence and wit, a deep interest in domestic life and matters of social class, an agreeably old-fashioned commitment to the art of sto-rytelling and a preference for the miniature over the grandiose. Though women's lives, opportunities, difficulties and rights are important to all of them, none is reflexively ideological or feminist. They speak their minds, but they decline in all instances to hector the reader, which cannot be said for the most famous British woman writer of their generation, Doris Lessing, who is of course (the world being such as it is), the one to whom a Nobel Prize in Literature was awarded.

Among the many books by these writers that I have read, a particular favorite is Colegate's *The Shooting Party*. Published in this country in the spring of 1981, it came to my attention in a most unlikely fashion. For seven years I had been moonlighting from my newspaper jobs (first at the *Miami Herald*, then at the *Washington Star*) as a "special contributor" to *Sports Illustrated*, for which I was, in effect, chief book reviewer. It was (for me at least) a most enjoyable relationship, not least because I made some treasured friendships and was paid exceptionally well by book-reviewing standards, but the choice of books to review was limited and often frustrating.

As a result I was forever on the prowl for books that weren't "sports books" per se but that might be of interest to *Sports Illustrated*'s editors and readers. Five years earlier I had chanced upon *Beautiful Swimmers: Watermen, Crabs and the Chesapeake Bay,* by a first-time author named William W. Warner: It was about fishing, and fishing is a sport, right? The book went on to win a Pulitzer Prize and to become a regional, if not national, classic. So when I saw the galley proofs of a novel by an English writer about a shooting party—hunting, I thought at once, and hunting is a sport, right?—I leaped at it.

Precisely what I said about it in my review I do not recall, as my copy has long since vanished, but I know that I spoke admiringly about its wit and its keen delineation of British class lines. Rereading it now, I remain deeply impressed by those qualities, but also by the way in which Colegate evokes pre-World War I England, teetering at the brink of catastrophe yet utterly unaware of what lay ahead. This period has been the subject of many evocative works of nonfiction, but I can think of no work of fiction that brings it to life so fully and subtly as does *The Shooting Party*.

It was Colegate's ninth novel—she has since published five more—and it remains her best-known, in part no doubt because a first-rate movie adaptation was released in 1985, with one of those breathtakingly all-star casts that only the Brits can regularly assemble: James Mason, in what turned out to be his last role, as Sir Randolph Nettleby, proprietor of the estate on which the shoot takes place; Dorothy Tutin as his wife, Minnie; Edward Fox as the haughty champion marksman Lord Gilbert Hartlip; and John Gielgud, in yet another of his autumnal cameo star turns, as the animal-rights protester Cornelius Cardew. It is one of the few cinematic adaptations of a literary novel that somehow manages to be true to the original without diminishing it.

The novel takes place "in the autumn before the outbreak of what used to be known as the Great War," in Nettleby Park, which "was very large in those days, nearly a thousand acres (an eighth of the whole estate)," all of it the property of Sir Randolph, a gentleman of conservative leanings who laments the coming of a new age of "striking industrial workers, screaming suffragettes, Irish terrorists, scandals on the Stock Exchange, universal suffrage." It outrages him that "the politicians are determined to turn this country into an urban society instead of a rural one" and to "take away the power of the landed proprietor." He may seem at first a caricature of the British upper class, but he is simply a man of another time, a paternalistic patrician who believes it his duty to care for the men and women who work on his farm. His instincts are kind and his sense of humor is fully functional, including when it is self-directed.

We know almost from the outset that someone will die during the shoot, though who that will be remains the chief matter of suspense as the story unfolds. One likely candidate is a duck rescued by Osbert, Sir Randolph's ten-year-old grandson. A John Bull type named Charles Farquhar, laughing at his own rich humor, tells the duck, "If I see you flying over me I can tell you you haven't a hope. Bang, bang and it will be all over," to which Osbert replies: "If you kill her, I will kill you." The possibility that at least one of these calamities will come to pass is very real, as one of the housemaids understands:

Ellen knew as well as anyone that the last day of a big shooting party ended with a duck shoot by the river at dusk. She also knew that the rules of sport and the rules of entertaining were both inexorable. Even Sir Randolph could not be expected to refuse to offer his guests the opportunity of shooting at wild duck just because a child's tame duck might have chanced to be among them.

The guests are a populous and mostly clamorous lot. Gilbert Hartlip is a "superlative sportsman"—i.e., expert at killing fat pheasants on the fly, if that fits one's definition of sport—but, in Sir Randolph's judgment, "an odd, cold, proud fish of a fellow." Lionel Stephens is a successful lawyer no doubt on the way to becoming a prominent judge, an open-minded and handsome man who finds himself, to his joy and consternation, falling in love with Olivia Lilburn, the beautiful, intelligent and good-hearted wife of a man who does not deserve her. The sparks that begin to fly between Lionel and Olivia are seen by Minnie Nettleby, who contrives to seat them together as often as possible, because she "loved beauty, and considered the furtherance of romance between the possessors of it the least of the services she could perform for it."

Then there are the people of the lower orders. These include the gamekeeper, Glass, and his bright, ambitious, devoted teenage son, Dan, but most particularly they include Tom Harker, "a thatcher by trade" whom Glass enlists as a beater—one of the men who rouse the birds from their nests for their flight to death—when a more reliable man proves unavailable. Tom "was known to do a bit of poaching, [but] he was looked on as a respectable man, a good son to his mother and a man of his word, kind to the children who stole apples from his three prolific old trees and—had they not all heard him say so a hundred times?—never in his life the worse for drink." Tom has his full share of class resentment, yet he greatly admires the shooting skill of Gilbert Hartlip: "You wouldn't see better sport anywhere in

England, Tom Harker thought, finding no difficulty in accommodating that notion in his mind along with his views about the stranglehold of the rich on the life-blood of the working man."

The tensions of class are very much present in *The Shooting Party*, but Colegate never bludgeons the reader with them, nor does she ever get heavy-handed about two other themes—the situation of women and the rights of animals—that flow through the novel. These last two are interwoven as Olivia talks quietly with Lionel moments after Osbert's duck has made a surprise appearance in the manor house. She expresses sympathy for Osbert, and goes on:

> . . . you can see he has such strong emotions, and he will have to be educated and taught the ways of the world and made to be on the side of the guns and against the ducks. It seems such a pity. . . . Who says it's the height of heroism to kill? For every hero does there have to be a living sacrifice? . . . I am often aware at shooting parties how differently I feel from a man and how, more than that, I really would like to rebel against the world men have made, if I knew how to. I see the beauty of a good shoot of course and the charm of country sports and traditions, but I can't help feeling the added solemnity the whole thing gets from that sacrificial note, the note of death, of blood. Why do we have to have that, to complete our pleasure?

The question is at the core of the novel, never more so than at the release of the pheasants, "forced to take to the air reluctantly—heavy birds, a flight of more than a few feet exhausts them—forced up and out to meet a burst of noise and a quick death in that bright air." The same fate, of course, awaits some of the men in the shooting party in the years to come, as Europe collapses into a mad four-year fit of self-destruction. Once again, Colegate declines to beat the reader over the head with the point, but it clearly is there to be contemplated. That she has managed to take on these very large subjects in a book of fewer than 200 pages, and to consider them through a cast of wholly human characters, is a remarkable accomplishment.

THE ELEMENTS OF STYLE
by William Strunk and E.B. White

One of the never-ending frustrations of my otherwise enjoyable half-century newspaper career has been what newspapers call "style." Newspapers have many good qualities, but "style" most certainly is not among them. Newspaper "style" consists mainly of ungrammatical, unlovely attempts to compress as much information as possible into as little space as possible. Thus instead of the elegant "Senator Nonesuch, Republican of Transylvania," we are required to write, "Sen. Nonesuch (R-Tr.)"; instead of "Rockville, Maryland," we must suffer with "Rockville, Md."; and poor "William Strunk, Jr.," must sacrifice his comma and become "William Strunk Jr."

That, believe you me, would not have sat well with William Strunk, Jr., who on page three of his immortal *The Elements of Style* writes: "The abbreviations etc. and jr. are parenthetic and are always to be so regarded," as in (the example is his), "James Wright, Jr." This is the same William Strunk, Jr., who two pages earlier writes, "In a series of three or more terms with a single conjunction, use a comma after each term except the last," as in "red, white, and blue," this second comma being "often referred to as the 'serial' comma," except in newspaper offices, where it is often referred to as the "space-eating" comma.

I have been a Strunkaholic for almost as long as I have been a journalist, though no doubt there have been times when one would never have known it from my prose. *The Elements of Style, With Revisions, an Introduction, and a New Chapter on*

304 · JONATHAN YARDLEY

Writing by E.B. White, was published in 1959, two years after White had written an article in the *New Yorker* about this privately published (in 1918) textbook "I had used when I was a student at Cornell." Editors at Macmillan immediately decided they wanted to publish it, and contracted with White "to make revisions in the text and write a chapter on style," not newspaper style, needless to say, but real style, of which White was a master.

When what Strunk "sardonically and with secret pride" called "the little book" made its public appearance, I was at Chapel Hill, pretending to be a college student but actually working full time on the university newspaper, the *Daily Tar Heel*. I must have rushed out to get a copy, because my heavily worn little hardcover is a first edition with a price of one dollar. The book has accompanied me to Washington, New York, North Carolina, Massachusetts, Florida, Baltimore and finally back to Washington, and has been what White probably would not have called my vade mecum, since in his "Approach to Style" he counsels, "Avoid foreign languages. . . . It is a bad habit. Write in English." So: For half a century *The Elements of Style* has been my constant companion, vade mecum being Latin (O lost!) for "go with me."

It is that to this day, and if someone wants to toss it in the box with me when I go six feet under, that would be fine; it might actually assure my passage through the Pearly Gates, since Saint Peter no doubt is a gentleman of impeccable grammatical taste, not to mention style. In the half-century of its public life "the little book" has been a constant companion for millions of people, most of whom know it simply as *Strunk and White*. It is scarcely so encyclopedic as H.W. Fowler's *A Dictionary of Modern English Usage* (1926, revised 1965 by Sir Ernest Gowers) but it is distinctly and distinctively American, and its brevity renders it both portable and accessible.

Strunk (1869-1946) spent his entire teaching career at

Cornell and was little known beyond the campus. White describes him as "a memorable man, friendly and funny." He "scorned the vague, the tame, the colorless, the irresolute. He felt it was worse to be irresolute than to be wrong." In his forty-six years at Cornell he seems to have been widely respected, even loved, yet his book "passed into disuse" not long after his death and probably would have vanished for good had not someone purloined one of two copies in the Cornell library and mailed it to White, who "had not laid eyes on it in thirty-eight years, and . . . was delighted to study it again and rediscover its rich deposits of gold."

Of Strunk's many emphatic grammatical dicta, the most famous and surely the most frequently violated is, "Omit needless words." Strunk eschewed an exclamation point therein, but it cries out for one, for the exclamation point "is to be reserved for use after true exclamations or commands," which "Omit needless words!" most certainly is. The command is followed by what White calls "the masterly Strunkian elaboration of this noble theme," to wit:

> Vigorous writing is concise. A sentence should contain no unnecessary words, a paragraph no unnecessary sentences, for the same reason that a drawing should have no unnecessary lines and a machine no unnecessary parts. This requires not that the writer make all his sentences short, or that he avoid all detail and treat his subjects only in outline, but that every word tell.

Thus in Strunk's hands "the question as to whether" mercifully becomes simply "whether" and "he is a man who" becomes "he." Then follows the stricture to which almost no one pays attention: "An expression that is especially debilitating is the fact that. It should be revised out of every sentence in which it occurs." Expunge "owing to the fact that" and use "since," ditto for "I was unaware of the fact that," because "I was unaware that" is so much better. I am pleased (and relieved) that a search of the *Washington Post*'s electronic library for "Yardley" and "the fact that" yields, on its first page, no appearance in my own prose of "the fact that" but several in quotations from books under review, including ones by William Styron, Toni Morrison and Joan Didion.

The point isn't that I'm a grammatical paragon but that even the best writers can fall into sloppy habits. The price of being a Strunkaholic is eternal vigilance, for it is easy to let participial phrases dangle (my favorite, from Strunk, is, "Being in a dilapidated condition, I was able to buy the house very cheap"), to use "disinterested" when you mean "uninterested," to ignore the difference between "farther" ("distance") and "further" ("time or quantity"), to use "less" when you mean "fewer," to use a plural verb with "none," which "takes the singular verb," to confuse "that" and "which." A particular bugaboo of my own is the use of "like" for "as," which is now near-universal and is almost always wrong:

> The use of like for as has its defenders; they argue that any usage that achieves currency becomes valid automatically. This, they say, is the way the language is formed. It is and it isn't. An expression sometimes merely enjoys a vogue, much as an article of apparel does. Like has always been widely misused by the illiterate; lately it has been taken up by the knowing and the well-informed, who find it catchy, or liberating, and who use it as though they were slumming. If every word or device that achieved currency were immediately authenticated, simply on the grounds of popularity, the language would be as chaotic as a ball game with no foul lines. For the student, perhaps the most useful thing to know about like is that most carefully edited publications regard its use, before phrases and clauses, as simple error.

It was, of course, an advertisement that nailed the coffin on proper usage—"Winston tastes good like a cigarette should"—and, as White says in his essay, "the language of advertising enjoys an enormous circulation," hardly to the betterment of us all. This isn't to argue that the language shouldn't change. To the contrary, many new words that enter common usage from unlikely sources are useful and uniquely describe specific meanings; think, for example, of "geek" and "dis" and "spam," all of which I use with pleasure because they are, quite simply, good words. I shudder to think, though, of what Strunk and White would say about "author" and "reference" and "friend" used as verbs, of "presently" used as a synonym for "currently" or "now," of "interface," a word with a specific technological meaning, used as a synonym for "meet," as in: "Let's interface in the conference room at noon." Perhaps the day is not far off when it will become a synonym for "kiss," as in: "Interface me, baby!"

Et cetera. The language takes a daily beating, often from people who, as both Strunk and White point out, are more interested in appearing elegant and erudite than in actually being so, people who believe that pompous, inaccurate language is evidence of deep thought and noble purpose. The truth is the opposite. As White writes: "Avoid the elaborate, the pretentious, the coy, and the cute. Do not be tempted by a twenty-dollar word when there is a ten-center handy, ready and able." As both Strunk and White were aware, this is hard advice to follow, for it is much more difficult to be concise than to be verbose. Consider, if you will, the Gettysburg Address on the one hand and the rhetoric of William Jefferson Clinton (or, to be bipartisan, George W. Bush) on the other. It is the difference between eloquence and bloviation, but as Warren Gamaliel Harding well knew, bloviation is a presidential prerogative.

ACT ONE
by Moss Hart

Moss Hart had one of the most spectacular show business careers of the twentieth century. Born in New York City in 1904 to parents who existed at or barely above the poverty line, he had his first hit show, *Once in a Lifetime*, written with George S. Kaufman, shortly before his twenty-sixth birthday. He and Kaufman wrote five other hits, two of which—*You Can't Take It With You* and *The Man Who Came to Dinner*—are still mainstays of the amateur and professional repertoire. On his own he wrote *Lady in the Dark*, with haunting music by Kurt Weill and Ira Gershwin, and the screenplay for Judy Garland's finest movie, *A Star Is Born*. He was, to boot, the director of the most successful musical in Broadway history, *My Fair Lady*, and of *Camelot*.

On top of all that, his autobiography, *Act One*, published in 1959—two years before his sudden death from a heart attack—was, according to his biographer Steven Bach, "a runaway bestseller on the *New York Times* list for almost a year and number one for twenty-two weeks." Yet today, half a century after his death, Hart seems almost completely forgotten outside theater circles. Perhaps this is because, unlike his contemporaries and friends Noel Coward, Cole Porter and George Gershwin, he wrote only words, not music that can be sung, hummed and remembered. Perhaps it is because even the best and most durable of his plays have, today, a touch of the period piece. Whatever the explanation, it is a great injustice, for as a re-reading of *Act One* reminds us, he was an amaz-

ing man with an amazing story—a "Dazzler," to use the title of
Bach's superb book.

When *Act One* came out I had just turned twenty and was
in the grip of an infatuation with show business that has never
quite gone away, though I've never acted on it in any significant way beyond buying too many original-cast Broadway
recordings. I don't recall what steered me to the book. It might
have been my mother, but it certainly wasn't my father, who
loathed showbiz. Probably it was the Modern Library volume
Six Plays by Kaufman and Hart, which I'd read over and over
and have kept to this day, through more moves and library
purges than I care to recall.

Whatever got me to *Act One*, it knocked me out when I first
read it, and it knocks me out now. Many people knowledgeable about such matters regard it as the finest of all twentieth-
century theatrical memoirs; I'd say its only competition is
Present Indicative, by Noel Coward. A thoroughgoing showbiz
veteran by the time he wrote it in the 1950s, Hart knew how to
play the emotions of readers just as he knew how to play those
of an audience, and he plays mine to a fare-thee-well. I admit
without the slightest embarrassment that in its closing pages
"my eyes were blurred," as Hart's were when, at the opening
night of *Once in a Lifetime,* his celebrated collaborator went
onstage to say, "I would like this audience to know that eighty
per cent of this play is Moss Hart." Hart writes:

> I stood staring at the stage and at George Kaufman. Generosity
> does not flower easily or often in the rocky soil of the theatre. Few
> are uncorrupted by its ceaseless warfare over credit and billing, its
> jealousies and envies, its constant temptations toward pettiness
> and mean-spiritedness. It is not only a hard and exacting profes-
> sion but the most public one as well. It does not breed magna-
> nimity, and unselfishness is not one of its strong points. Not often
> is a young playwright welcomed into it with a *beau geste* as gallant
> and selfless as the one that had just come over those footlights.

That paragraph, touching though it most certainly is, comes toward the end, but we must begin at the beginning, which occurs with Hart's birth in a tenement at Seventy Four East 105th Street, a fashionable neighborhood now but then, as Bach reports, one "of dray wagons, pushcarts, and immigrants." His father was a feckless and rather shiftless cigarmaker with whom he was often impatient, and Hart quite actively disliked his mother, though he plays down these sentiments in *Act One*, whether out of kindness to their memories or some less elevated motive, I do not know. The most important people in his early life were his grandfather, "the black sheep of a large and quite wealthy family of English Jews" who "towered over my first seven years like an Everest of Victorian tyranny," and his Aunt Kate, a "touching combination of the sane and the ludicrous along with some secret splendor within herself," who did him the great favor of his life by introducing him to the theater and encouraging his interest in it.

Hart came to believe "that the theater is an inevitable refuge of the unhappy child," who "perceives that his secret goal is attainable—to be himself and yet be somebody else, and in the very act of doing so, to be loved and admired; to stand gloriously in a spotlight undimmed by the rivalry of brothers or sisters and to be relieved of his sense of guilt by the waves of applause that roll over the footlights to those wonderful creatures on the stage." No doubt there is much truth to this. Not merely was Hart oppressed by the poverty in which he grew up, but two other conditions weighed heavily on him; he was tormented by doubts about his sexual identity—a subject he does not explore in *Act One* but was common knowledge in his circle, though eventually he had a happy marriage to Kitty Carlisle—and by what we now know as bipolar disorder, which led to fits of depression that afflicted him to the end of his life. Poverty, though, was what tormented him most, as he recalls of a point in his teens when he secured a night job:

> The mere idea, little enough in itself, of not returning home each evening and walking those four flights up the grimy stairway to our apartment, filled me with an almost unbearable sense of exhilaration and freedom such as I had never before known. It is hard to describe or to explain concisely the overwhelming and suffocating boredom that is the essence of being poor. A great deal has been written about the barren drudgery of poverty; but I do not recall that the numbing effect of its boredom has been much written or talked about. Yet boredom is the keynote of poverty—of all its indignities, it is perhaps the hardest of all to live with—for where there is no money there is no change of any kind, not of scene or of routine. To be able to break out of its dark brown sameness, out of the boredom of a world without movement or change, filled me with a deep excitement.

By then Hart had begun spending his summers as an actor and social director at a succession of summer camps in what eventually became known as the Borscht Belt. He claims to have done this for six years and mostly to have hated it mightily, but Bach says the ordeal lasted only four summers and wasn't really quite so awful as Hart depicts it. Even Hart acknowledges that "some of the lessons I learned at camp served me very well later on in the professional theatre, for certain absolutes obtain in the amateur as well as in the professional theatre," among them that "talent by itself is not enough," that talent must be translated into performance, that exhaustion is inevitable in the theater and must be dealt with as a matter of professionalism.

Summer camp also taught him that he wasn't good enough as an actor to make it on Broadway, that "the only way for me to get past a stage door again was to write a play," which he proceeded to do each winter. His efforts, all of them serious if not downright solemn, were repeatedly rejected. One producer suggested he write a comedy, which he resisted because "I was a full-blown snob so far as comedy was concerned," yet soon he began writing a satire of Hollywood, and the words positively flew across the page; the play "was finished in something under three weeks' time." Being new to comedy, he had no idea whether it was any good, but he soon found himself welcomed by the universally beloved producer Sam Harris, who saw great potential in it, took it to Kaufman in the hopes of persuading him to collaborate, and put Hart on the path to theatrical stardom.

The story of the evolution of *Once in a Lifetime* is a classic of theater lore, played out by Hart herein for everything it's worth. Collaborating with Kaufman wasn't always easy, but the two quickly clicked and Hart came to understand the decidedly quirky habits of his partner, who was fifteen years older and one of the most established presences in the American theater. Hart learned that "the process of collaboration is exactly what the dictionary says it is: a union of two people working in agreement on a common project," and that "it requires no special gift except the necessary patience to accommodate one's own working method harmoniously to that of one's collaborator."

We know how the story ends, but Hart still manages to build suspense as he and Kaufman lurch toward that night at New York's Music Box Theatre. The play starts out with a solid first act, half of a second act and not a word of a third. The drama takes on *Perils of Pauline* dimensions as one rewrite after another fails to deliver the goods, and only at the last minute is Hart struck by an inspired solution that enables the collaborators to fix the play. Along the way he gives the reader an unparalleled look inside the theater world, at how it really works, at how much failure and heartbreak go into even the most successful plays and musicals.

For proof, read Bach's account of the making of *My Fair Lady*. At its opening in March 1956 it seemed sheer perfection, seamless in every way, but the road to perfection was long and hard. You'll want to read Bach anyway, because at the end of *Act One* you'll be eager to know the rest of the story. Hart, consummate pro that he was, knew to leave the audience wanting more. That is just what he does at the end of *Act One*, which itself comes not far short of perfection and over half a century has lost absolutely none of its glow.

BLACK BOY
by Richard Wright

I n 1944 Richard Wright, already celebrated, and in some
quarters reviled, for his novel about African-American life,
Native Son (1940), delivered the manuscript of a memoir
to Harper and Brothers, his publisher. It was submitted in turn
to the Book-of-the-Month Club, which rejected its second section, dealing with Wright's life in Chicago and his involvement
with the Communist Party. So the next year, Harper published
only its first section, about Wright's youth in the segregated
South, and called it *Black Boy*.

The book went almost immediately onto the bestseller
lists—it held the Number One position for several weeks—
and was widely received as an American classic. It remains one
to this day, kept steadily in print over more than six decades,
taught in classes at many levels and read in book clubs,
enshrined (though "entombed" often seems more like it) in the
Library of America. It is no exaggeration to call it an essential
American document, because it so powerfully depicts the lives
of rural Southern blacks in the Jim Crow era and even more
important because it tells a quintessential American story, of a
youth pulled out of poverty and despair by his own fierce insistence on making the most of himself.

I quite clearly remember when I first read it. In the winter
of 1962-63, I was put out of work by the infamous printers'
strike against the New York newspapers—I was working then
at the *New York Times*—and decided to try to write a magazine
article about the increasing militancy of the civil rights move-

ment and its accompanying rhetoric. I read everything I could get my hands on, from W.E.B. Du Bois to Gunnar Myrdal to James Baldwin, and spoke to a number of people active in the movement. The article that I wrote never saw the light of day—I was much too young and inexperienced to have a firm grasp on the subject—but I learned a lot, and have been grateful ever since for having read everything that I did.

The trouble with a reading binge, of course, is that you take in too much. It all becomes a big blur in which individual books tend to get lost. That was, for me, the case with *Black Boy.* I was deeply impressed by it, but I was also deeply impressed by *The Souls of Black Folk* and *An American Dilemma* and *The Fire Next Time*. Reading it in isolation forty-five years later, I am far more moved by it than I was then. To be sure, it is a different book now, for the rejected second section, "The Horror and the Glory," has been restored and the book is finally what Wright meant it to be. But for me it is that first section, "Southern Nights," that is the heart of the story and probably the great achievement of his career.

Wright was born in rural Mississippi in 1908. The family moved to Memphis, where his father "worked as a night porter in a Beale Street drugstore" but abandoned his wife and two young sons for another woman when Richard was about five years old. His mother, Ella Wilson Wright, set off on a series of moves through Arkansas and Mississippi, in a desperate attempt to support her little family despite her own fragile health. Richard's schooling was erratic, but he was enchanted by storytelling and determined, at a very young age, to become a storyteller himself. He read constantly and perceptively, distancing himself from the world of bigotry and hatred into which he had been born. He made his way to Chicago when he was nineteen, and a dozen years later published *Native Son.* He died of a heart attack in 1960 in Paris, where he had lived for many years.

Wright's literary reputation was not without its challengers, most particularly Baldwin, who in a withering essay called "Many Thousands Gone" (collected in *Notes of a Native Son* in 1955), attacked Wright for linking "the Negro" and "the worker" and turning one man's story into a parable of "that fantasy Americans hold in their minds when they speak of the Negro: that fantastic and fearful image which we have lived with since the first slave fell beneath the lash." It is indeed true that Wright was strongly drawn to social and political protest in the various forms it took during his lifetime, and though he eventually left the Communist Party, it was not a complete cutting of the cord. "I wanted to be a Communist," he says in the second section of *Black Boy*, "but my kind of Communist. I wanted to shape people's feelings, awaken their hearts."

This he most certainly does in the "Southern Nights" section, i.e., the complete book as originally published. It is difficult to imagine how forcibly this 250-page narrative must have struck readers in 1945, when most of the nation was only dimly aware of the terrible conditions in which Southern blacks lived, but it strikes today's reader not significantly less so. Race relations in this country have scarcely reached millennial perfection and African-Americans still frequently face daunting obstacles in their quest for better lives, but it comes as a shock nonetheless to be reminded of just how debased their condition was a mere eight or nine decades ago, especially when that reminder is couched in language as eloquent and passionate as Wright's.

At one point, when Wright was still a small boy, his mother worked as a cook for a white family. "Watching the white people eat would make my empty stomach churn," he writes, "and I would grow vaguely angry. Why could I not eat when I was hungry?" Hunger, both physical and intellectual, is a persistent theme in this memoir, "hunger that made my body aimlessly restless, hunger that kept me on edge, that made my temper flare, hunger that made hate leap out of my heart like the dart of a serpent's tongue."

While living in Memphis, Wright "first stumbled upon the relations between whites and blacks, and what I learned frightened me," but once his family moved to the country "a dread of white people now came to live permanently in my feelings and imagination." An uncle was murdered by whites "who had long coveted his flourishing liquor business," and the brother of a friend was killed by whites who "said he was fooling with a white prostitute."

Violence and death were all around him, but Wright had a means of escape. Living with his grandmother, he met a schoolteacher boarding there who told him the story of Bluebeard. His imagination was fired, and he was filled with "sharp, frightening, breathtaking, almost painful excitement." For a while he delivered newspapers that contained serialized stories by Zane Grey and others, which he read with wonder and delight: "For the first time in my life I became aware of the life of the modern world, of vast cities, and I was claimed by it; I loved it. Though they were merely stories, I accepted them as true because I wanted to believe them, because I hungered for a different life, for something new."

He had no encouragement from his grandmother, a hard, unforgiving religious zealot, and not much from his mother, who "had suffered a stroke of paralysis" when he was ten or eleven, but a couple of years later he was able to attend school regularly and "suddenly the future loomed tangibly for me, as tangible as a future can loom for a black boy in Mississippi." He studied hard, did well. As his education progressed, as he read more and more, as he wrote his own first stories and even had one published in "the local Negro newspaper," his sense of possibility was strengthened:

> I was building up in me a dream which the entire educational system of the South had been rigged to stifle. I was feeling the very thing that the state of Mississippi had spent millions of dollars to make sure that I would never feel; I was becoming aware of the

thing that the Jim Crow laws had been drafted and passed to keep out of my consciousness; I was acting on impulses that southern senators in the nation's capital had striven to keep out of Negro life; I was beginning to dream the dreams that the state had said were wrong, that the schools had said were taboo.

In the fall of 1925, Wright left Mississippi and began his slow northward trek. Two years later, while working in Memphis, he encountered the world of H.L. Mencken, then at the height of his fame and influence. He was jarred and shocked by the style, the clear, clean, sweeping sentences. What "amazed me was not what he said, but how on earth anybody had the courage to say it." Coming to the end of *A Book of Prefaces*, he felt that "I had somehow overlooked something terribly important in life" and he "hungered for books, new ways of looking and seeing." He read Sinclair Lewis, Theodore Dreiser, everything he could get his hands on, and soon he "had a new hunger," to set down words of his own, and to do that he had to get away from everything he had known:

> I held my life in my mind, in my consciousness each day, feeling at times that I would stumble and drop it, spill it forever. My reading had created a vast sense of distance between me and the world in which I lived and tried to make a living, and that sense of distance was increasing each day. My days and nights were one long, quiet, continuously contained dream of terror, tension, and anxiety. I wondered how long I could bear it.

So he moved north, to Chicago, where he "felt lonely." He "had fled one insecurity and had embraced another." He found work, made friends, had his flirtation with communism, but his real world was "within the walls of my consciousness, contained and controlled." It was within this world that he began to write, trying to set down on paper the lives of African-Americans. Success was slow in coming, but come it did, first with *Native Son* and then with *Black Boy*, an extraordinary book that remains to this day a shock and an inspiration.

The Young Lions
by Irwin Shaw

In the years immediately after World War II, four immensely long and immensely popular novels were published that seemed, at the time, to change forever the American literary landscape. Two—Norman Mailer's *The Naked and the Dead* and Irwin Shaw's *The Young Lions*—were published in 1948, while James Jones's *From Here to Eternity* and Herman Wouk's *The Caine Mutiny* appeared in 1951. All four became huge best-sellers and were made into highly popular movies, only one of which, *From Here to Eternity*, has proved to possess much staying power. Today, at a remove of well over half a century, it is difficult to conjure the incredible excitement these books created, not merely the sense that the terrible war had inspired fiction of lasting importance but also the belief that the "Great American Novel" at last was within reach.

We know now that both assumptions were wrong. Some excellent fiction was indeed written about the war, but it came later and today even the best of it—I think in particular of Jones's visceral novel about combat, *The Thin Red Line*, and his taut novella *The Pistol*—is on the literary margins. It further developed that this brief outburst was pretty much the last gasp of the competition to write the "Great American Novel," as writers turned inward if not outright narcissistic and became more interested in the esteem of their peers than in that of the mass readership. Though all four of these books remain in print and enjoy occasional sales, they have more value now as documents about the war than as literary accomplishments.

Still, I remember all four with affection and no small measure of gratitude. I entered my teens in the early 1950s and cut my literary eyeteeth with a vengeance. Young though I was, I was old enough to have memories of wartime: Three of my uncles had been in the service, I had known a young man who was killed in combat, and I was endlessly curious about how the war had been fought by ordinary soldiers and what the experience had done to them.

Though today's reconsideration of *The Young Lions* marks the first time I've reread any of the four, for a long time they occupied a large piece of real estate in my private literary landscape. However pronounced their shortcomings may seem to me now—in particular those of *The Naked and the Dead*, a book whose clumsy prose I cannot imagine rereading—they taught me lessons about manhood and courage, betrayal and deceit, that remained long after my memory of them had faded. They were as important to me as were Tim O'Brien's novels about Vietnam to a later generation of young readers.

Still, one of the built-in liabilities of doing a series of literary reconsiderations is that it exposes one's treasured youthful tastes to the cold light of a more mature reading. I came to *The Young Lions* for the second time with high expectations but found them, if not exactly dashed, considerably disappointed. This long story (nearly 700 pages!) of three soldiers in the European Theater, two Americans and one German, retains considerable force, but it underscores the central truth about Shaw's writing: Though many of his elephantine novels, in particular *Rich Man, Poor Man*, were great popular hits, his best work was done in his short stories, which you can—and should—read in *Short Stories: Five Decades* (University of Chicago Press paperback, $20). At least two of those stories, "The Eighty-Yard Run" and "The Girls in Their Summer Dresses," are minor classics. Though moments in *The Young Lions* approach this level, overall it is too prolix and flabby to fulfill the high ambitions Shaw obviously had for it.

Shaw, who was born in New York City in 1913, achieved early success with his short stories and a play, *Bury the Dead* (1936), all of which had made him, as James Salter says in his excellent introduction to the University of Chicago edition, "one of the principal voices of his generation." In the war he served as a photographer for the Signal Corps, but there can be little question that he was really gathering material for the novel he so badly wanted to write. After *The Young Lions* he published seven more novels (most of them bestsellers), several story collections and plays, and a couple of volumes of nonfiction, including a tribute to his beloved Paris. He was, Slater writes, "manly, moral, sentimental, observant, with an immodest impulse for the dramatic," and he had many friends. At his death in 1984 he was widely mourned.

Clearly he had "Great American Novel" in mind as he wrote *The Young Lions*. It begins in prewar America and Germany, marches resolutely through many of the war's most dramatic moments, and ends with the Allies on the brink of victory, the ironic aspects of which Shaw does not shy away from making clear. It is loaded with, and weighed down by, extended ruminative passages in which Shaw expresses his views on various moral and other questions provoked by the war, and though the sincerity of these sections is beyond dispute, their overall effect is more soporific than enlightening. By the testimony of his friends—among whom were James Jones, Willie Morris and William Styron, for he was very much a man's man—he was a delightful and thoughtful conversationalist, but this does not come across in the philosophical musings of *The Young Lions*.

The novel's strengths, and they are considerable, lie in its depiction of America on the brink of war, of the brutal training conditions in the U.S. Army, of warfare itself, and of the evolving lives of the three young men who are its protagonists. These are Christian Diestl, a sergeant in the German army, a loyal but scarcely fanatical Nazi; Michael Whitacre, a stage manager for Broadway productions and, according to Salter, "in many respects, Shaw's representative in the novel"; and Noah Ackerman, a young Jewish American whose life has been "wandering and disordered" but who has begun to put things together after moving to New York. Each in his different way is an exceptionally attractive person; they are of course fated to arrive at the same point in the book's final pages, but the obviousness of this narrative device does not diminish the poignancy of those pages.

Shaw was an interesting mix of macho man and antiwar moralist, and both aspects are on display in *The Young Lions*. He knew, as virtually all Americans did, that the war against the Axis was both necessary and "good," but he deplored much of the leadership on both sides and found the Army stultifying, bigoted and claustrophobic. Michael, speaking for Shaw, says:

> When I went into the Army, I made up my mind that I was putting myself at the Army's disposal. I believe in the war. That doesn't mean I believe in the Army. I don't believe in any army. You don't expect justice out of an army, if you're a sensible, grown-up human being, you only expect victory. And if it comes to that, our Army is probably the most just one that ever existed. . . . I expected the Army to be corrupt, inefficient, cruel, wasteful, and it turned out to be all those things, just like all armies, only much less so than I thought before I got into it. It is much less corrupt, for example, than the German Army. Good for us. The victory we win will not be as good as it might be, if it were a different kind of army, but it will be the best kind of victory we can expect in this day and age, and I'm thankful for it.

One of several characteristics that *The Young Lions* shares with the three other big postwar novels is that it is written from the point of view of the rank-and-file serviceman and expresses all the cynicism that was prevalent in the ranks. Today we wax egregiously sentimental about "the Greatest Generation," and more than a few of its surviving members have turned sentimental about themselves, but at the time there was much less talk about noble causes and heroic deeds than about the indignities to which men were subjected, the arbitrariness of officers at all levels, the bureaucratic ineptitude, the daily struggle for survival in dreadful conditions. There was also precious little talk among non-Jews about the routine, quotidian bigotry to which Jewish Americans were subjected. Noah, sent to boot camp in the South, finds himself quartered with a gang of bullies who subject him to psychological and physical abuse. He resists it bravely and forcibly, but the odds against him are overwhelming, and he absorbs beating after beating.

The Young Lions was published one year after *Gentleman's Agreement*, by Laura Z. Hobson, the first widely read novel about anti-Semitism in America. I have no idea whether it had a comparable effect on readers, though since it usually is described as a "war novel," that seems unlikely. Still, at least some readers must have been shocked to realize that Hitler did not have a monopoly on bigotry, that it was widespread and often unchecked by authority in our own country's armed forces: a reflection, needless to say, of anti-Semitism in the country itself, as embodied by the Georgia landlady who turns away Noah and his bride because "we were Jewish."

The country has changed significantly in that regard and so has the Army, in both cases much for the better. Today's reader of *The Young Lions* will also have to shift gears to comprehend that the vast majority of Americans who fought in World War II were civilians, draftees or volunteers; the Army was essentially amateur rather than professional, and thus quite different from what it is today. This is another way in which *The Young*

Lions will seem something of a period piece to readers in the early twenty-first century, but the portrait it paints of those distant days is in most important respects accurate, so we still have much to learn from it.

NEWSPAPER DAYS
by H.L. Mencken

Henry Louis Mencken was in his late fifties when he began writing a series of autobiographical recollections that eventually became three volumes of memoirs published between 1940 and 1943: *Happy Days, Newspaper Days* and *Heathen Days.* Coming as they did from the typewriter of America's most notorious journalistic curmudgeon, these books delighted readers with their rich humor, a salient characteristic of Mencken's prose since he began writing as a teenager in the 1890s, but also surprised them with sunny nostalgia. Here was a Mencken whom almost no one had known, and readers by the uncountable thousands warmed to him at once.

Any of these books would be a worthy candidate for reconsideration, but in the present moment *Newspaper Days* seems especially appropriate. At a time when newspapers are busily if not obsessively composing their own obituaries, it is a joy to recall "the gaudy life that young newspaper reporters led in the major American cities at the turn of the century . . . the maddest, gladdest, damndest existence ever enjoyed by mortal youth," a time when "life was arduous, but it was gay and carefree," when "the days chased one another like kittens chasing their tails." It is a time that had vanished long before my own newspaper career began in 1961, but from time to time I glimpsed evanescent traces of it, and reading *Newspaper Days* for the third or fourth time brings back, in a way, the days of my own youth.

Too often books about newspapers, like articles about newspapers' imminent demise, are of interest only to newspaper people, but *Newspaper Days* certainly is an exception, and so, too, are others of a more recent vintage. Two of Mencken's fellow Baltimoreans have written deservedly popular books about newspapering in that city: Russell Baker in his evocative memoir, *The Good Times*, and Laura Lippman in her spunky, irreverent series of novels about newspaper reporter turned private detective Tess Monaghan. John Darnton's *Black and White and Dead All Over* (2008), is a deliciously acerbic roman à clef about the *New York Times*, and Philip Norman's *Everyone's Gone to the Moon* (1996) is the funniest novel about London's Fleet Street since Evelyn Waugh's classic *Scoop*.

Still, *Newspaper Days* is in a class by itself. I did not come to it until 1980, the centennial of Mencken's birth, but when I did it was as though the clouds had finally parted and the sun at last shone forth in all its glory. I was swept away by Mencken's prose—firm, confident, inventive, blunt, hilarious—as well as by the mixture of unabashed nostalgia and fierce irreverence with which he wrote, not to mention the extraordinary intelligence of every sentence. This, I realized, was writing that far transcended anything ever done by any other American journalist, indeed writing that far transcended mere journalism and strode confidently into the temple of literature.

Newspaper Days begins in January 1899 when Mencken, eighteen years old, entered the newsroom of the *Baltimore Morning Herald* to apply for a job; it ends in June 1906 with the end of the *Herald* itself. In those seven years Mencken rose, astonishingly, from cub reporter to star reporter to Sunday editor, city editor, managing editor and, finally, editor of the paper and secretary of the company. He had attained this eminence at the ripe age of twenty-six, and of course that was only prelude. He went on "to the various Sunpapers— morning, evening and Sunday," and then to a parallel career as magazine editor, author of dozens of books, crusader against literary and cultural Puritanism, the most influential American journalist of his or any other day. By his death in 1956 his star had faded—a stroke in 1949 had weakened his speech and other faculties—but it still glows, and the magnificence of his prose is undiminished.

That Mencken was able, as he neared his sixtieth birthday, to recapture in full the exuberance of newspaper days four decades behind him is testimony to the powerful hold his memories of those days had on him. As he says, "When I project my mind back into space and time it gathers in more pictures from my days as a police reporter than from any other period, and they have more color in them, and a keener sense of delight." He was convivial but not demonstrative and kept his emotions pretty much to himself, especially the sentimental ones, but here—far more than in the boyhood recollections of *Happy Days* or the miscellaneous ones of *Heathen Days*—he gives full, gleeful vent to the joy he had contained for so long.

Mencken had wanted to be a newspaperman throughout his teens, and immediately after the death of his father—which freed him from the obligation to labor in the family cigar factory—he showed up at the *Herald*. The city editor, Max Ways, was skeptical but open-minded and eventually offered him a job at the grand salary of seven dollars a week. Ways soon became the first of several older men who saw Mencken's abilities and steered him through his apprenticeship, for which Mencken remained eternally grateful. He grew to know Baltimore intimately, in all its variety, corruption and eccentricity, and came to love it so much that "I stuck to living in Baltimore, which suited me, and still suits me, precisely."

Newspaper Days takes the reader into the bowels of Baltimore's police stations, courts, city hall, saloons, whorehouses, burlesque theaters and concert halls. Wherever he went, Mencken was a keen, irreverent observer and never more so than in the newsroom itself. He loved newspapering but had no illusions about it or those who practiced it. Editorial writers, for example, were "copy-readers promoted from the city-room to get rid of them, alcoholic writers of local histories and forgotten novels, former managing editors who had come to grief on other papers, and a miscellany of decayed lawyers, college professors and clergymen with whispered pasts."

There's a wonderful chapter about "a notable series of giants who flourished in Baltimore at the turn of the century"—heroic drunks whose feats provoked awe among their less talented contemporaries—but it is with "the great Baltimore fire of 1904" that *Newspaper Days* reaches its climax. The fire "burned a square mile out of the heart of the town and went howling and spluttering on for ten days." The beginning of this chapter demands to be quoted at length:

> It delights me, in my autumnal years, to dwell upon it, for it reminds me how full of steam and malicious animal magnetism I was when I was young. During the week following the outbreak of the fire the *Herald* was printed in three different cities, and I was present at all its accouchements, herding dispersed and bewildered reporters at long distance and cavorting gloriously in strange composing-rooms. . . . It was brain-fagging and back-breaking, but it was grand beyond compare—an adventure of the first chop, a razzle-dazzle superb and elegant, a circus in forty rings. When I came out of it at last I was a settled and indeed almost a middle-aged man, spavined by responsibility and aching in every sinew, but I went into it a boy, and it was the hot gas of youth that kept me going.

Almost forty years after the fact, Mencken was still reduced to ecstasies by it: "We had a story, I am here to tell you! There have been bigger ones, of course, and plenty of them, but when and where, between the Chicago fire of 1871 and the San Francisco earthquake of 1906, was there ever one that was fatter, juicier, more exhilarating to the journalists on the actual ground?" Clearly, Mencken was running on sheer adrenaline by the second or third day, but he never skipped a beat. He was delighted when the *Herald* was printed at the presses of the *Baltimore World*, "a small, ill-fed sheet of the kind then still flourishing in most big American cities," even though the resulting paper "looked as if it had been printed by country printers locked up in a distillery."

For five weeks the *Herald* was printed by the *Philadelphia Evening Telegraph*, the B&O Railroad running back and forth between the two cities at record speeds. When, at the end of the adventure, Mencken went to the railroad's president to settle up, Oscar G. Murray said, "We had some fun together, and we don't want to spoil it now by talking about money." For the rest of his life it was a point of pride with Mencken that "we were printing a daily newspaper 100 miles from base—a feat that remains unparalleled in American journalism, so far as I know, to this day."

Possibly so, though half a century after Mencken's death, the staff of the *New Orleans Times-Picayune* could claim comparable distinction for its heroics during and after Hurricane Katrina. But *Newspaper Days* itself is unparalleled. It is the ultimate newspaper book, a brassy reminder that every once in a while the good old days really were good, and a grand monument to its author, the greatest journalist there ever was.

A Connecticut Yankee in King Arthur's Court
by Mark Twain

By 1889, when Mark Twain published *A Connecticut Yankee in King Arthur's Court*, he was in his mid-fifties and the most famous writer in the United States, not merely author but also book publisher, lecturer, and enthusiastic but invariably failed investor. Two more decades of writing and performing lay ahead of him, but *Connecticut Yankee* brought to an end the period of his greatest work, which had started in 1867 with *The Celebrated Jumping Frog of Calaveras County, and Other Sketches* and continued apace with *Innocents Abroad, Roughing It, Life on the Mississippi, The Prince and the Pauper* and of course, most famously, *The Adventures of Tom Sawyer* and *The Adventures of Huckleberry Finn*.

For most of the way, *Connecticut Yankee* is a wonderfully funny and wildly improbable romp through Arthurian England, but toward the end it turns dark, with a bloody massacre that, as Justin Kaplan suggests in his introduction to the Penguin Classics edition, reflects Twain's own disenchantment with the mechanized modern world for which he had once held such high hopes. We now know, from the convenient vantage point of hindsight, that the darkness that had descended upon Twain never really lifted, and his writing became more eccentric and even angry as he railed against Christianity, despotism, humanity itself and anything else that aroused his considerable capacity for invective.

When I first began reading Twain, as a boy of eight or ten in the late 1940s, I knew nothing of his dark side. Twain had been dead for less than four decades and was still a palpable presence in the country's life. Boys perhaps more than girls read *Tom Sawyer* and *Huckleberry Finn* for the sheer fun of it, most of them myself certainly included doubtless failing to recognize that while the first was a wonderful book for young readers, the latter was a literary masterpiece of immense depth and complexity. More sophisticated readers had long understood that Twain, celebrated and loved as humorist and journalist, was America's first truly great writer and had engineered his way into the classroom, which today is probably the place where people first encounter him.

My own first encounter with *Connecticut Yankee* was at the movies. Adaptations had been filmed in 1921 and 1931, and soon forgotten. Then in 1949 a new version appeared, in the full (and still novel) glory of Technicolor, starring Bing Crosby as the Hartford mechanic who, "during a misunderstanding conducted with crowbars with a fellow we used to call Hercules," is knocked for a loop and wakes to find himself in sixth-century England. I was enchanted and much amused by the movie, which takes vast liberties with the novel and now seems fairly dated, though Crosby is charming and some of the secondary characters, notably Cedrick Hardwicke as King Arthur, are terrific.

The movie led me to the book, but at this remove I remember absolutely nothing about how, as a ten- or eleven-year-old, I responded to it. My hunch is that parts of it must have puzzled me, because what may seem at first glance to be a book for young readers is in fact a singularly adult novel. There are scenes a young reader can enjoy, and after well over a century the novel's language remains remarkably fresh and accessible, but behind all the fun lurks a grown-up's book that deals with grown-up themes, among them freedom and oppression, democracy and autocracy, religion and superstition.

Hank Morgan is "a practical Connecticut man" who quickly

determines that the Knights of the Round Table are "big boo-bies" who pick fights with strangers and then boast endlessly about their triumphs, though he also finds "something very engaging about these great simple-hearted creatures," because "there did not seem to be brains enough in the entire nursery, so to speak, to bait a fish-hook with; but you didn't seem to mind that, after a little, because you soon saw that brains were not needed in a society like that, and indeed would have marred it, hindered it, spoiled its symmetry—perhaps rendered its existence impossible." It is a society that this freedom-loving Yankee finds utterly incomprehensible:

> The most of King Arthur's British nation were slaves, pure and simple, and bore that name, and wore the iron collar on their necks; and the rest were slaves in fact, but without the name; they imagined themselves men and freemen, and called themselves so. The truth was, the nation as a body was in the world for one object, and one only: to grovel before king and Church and noble; to slave for them, sweat blood for them, starve that they might be fed, work that they might play, go naked that they might wear silks and jewels, pay taxes that they might be spared from paying them, be familiar all their lives with the degrading language and postures of adulation that they might walk in pride and think themselves the gods of this world. And for all this, the thanks they got were cuffs and contempt; and so poor spirited were they that they took even this sort of attention as an honor.

That is an authentic American voice as immediately recognizable today as in 1889: the voice of the small-d democrat. Hank is a nineteenth-century American who has been plopped down in the Dark Ages and resolves to do what any good Yankee would do: Fix them. He is "the best-educated man in the kingdom by a matter of thirteen hundred years," and he resolves to use his superior knowledge to "boss the whole country." Knowing the specific day and hour that an eclipse had appeared in the sixth century, he predicts the disappearance of the sun and, when it happens as advertised, the entire land is in fear and awe of him. Merlin, the royal wizard, is revealed as a fraud, and Hank is dubbed the Boss, "the second personage in the Kingdom, as far as political power and authority were concerned."

So at once Hank sets about turning Arthurian England into nineteenth-century America. The first thing he establishes is a patent office, then a school system, then a newspaper, then onward to "the destruction of the throne, nobility abolished, every member of it bound out to some useful trade, universal suffrage instituted, and the whole government placed in the hands of the men and women of the nation, there to remain." After a mere three years, Camelot has become Connecticut:

> Slavery was dead and gone; all men were equal before the law; taxation had been equalized. The telegraph, the telephone, the phonograph, the type-writer, the sewing machine, and all the thousand willing and handy servants of steam and electricity were working their way into favor. We had a steamboat or two on the Thames, we had steam war-ships, and the beginnings of a steam commercial marine; I was getting ready to send out an expedition to discover America.

Along the way to this nirvana (which of course doesn't last, but how and why is for you to discover), Hank acquires the companionship of Demoiselle Alisande la Carteloise, who is as chatty as she is lovely. This is discussed in a paragraph that must be savored in full, as it is quintessential Twain:

> I was gradually coming to have a mysterious and shuddery reverence for this girl; nowadays whenever she pulled out from the station and got her train fairly started on one of those horizonless transcontinental sentences of hers, it was borne in upon me that I was standing in the awful presence of the Mother of the German Language. I was so impressed with this, that sometimes when she began to empty one of these sentences on me I unconsciously

took the very attitude of reverence, and stood uncovered; and if words had been water, I had been drowned, sure. She had exactly the German way: whatever was in her mind to be delivered, whether a mere remark, or a sermon, or a cyclopedia, or the history of a war, she would get it into a single sentence or die. Whenever the literary German dives into a sentence, that is the last you are going to see of him till he emerges on the other side of the Atlantic with his verb in his mouth.

Having spent more of my teenage years than I care to remember wrestling with, and losing to, the intricacies of the German language, I can testify that in this one paragraph Twain nails it on the head and leaves it for dead. But then, when Twain was at his absolute best, he did that all the time. Long after his death in 1910 his humor remains as fresh as ever, and it is as a humorist that he lives on. Yes, it certainly is true that in *Huckleberry Finn* he went far beyond humor to depict this country with astonishing acuity, yet even there it is the humor that sets the novel's basic tone.

The same goes for *Connecticut Yankee*, though the change of mood in its closing pages comes as a surprise, by no means a welcome one. I still love the book, and I understand it far better than I did those many years ago, but *Huckleberry Finn* remains the greatest achievement of Twain's stupendous career.

POMP AND CIRCUMSTANCE
by Noël Coward

First published in 1960, reissued in paperback in 1982, now out of print but not at all difficult to find in used copies, Noël Coward's first and only novel is a small gem. It must have caught everyone by surprise when it appeared. Coward was in his early sixties and really didn't need to go to the trouble. He was one of the world's most famous and beloved entertainers, the author of dozens of plays and hundreds of songs, an actor of surprisingly broad range and a hugely popular cabaret performer. That he actually wanted to write a novel at this stage of his life is remarkable; that he found the time and energy to do it is even more so.

But write it he did. It is called *Pomp and Circumstance* and it is Coward to the core: a deliciously witty and ingenious entertainment that puts on full display his "talent to amuse" (his own phrase, from the song "If Love Were All") and his deep affection for distant, exotic and preferably sun-drenched parts of the world. It was received with considerable enthusiasm when it appeared, and—this will come as no surprise to anyone who knows Coward's work—holds up very well indeed.

I first read it in the 1982 paperback edition. That I had been unaware of it before then is an utter mystery, for I had loved Coward's work since the 1950s. His famous plays—*Hay Fever, Private Lives, Present Laughter, Blithe Spirit*—were staples of the professional and amateur repertory during my youth (and remain so to this day) and I so passionately loved his 1955 cabaret recording, *Noël Coward at Las Vegas*, that I have (and still have) every syllable of it memorized. Available on CD in expanded form as *The Noël Coward Album*, it too is quintessential Coward, at once openly sentimental ("I'll See You Again," "I'll Follow My Secret Heart") and wickedly naughty ("A Bar on the Piccolo Marina," "Alice Is at It Again"). I can't imagine life without it.

Long after his death in 1973 at age seventy-three, Coward remains a highly visible presence, so it isn't necessary to give a detailed account of his life. He was born in 1899 into a middle-class British family, showed various talents as a boy, charmed members of the upper crust and soon made himself comfortable among them, poured forth plays and songs in a seemingly endless torrent. He was by all accounts a kind man who was especially generous to others in the theater. He was homosexual but, as a child of the times, kept his private life to himself and his intimates. Like other gay composers and lyricists of the period (Cole Porter, Lorenz Hart), he channeled his erotic impulses into heterosexual settings, which lent the results a particular poignancy.

Pomp and Circumstance, according to Philip Hoare, one of his many biographers, originated in a play drafted in the late 1940s and eventually presented in the 1950s as *South Sea Bubble*. Hoare says the play was written with Gertrude Lawrence, Coward's favorite actress and frequent co-star, in mind for the role of "Lady Alexandra, or Sandra, a Diana Cooper-Edwina Mountbatten figure," i.e., a titled Englishwoman of blithe spirits and an active, highly unconventional amatory life. In the novel, though, Sandra moves away from center stage, which is occupied by its narrator, a fortyish wife and mother with the rather odd name of Grizelda Craigie.

Too much should not be read into Coward's decision to tell the story through the voice of a woman, but it's an interesting choice and Coward brings it off. She lives with her husband, Robin, who runs a banana plantation, and their two children on Samolo, a British colonial possession in the South Seas, a "beautiful but stagnant pond" where almost nothing ever happens and where the natives are, as Coward always preferred them to be, anything except restless:

> There are no dope addicts or nymphomaniacs or pathological sex murderers in Samolo. There is a great deal of sex which goes on all the time with a winsome disregard of gender, but there are very few "sex crimes." In England we know that no little girl can hope to get across Wandsworth Common after dark without being "interfered with," whereas here she could prattle her way across the whole length and breadth of the island without anything happening to her at all beyond possibly being stuffed with guavas and mangoes by kindly villagers and given indigestion.

Now, however, something is about to happen on Samolo. Something big. Sandra, who is married to the colonial governor, confides to Grizel (as she is called) in a fit of confidentiality: "They're coming in June." Who? "The Queen of course. And Prince Philip. They're arriving in a warship on the twenty-first and going to spend three days. Three whole days and three whole nights, and long long before those three whole days and nights I shall be led away in a straitjacket like that poor beast in *Streetcar Named Desire*." The news is supposed to be top secret, but it quickly develops that everyone on the island is telling it to everyone else and saying how wonderfully good it will be for the island: for the economy, for morale, for anything else that comes to mind.

Well, says Sandra, "We must all bend our minds to think of different ways of boring our royal visitors to death," with the result that every amateur actor, director, composer and writer on the island sets about creating a water pageant to regale their majesties. Grizel mostly watches from the sidelines, but she is scarcely a cynic when it comes to the royals. We need to remember that at the time Elizabeth and Philip were still young and, respectively, pretty and handsome, and that the disillusionments of the past quarter century had yet to set in. It also should be borne in mind that Coward, for all his irreverence and flippancy, was a devoutly patriotic Englishman. He served his country with distinction during World War II, wrote a heartfelt song, "London Pride," to celebrate the city in wartime, and made the film *In Which We Serve* to help the war effort. There can be no doubt that Grizel speaks for him:

> Royal snobbery, in moderation, is rather a good thing, I think, and I am all in favour of it. The crown is a symbol and as such is, or should be, of tremendous importance. We are used to the tradition of royalty and have been brought up to believe in it and respect it and love it. I, being thoroughly British and sentimental to the core, would hate to live in a country in which there was no royal pageantry and no chance of suddenly seeing the Queen drive by. This I know can be described as reactionary emotionalism which perhaps it is, but reactionary or not I feel it very strongly, and when the gutter press alludes to our royal personages by their Christian names and smears their private affairs with its grubby little clichés, I feel deeply angry and somehow ashamed. I want the symbol to go on shining, to go on being out of reach, and I am thankful to say that in our country and its colonies and dominions, it still does, in spite of all efforts to belittle it.

As preparations progress, Grizel's life is suddenly complicated by a request from her friend Bunny Colville, whom Robin calls "a monster where women are concerned," who asks if his current lover, the very-much-married Countess Eloise Fowey, can stay with the Craigie family while sneaking off to trysts in Bunny's isolated bungalow. Eloise is not very bright but is a total bombshell, "endowed with every conceivable physical attribute that the female heart could ever wish for," though "beautiful and alluring and amiable as she was there was an inherent silliness in her character." Back in London, she inhabits a world that Coward knew well, people who "mostly, as far as I could gather, came under the ambiguous heading of

'The International Set,' who wandered aimlessly back and forth between London, Paris, Rome, Cannes, and Deauville, and wandered, equally aimlessly, in and out of bed with one another and in and out of the divorce courts with their lawyers."

Eloise arrives in good spirits, "obviously well disposed and willing to behave with as much discretion as possible in the circumstances, but the basic trouble was of course that the circumstances never should have occurred. Bunny shouldn't have been idiotic enough to have asked her to come out in the first place, and in the second place she should have had more sense than to have agreed to come. The immediate future bristled with evasions and deceits and appalling complications . . . ," all of which amount to a huge headache for Grizel and loads of fun for the reader. When chickenpox rears its head, everyone is off to the races.

Pomp and Circumstance reminds us, as if any reminder were necessary, that Coward was a master entertainer in the very best sense: an immensely intelligent, witty, resourceful man who took endless delight in the human comedy and managed to make it even funnier than it already is. He brought a great deal of light to what was in many respects a dark century, and that light shines on.

THE BRIDGE OF SAN LUIS REY
by Thornton Wilder

In the summer of 1926 a twenty-nine-year-old teacher at a
private school for boys in New Jersey began to write a
novel. It was set in Peru (a place he had never visited) in
the early eighteenth century and was inspired by certain people and events in the country's past, but most particularly it
was inspired by a sentence from the Gospel According to
Luke: "Or those eighteen upon whom the tower of Siloam fell
and killed them, do you think that they were worse offenders
than all the others who dwelt in Jerusalem?"

It is a question that has haunted humankind throughout
history: Is our fate random or is it planned and controlled by
some higher power? Thornton Wilder, the young man who
sought to address the question in fiction, did not pretend to
have the answer, but he wrote, as he subsequently said in a letter, in the spirit of Chekhov: "The business of literature is not to
answer questions, but to state them fairly." That is exactly what
Wilder did in the book he called *The Bridge of San Luis Rey*. It
was published in November 1927, greeted with ecstatic reviews
and impressive sales, and awarded a Pulitzer Prize in May 1928.

The novel—at 34,000 words it's really a novella—has been
a classic of American and world literature ever since, which
explains why at some point in my long slog through the edu-
cational system I was required to read it, which in turn
explains why it almost immediately vanished from my memory.
There's nothing to kill off a book like being force-fed it, especially if the book is a moral fable that poses questions rather

too advanced and complex for the teenaged mind. I filed it away and forgot it, until a few months ago when a friend told me he'd reread it and been pleasantly surprised.

I decided to follow suit, in part out of curiosity, in part because in recent years I have become a part-time resident of Peru and thus was curious about Wilder's depiction of a place I have come to love. It is no exaggeration to say that on second reading I was completely in awe, not so much of Wilder's sensitive treatment of his central theme as of the richness and power of his prose.

We know from Gerald Martin's biography of Gabriel García Márquez that the great Colombian writer read Wilder's *The Ides of March* while working on his own *The Autumn of the Patriarch*, but I am now convinced that he must have read *The Bridge of San Luis Rey* long before, so eerily do many passages in it anticipate his own mature prose style as it emerged in *One Hundred Years of Solitude*. By the time that novel appeared in 1967, Wilder was one of the world's most famous and admired writers. None of his six other novels enjoyed the acclaim of *Bridge*, but his success as a playwright was stupendous. *Our Town* won his second Pulitzer in 1938 and in 1943 *The Skin of Our Teeth* took his third. *The Matchmaker* (1954) was another success, but far more so in its musical adaptation as *Hello, Dolly!* Apart from his three Pulitzers, Wilder was festooned with prizes at home and around the world, and *Our Town* lives on as the most beloved and most frequently performed of American plays. Wilder died in 1975 at age seventy-eight.

The opening sentence of *Bridge* is deservedly famous: "On Friday noon, July the twentieth, 1714, the finest bridge in all Peru broke and precipitated five travelers into the gulf below." The incident is witnessed by Brother Juniper, a Franciscan from Italy who "happened to be in Peru converting the Indians" and asks himself: "'Why did this happen to *those* five?' If there were any plan in the universe at all, if there were any pattern in a human life, surely it could be discovered mysteriously latent in those lives so suddenly cut off. Either we live by accident and die by accident, or we live by plan and die by plan. And on that instant Brother Juniper made the resolve to inquire into the secret lives of those five persons, that moment falling through the air, and to [surmise] the reason of their taking off."

The five are: Doña María, Marquesa de Montemayor, whose letters after her death were to "become one of the monuments of Spanish literature"; her young maid, Pepita; Esteban, a young man whose twin brother has recently died; Uncle Pio, an adventurer possessed of "a reluctance to own anything, to be tied down, to be held to a long engagement"; and Jaime, the little son of Camila Perichole, the best and most famous actress in Peru. Brother Juniper's six years of research are intended to prove that "each of the five lost lives was a perfect whole" and that each had been ended with "a sheer Act of God."

It doesn't quite turn out that way, and when Brother Juniper finally reveals his results he pays a heavy price. The Spanish Inquisition is still very much in operation. "The book being done fell under the eyes of some judges and was suddenly pronounced heretical. It was ordered to be burned in the Square with its author." The last word belongs to Wilder, in four sentences that have been quoted over and over again: "But soon we shall die and all memory of those five will have left the earth, and we ourselves shall be loved for a while and forgotten. But the love will have been enough; all those impulses of love return to the love that made them. Even memory is not necessary for love. There is a land of the living and a land of the dead and the bridge is love, the only survival, the only meaning."

Whether the next two sentences have ever before been quoted I do not know, but they leaped off the page at me. The first involves the Viceroy of Peru: "Don Andrés had contrived to make exile endurable by building up a ceremonial so complicated that it could be remembered only by a society that had nothing else to think about." The second involves Doña María: "Twice she lay back, refusing to seize the meaning, but at last, like a general calling together in a rain and by night the dispersed division of his army she assembled memory and attention and a few other faculties and painfully pressing her hand to her forehead she asked for a bowl of snow."

Discussing his prose style long after the book's publication, Wilder cited "the 'removed' tone, the classical, the faintly ironic distance from the impassioned actions" and called it "the expression—even a borrowing—from the latin thought world." Apparently he meant, among others, the Spanish playwrights Lope de Vega and Calderón, as well as Cervantes, and in that sense he was connecting his own work to that of the Spanish giants. But he was also, all unwittingly, looking to the future, for either of those sentences could have been written by García Márquez or, for that matter, the great Peruvian writer Mario Vargas Llosa, with their very modern wit, irony and elaborate structure. For more of the same, consider this:

> There was something in Lima that was wrapped up in yards of violet satin from which protruded a great dropsical head and two fat pearly hands; and that was its archbishop. Between the rolls of flesh that surrounded them looked out two black eyes speaking discomfort, kindliness and wit. A curious and eager soul was imprisoned in all this lard, but by dint of never refusing himself a pheasant or a goose or his daily procession of Roman wines, he was his own bitter jailer. He loved his cathedral; he loved his duties; he was very devout. Some days he regarded his bulk ruefully, but the distress of remorse was less poignant than the distress of fasting and he was presently found deliberating over the secret messages that a certain roast sends to the certain salad that will follow it. And to punish himself he led an exemplary life in every other respect.

The stately procession of that paragraph is balanced by the underlying tongue-in-cheek tone. An archbishop in García

Márquez's Cartagena or Vargas Llosa's Miraflores could easily be described in the same words. One expects, though, that these native South Americans would get their facts right. Pheasant may be a priestly dish in England, but it is virtually unknown in Peru. Peruvians love their chicken and cook it as well as anyone in the world, but wild game is not on the menu. Wilder seems to have thought that it rains often in Lima, a city where to all intents and purposes it never rains at all. He says that "tidal waves were continually washing away cities," when in fact tidal waves are exceedingly rare, occurring only as the consequence of powerful earthquakes.

So it probably wouldn't have been a bad idea if Wilder had visited Peru in 1925 rather than in 1941, when he did for the first time, but in truth that is neither here nor there. In his broader strokes Wilder has created a Peru that I recognize and Peruvians who remind me in some ways of Peruvians whom I know. In any event *The Bridge of San Luis Rey* deals in universals and just happens to be set in Peru. It is an entirely remarkable book, it has lost none of its pertinence in the eight decades since its publication, and I'm very glad indeed that my old friend sent me back to it.

In 1969 I did something I never do: I wrote a letter to the editor. I was an editorial writer and book editor in North Carolina, so I was accustomed to being the recipient rather than the author of such letters. This time, though, I was deeply upset by a book review that had just appeared in a national publication I much admired, and I was determined to protest it. I had nothing in mind except to try to correct the record, but as it turned out the letter had consequences that changed my life, setting off developments that a dozen years later led to my becoming the book critic of the *Washington Post*.

I'm returning today to the book that inspired that letter because this is the last of these Second Readings. The book was *The Collected Stories of Peter Taylor* and the review that so disturbed me, written by someone previously unknown to me named Barbara Raskin, was in the *New Republic*, which I then regarded as the best magazine of political and literary commentary in the country. Precisely why Raskin had been chosen to review the book I do not know, but the world of Peter Taylor was terra incognita to her. This was the fall of 1969, leftist radicalism was all the rage, and Raskin, who was in her early thirties and married to a prominent activist named Marcus Raskin, was totally caught up in all the causes of the moment.

Taylor, by contrast, was in his early fifties and writing, as he had for three decades, about the lives of genteel whites of the Upper South and the blacks with whom they coexisted uneasily and intimately. He was almost entirely unknown outside a small circle of ardent admirers, many of them fellow writers, so the publication of *The Collected Stories* in 1969 clearly was an attempt to get critical recognition in the mainstream press and perhaps even to sell a few books. The notices generally were positive, in some cases rhapsodic, but Raskin took off the gloves. She said that Taylor dealt in Southern stereotypes and that his work was "a return to the same insipid, if not insidious, situations, events, remembrances, and nostalgia that finally implicates and indicts the author as much as his work."

As it happens, I had only recently returned to the newspaper in Greensboro after a year of postgraduate study in which I had read deeply in Southern literature. I felt that Raskin's depiction of Taylor and his work was utterly wrongheaded. I fired off a long letter to the *New Republic* in which I noted "the fundamentally untenable premise that all Southern fiction is alike" and took Raskin to task for "racing Dixiephobia." I put the letter in the mail and went about my business, but that was only the beginning. A few days later I received a letter from Reed Whittemore, the distinguished poet who was then the magazine's literary editor, saying that he liked my letter, that it would be published in full, and that he wondered if I'd be interested in doing some reviews for him.

You could have knocked me over with a page from the *New Republic*. *Would I be interested?* I had just turned thirty years old, I had recently realized that book reviewing interested me far more than editorial writing, and here the best literary section in the country had invited me to become a contributor. It was my big opportunity, and I seized it with glee and determination. I began contributing regularly to the magazine, and the way of the world being such as it is, soon I was also contributing regularly to newspapers and magazines around the country, making a small name for myself in a very small corner of journalism that over the next dozen years led to a couple of book-reviewing jobs—first at the *Miami Herald*, then at the

Washington Star—before landing me at the *Washington Post* in the summer of 1981.

The rest of the story is just a lot of work done pretty much in isolation, but a footnote must be added. Sometime in 1998, after I'd finally taken up residence in the District of Columbia, I met Barbara Raskin at a dinner party. I shook her hand, smiled and said, "I owe you a lot." She laughed and replied, "I know you do!" It was the beginning of a friendship that I valued enormously. Barbara was earthy, great-hearted, funny, loyal, smart and proud yet self-mocking. Alas, our friendship turned out to be far too brief. Barbara died suddenly the next year, aged sixty-three, from post-operative complications. The informal memorial service that was held for her a few days later was jammed with people who were heartbroken by her death but joyful about her exuberant life.

More than once Barbara told me that she had been the wrong person to review Taylor's stories—I don't recall her exact words, but they were along the lines of: What's a nice Jewish girl from Minneapolis doing writing about a genteel man from Tennessee?—but she was kind enough to say that if her review helped jump-start my career, she was glad of it. So you can imagine that she was uppermost in my mind when, for the first time in four decades, I sat down to reread Taylor's *Collected Stories*. Nothing that I rediscovered there changed my mind about either her review or Taylor's stories, but I was reminded that a great deal happened between 1969 and Taylor's death a quarter-century later. I realize now that *The Collected Stories*, wonderful though the best of them are, were not the climax of Taylor's writing career, as at the time his publisher may have thought them to be, but the prologue to his finest work, the short stories and novels that secured his place among this country's greatest writers.

Certainly the twenty-one stories gathered here are far more than apprentice work, as among them are "Dean of Men,"

"What You Hear From 'Em?," "A Wife of Nashville," "The Elect" and "Miss Leonora When Last Seen," all of which rank with the finest work of his mature years. The themes that characterize his work are all to be found here: the confusion, uncertainty and self-doubt faced by people in times of great social, economic and cultural change, the longing for "the old ways, the old life, where people had real grandfathers and real children, and where love was something that could endure the light of day"; the tangled, strangely loving relationship between white middle-class women and the black women who served them; loneliness, "the loneliness from which everybody, knowingly or unknowingly, suffered"; the life of small towns, epitomized by the fictional Thornton, and of the big cities, Memphis and Nashville, to which Taylor was drawn over and over again.

In the story "There," Taylor writes about a shipboard encounter between an "old gentleman" and the younger narrator, who turns out to come from the same small Southern town. The older man is a gifted raconteur. "He had a way of making you feel that he couldn't say what he was saying to anyone but you," Taylor writes. "From the outset I observed in him what seemed a mixture of masculine frankness and almost feminine gossipiness. It was this mixture which must always have constituted his charm for people." That story was written in the early 1960s, when Taylor was still in his forties, and there is no way of knowing how much if any self-awareness went into those words, but one would be hard put to depict Taylor himself more accurately. He was a thoroughly masculine man, but he had a strong feminine side that resulted in, among other things, his delight in gossip and secrets and stories.

Thus *The Collected Stories* is dedicated to Taylor's mother, "who was the best teller of tales I know and from whose lips I first heard many of the stories in this book." Taylor was the most domestic of men, who shared with his wife, Eleanor Ross Taylor, herself a poet of high reputation, a love for houses and gardens and all the accouterments of domesticity. Over the many years of their marriage they bought, renovated and sold something on the order of two dozen houses, and apparently they loved every one of them.

The stories in this collection are suffused with these things that Taylor loved, as is everything else he wrote before his death in 1994. Marvelous though the early stories are, it is this later work that will bring readers to him for generations to come. I think in particular of "The Old Forest," which I consider the greatest short story ever written by an American, and *A Summons to Memphis*, the novel that at last he wrote—people had been wondering for years why he hadn't written one, beyond the rather slight *A Woman of Means* (1950)—and for which he was awarded a Pulitzer Prize in 1987. Throughout the years before these two triumphs Taylor bemoaned the obscurity in which he had for so long labored, but I believe that this freed him from the distractions of such celebrity as literary success offers and gave him time and space in which to grow. Unlike so many American writers, who soar early and then flame out, Taylor was at his best at the end of his writing life.

THE REST OF THE LIST

The thirty-seven Second Reading columns not collected here can be read at the excellent Neglected Books Website: http://neglectedbooks.com. In alphabetical order, the missing pieces are:

About Three Bricks Shy of a Load, by Roy Blount, Jr.
And Then We Heard the Thunder, by John Oliver Killens
Appointment in Samarra, by John O'Hara
Black Like Me, by John Howard Griffin
Bleak House, by Charles Dickens
Cheaper by the Dozen, by Frank B. Gilbreth, Jr.,
    and Ernestine Gilbreth Carey
The Clock Winder, by Anne Tyler
Cockfighter, by Charles Willeford
The Count of Monte Cristo, by Alexandre Dumas
Dale Loves Sophie to Death, by Robb Forman Dew
The Daughter of Time, by Josephine Tey
The Earl of Louisiana, by A.J. Liebling
Fear and Loathing in Las Vegas, by Hunter S. Thompson
Generation of Vipers, by Philip Wylie
Giant, by Edna Ferber
Happy All the Time, by Laurie Colwin
The Heart Is a Lonely Hunter, by Carson McCullers
Instant Replay, by Jerry Kramer with Dick Schaap
Little House in the Big Woods, by Laura Ingalls Wilder
The Mountain Lion, by Jean Stafford

My Young Years, by Arthur Rubenstein
Never Love a Stranger, by Harold Robbins
No Left Turns, by Joseph L. Schott
Office Politics, by Wilfrid Sheed
The Ox-Bow Incident, by Walter Van Tilburg Clark
Penrod and Sam, by Booth Tarkington
Pride and Prejudice, by Jane Austen
The Proud Tower, by Barbara Tuchman
Scott Fitzgerald, by Andrew Turnbull
The Second Happiest Day, by John Phillips
The Spawning Run and *My Moby Dick*,
    by William Humphrey
St. Urbain's Horseman, by Mordecai Richler
The Stardust Road, by Hoagy Carmichael
Treasure Island, by Robert Louis Stevenson
Veeck—As in Wreck, by Bill Veeck with Ed Linn
Victory, by Joseph Conrad
The Year the Yankees Lost the Pennant,
    by Douglass Wallop

ABOUT THE AUTHOR

Jonathan Yardley has been a book critic and columnist at the Washington Post since 1981. He has been awarded the Pulitzer Prize for distinguished criticism and a Fellowship from the Nieman Foundation for Journalism at Harvard University. He is the author of six books of non-fiction, including *Ring: A Biography of Ring Lardner* (Random House, 1977) and *Misfit: The Strange Life of Frederick Exley* (Random House, 1997). Yardley lives in Washington DC.

Europa Editions publishes in the USA and in the UK. Not all titles are available in both countries. Availability of individual titles is indicated in the following list.

Carmine Abate
Between Two Seas
"A moving portrayal of generational continuity."
—*Kirkus*
224 pp • $14.95 • 978-1-933372-40-2 • Territories: World

Salwa Al Neimi
The Proof of the Honey
"Al Neimi announces the end of a taboo in the Arab world: that of *sex!*"
—*Reuters*
144 pp • $15.00 • 978-1-933372-68-6 • Territories: World

Alberto Angela
A Day in the Life of Ancient Rome
"Fascinating and accessible."
—*Il Giornale*
392 pp • $16.00 • 978-1-933372-71-6 • Territories: USA & Canada

Muriel Barbery
The Elegance of the Hedgehog
"Gently satirical, exceptionally winning and inevitably bittersweet."
—Michael Dirda, *The Washington Post*
336 pp • $15.00 • 978-1-933372-60-0 • Territories: USA & Canada

Gourmet Rhapsody
"In the pages of this book, Barbery shows off her finest gift: lightness."
—*La Repubblica*
176 pp • $15.00 • 978-1-933372-95-2 • Territories: World (except UK, EU)

www.europaeditions.com

Stefano Benni
Margherita Dolce Vita
"A modern fable...hilarious social commentary."—*People*
240 pp • $14.95 • 978-1-933372-20-4 • Territories: World

Timeskipper
"Benni again unveils his Italian brand of magical realism."
—*Library Journal*
400 pp • $16.95 • 978-1-933372-44-0 • Territories: World

Romano Bilenchi
The Chill
120 pp • $15.00 • 978-1-933372-90-7 • Territories: World

Massimo Carlotto
The Goodbye Kiss
"A masterpiece of Italian noir."
—*Globe and Mail*
160 pp • $14.95 • 978-1-933372-05-1 • Territories: World

Death's Dark Abyss
"A remarkable study of corruption and redemption."
—*Kirkus* (starred review)
160 pp • $14.95 • 978-1-933372-18-1 • Territories: World

The Fugitive
"[Carlotto is] the reigning king of Mediterranean noir."
—*The Boston Phoenix*
176 pp • $14.95 • 978-1-933372-25-9 • Territories: World

(with Marco Videtta)
Poisonville
"The business world as described by Carlotto and Videtta
in *Poisonville* is frightening as hell."
—*La Repubblica*
224 pp • $15.00 • 978-1-933372-91-4 • Territories: World

Francisco Coloane
Tierra del Fuego
"Coloane is the Jack London of our times."—Alvaro Mutis
192 pp • $14.95 • 978-1-933372-63-1 • Territories: World

Giancarlo De Cataldo
The Father and the Foreigner
"A slim but touching noir novel from one of Italy's best writers
in the genre."—*Quaderni Noir*
144 pp • $15.00 • 978-1-933372-72-3 • Territories: World

Shashi Deshpande
The Dark Holds No Terrors
"[Deshpande is] an extremely talented storyteller."—*Hindustan Times*
272 pp • $15.00 • 978-1-933372-67-9 • Territories: USA

Helmut Dubiel
Deep in the Brain: Living with Parkinson's Disease
"A book that begs reflection."—*Die Zeit*
144 pp • $15.00 • 978-1-933372-70-9 • Territories: World

Steve Erickson
Zeroville
"A funny, disturbing, daring and demanding novel—Erickson's best."
—*The New York Times Book Review*
352 pp • $14.95 • 978-1-933372-39-6 • Territories: USA & Canada

Elena Ferrante
The Days of Abandonment
"The raging, torrential voice of [this] author is something rare."
—*The New York Times*
192 pp • $14.95 • 978-1-933372-00-6 • Territories: World

Troubling Love
"Ferrante's polished language belies the rawness of her imagery."
—*The New Yorker*
144 pp • $14.95 • 978-1-933372-16-7 • Territories: World

The Lost Daughter
"So refined, almost translucent."—*The Boston Globe*
144 pp • $14.95 • 978-1-933372-42-6 • Territories: World

Jane Gardam
Old Filth
"Old Filth belongs in the Dickensian pantheon of memorable characters."
—*The New York Times Book Review*
304 pp • $14.95 • 978-1-933372-13-6 • Territories: USA

The Queen of the Tambourine
"A truly superb and moving novel."—*The Boston Globe*
272 pp • $14.95 • 978-1-933372-36-5 • Territories: USA

The People on Privilege Hill
"Engrossing stories of hilarity and heartbreak."—*Seattle Times*
208 pp • $15.95 • 978-1-933372-56-3 • Territories: USA

The Man in the Wooden Hat
"Here is a writer who delivers the world we live in…with memorable and moving skill."—*The Boston Globe*
240 pp • $15.00 • 978-1-933372-89-1 • Territories: USA

Alicia Giménez-Bartlett
Dog Day
"Delicado and Garzón prove to be one of the more engaging sleuth teams to debut in a long time."—*The Washington Post*
320 pp • $14.95 • 978-1-933372-14-3 • Territories: USA & Canada

Prime Time Suspect
"A gripping police procedural."—*The Washington Post*
320 pp • $14.95 • 978-1-933372-31-0 • Territories: USA & Canada

Death Rites
"Petra is developing into a good cop, and her earnest efforts to assert her authority…are worth cheering."—*The New York Times*
304 pp • $16.95 • 978-1-933372-54-9 • Territories: USA & Canada

Katharina Hacker
The Have-Nots
"Hacker's prose soars."—*Publishers Weekly*
352 pp • $14.95 • 978-1-933372-41-9 • Territories: USA & Canada

Patrick Hamilton
Hangover Square
"Patrick Hamilton's novels are dark tunnels of misery, loneliness, deceit, and sexual obsession."—*New York Review of Books*
336 pp • $14.95 • 978-1-933372-06-8 • Territories: USA & Canada

James Hamilton-Paterson
Cooking with Fernet Branca
"Irresistible!"—*The Washington Post*
288 pp • $14.95 • 978-1-933372-01-3 • Territories: USA & Canada

Amazing Disgrace
"It's loads of fun, light and dazzling as a peacock feather."
—*New York Magazine*
352 pp • $14.95 • 978-1-933372-19-8 • Territories: USA & Canada

Rancid Pansies
"Campy comic saga about hack writer and self-styled 'culinary genius' Gerald Samper."—*Seattle Times*
288 pp • $15.95 • 978-1-933372-62-4 • Territories: USA & Canada

Seven-Tenths: The Sea and Its Thresholds
"The kind of book that, were he alive now, Shelley might have written."
—*Charles Spawson*
416 pp • $16.00 • 978-1-933372-69-3 • Territories: USA & Canada

Alfred Hayes
The Girl on the Via Flaminia
"Immensely readable."—*The New York Times*
164 pp • $14.95 • 978-1-933372-24-2 • Territories: World